"What Homeyer and Bennett have learned and lived out as practicing play therapists and university professors appears on the pages of this practical, detailed, essential, stress-relieving resource. They have anticipated everything a play therapist needs to know and do and provide a template for every form and document needed, from informed consent to termination summary. Completed forms provide examples to follow. This is a HOW TO book, unique in the field of play therapy, that will help play therapists become more efficient and effective. Don't miss the chapter on 'Parents Who Challenge Us' for new insights about what to do."

Garry Landreth, EdD, LPC, RPT-S, *Regents Professor at the University of North Texas, founder of the Center for Play Therapy*

"Using their years of experience as play therapists and as scholars, the authors have written the most comprehensive play therapy text in the field! Homeyer and Bennett provide guidance on everything from liability insurance, theory, case notes, and treatment planning with examples and templates ready to put directly into practice. Readers will be equipped with crucial guidance for working with parents, including addressing topics such as divorced parents, trauma, difficult conversations, and neurobiology. This is a must-have resource for the play therapist in training as they begin their career as well as for the experienced play therapist and supervisor."

Kristi Perryman, PhD, LPC-S, RPT-S, *Associate Professor at the University of Arkansas*

"This book is the definitive guide for play therapists in and out of the playroom. The authors freely share the deep knowledge that they have accumulated through their extensive experience as clinicians, educators, and supervisors. If I were to pick sand tray miniatures to represent this book, they would be a bridge that connects play therapists with a real-life experience and a treasure box that contains so many hidden and valuable materials."

Yumiko Ogawa, PhD, LPC-S, ACS, RPT-S, *Associate Professor in the Department of Counselor Education at the New Jersey City University*

The Guide to Play Therapy Documentation and Parent Consultation

The Guide to Play Therapy Documentation and Parent Consultation guides play therapists through the case-documentation process, from the initial inquiry for services through intake session, diagnosis, treatment planning, session notes, and termination summary. There's a special focus on writing session notes, one of the areas in which play therapists most often request additional training. Chapters also identify play themes, explore clinical theories and case conceptualization, and guide play therapists from the playroom to the paperwork. The authors include several examples of case notes and treatment plans completed from a variety of theoretical perspectives, and vignettes and case studies illustrate ways to connect with caregivers, strategies for working with challenging caregivers, addressing difficult topics at different ages and stages of parenting (how to talk about sex, screen time, co-parenting, etc.), and much more. The book also includes a thorough discussion of ways to structure parent consultations to facilitate the therapeutic process. Expansive appendices provide many case examples and tips to explain and demonstrate documentation, and the authors provide form templates in the text and on the book's website.

Linda E. Homeyer, PhD, LPC-S, RPT-S, after 30 years as play therapist, sandtray therapist, author, and professor at Texas State University, is semi-retired. She continues to write, provide professional consultations, and play in the clay in Texas.

Mary Morrison Bennett, PhD, LPC-S, RPT-S, has 20 years of experience in play therapy, is a former associate professor at Texas State University, and is now in private practice in Texas, where she continues to speak and write on play therapy.

The Guide to Play Therapy Documentation and Parent Consultation

Linda E. Homeyer and Mary Morrison Bennett

Routledge
Taylor & Francis Group

NEW YORK AND LONDON

Cover Photo by TedAlbracht.com

First published 2023
by Routledge
605 Third Avenue, New York, NY 10158

and by Routledge
4 Park Square, Milton Park, Abingdon, Oxon, OX14 4RN

Routledge is an imprint of the Taylor & Francis Group, an informa business

Library of Congress Cataloging-in-Publication Data
Names: Homeyer, Linda, author. | Bennett, Mary Morrison, author.
Title: The guide to play therapy documentation and parent consultation / Linda E. Homeyer, Mary Morrison Bennett.
Description: First edition. | New York, NY : Routledge, 2023. | Includes bibliographical references and index.
Identifiers: LCCN 2022038914 (print) | LCCN 2022038915 (ebook) | ISBN 9781032193458 (hbk) | ISBN 9781032193427 (pbk) | ISBN 9781003258766 (ebk)
Subjects: LCSH: Play therapy. | Child psychotherapy—Parent participation. | Parent and child. | Parenting.
Classification: LCC RJ505.P6 H655 2023 (print) | LCC RJ505.P6 (ebook) | DDC 616.89/1653—dc23/eng/20221122
LC record available at https://lccn.loc.gov/2022038914
LC ebook record available at https://lccn.loc.gov/2022038915

ISBN: 978-1-032-19345-8 (hbk)
ISBN: 978-1-032-19342-7 (pbk)
ISBN: 978-1-003-25876-6 (ebk)

DOI: 10.4324/9781003258766

Typeset in Palatino, Futura, and Rockwell
by Apex CoVantage, LLC

Access the Support Material: www.routledge.com/9781032193427

I dedicate this book to my parents, William and Adelaide Thorman, who instilled social interest; my siblings, Nancy, Frank, and Diane, with whom I shared our co-created family atmosphere with courage; and my colleagues who shared with me belonging. And my late husband, Dan, who balanced me with his Comfort.

Linda

I dedicate this book to Robbie, who knows my heart and encourages my dreams. To Goodhue and Eleanor who help me practice the core conditions each day. To my parents, Eddie and Ellie Morrison, who always support my endeavors. For Linda Homeyer, Sue Bratton, Dee Ray, and Garry Landreth, who saw my potential and have mentored me throughout my career. I am grateful for all of you.

Mary

▉ Contents

◼ About the Authors

Linda E. Homeyer, PhD, LPC-S, RPT-S™

After more than 30 years of work as a play therapist, sandtray therapist, and university professor, Linda retired from Texas State University and full-time clinical practice. She continues to write, provide professional consultations, a few teaching engagements, and play in the clay in Canyon Lake, Texas. Linda is a Licensed Professional Counselor Supervisor in Texas and a Registered Play Therapist Supervisor™.

In addition to keynotes and conference presentations in the United States, Linda has enjoyed traveling the globe and has taught play therapy, sandtray therapy, and clinical supervision in Turkey, Lebanon, Jordan, South Africa, Australia, Mexico, Canada, Great Britain, Ireland, Taiwan, Denmark, China, Italy, and even on a cruise ship! Her co-authored books include *Sandtray Therapy: A Practical Manual (4th ed.)*; *Advanced Sandtray Therapy: Digging Deeper Into Clinical Practice*; *The Handbook of Group Play Therapy*; *Play Therapy in Malaysia*; *The World of Play Therapy Literature*, numerous book chapters, and journal articles. Her work has been translated into Turkish, Chinese, Russian, Korean, and Spanish.

Linda is Distinguished Professor Emerita of Professional Counseling at Texas State University. The Association for Play Therapy named Linda as Director Emerita and awarded her their Lifetime Achievement Award. Linda helped form the Texas Association for Play Therapy and established their Dan E. Homeyer Research Award.

Linda is currently the international liaison and representative for the Association for Play Therapy on the Board of Directors for the International Consortium for Play Therapy Associations. She is also the editor of the *World Journal for Sand Therapy Practice*, the journal of the World Association for Sand Therapy Professionals.

Mary Morrison Bennett, PhD, LPC-S, RPT-S™

For more than 20 years, Mary has studied and practiced play therapy. She received her BS in special education at Texas Christian University and her MEd and PhD in counseling from the University of North Texas. For more than a decade Mary was part of the Professional Counseling faculty at Texas State University where she co-founded the Institute for Play Therapy.

Mary is a Licensed Professional Counselor Supervisor, Registered Play Therapist Supervisor™, Certified Child-Centered Play Therapy Trainer, and Child-Parent Relationship Therapy Trainer. Mary is past president of the Texas Association for Play Therapy and continues to provide supervision and training for play therapists at professional conferences. She has presented on play therapy across the United States, England, Ireland, and Russia.

Co-author of *Child-Parent Relationship Therapy—Toddler Model* and the *Child-Teacher Relationship Training Model*, Mary continues to write book chapters and for professional journals. She has been recognized for her professional contributions and was the recipient of the Dissertation Award from the Association for Play Therapy for her research on Child-Teacher Relationship Training and the Nancy Guillory Award from the Texas Association for Play Therapy. When not working in her private practice in Austin, Texas, Mary enjoys time with her husband and children and baking her world-famous chocolate chip cookies.

Part One

Documentation and Parent Consultation

Chapter 1

Introduction

Play therapy documentation and parent consultation are woven together throughout the entire therapeutic process with a play therapy client. From the initial inquiry contact through termination, both are integral to providing the standard of care. This guide will cover the details of often-overlooked aspects of our professional work. Often play therapists (and other mental health professionals) express their frustration and dislike of "*having to write notes.*" They like their work directly with the client but dislike the paperwork. The aim of this guide is to provide a structure to make this constant movement between people-paper-people-paper one that becomes natural, easy, and efficient. We make the case that effectively-completed paperwork protects the play therapist and maintains a clear focus on clinically sound therapy goals.

Creating thorough case documentation is an ethical and legal imperative. We typically begin learning about and practicing various parts of case documentation in a disjointed way while in graduate school. Perhaps initially understanding about and making a diagnosis in a psychopathology class. Treatment plans and progress notes are typically introduced in our first clinical course—a pre-practicum, advanced methods, or practicum class; wherever we encounter our first client. Perhaps we are introduced to writing case conceptualizations and summaries in practicum, internship, or field placement. Other components of documentation may be unique to our discipline or placement sites. Even more components of case documentation are learned on the job, either during our graduate-level internships or in our postgraduate positions. Often those positions have documentation protocols that are very specific to the agency or position.

Even with all these possible variations, there is a generally accepted protocol for client documentation. Obtaining a comprehensive understanding of all the components for a client case file is rarely taught or provided. Pulling together all the components of a *play therapy case* can seem even more unique and daunting. Finding and implementing a standard protocol that integrates documentation standards with the uniqueness of the play therapy process seems overwhelming and even unattainable. This guide will provide you, the play therapist, a way to look at a case from the initial inquiry contact to the termination summary.

Working with parents during the play therapy process (and documenting these consultations) is critical to effective intervention and change. This guide will also focus on the various stages of parent consultation, from the intake session to the termination session. Connecting with parents so they feel safe, secure, and understood is critical to the therapeutic process. Parents have their own unique needs and struggles. Play therapists must meet

DOI: 10.4324/9781003258766-2

parents where they are, to facilitate parental and family adjustments so the child client can thrive.

The reader will already notice that we are using the term *parents* rather than *caregiver*. We believe the term *parent* is inherently more relational; we believe children need relationships. While we understand the more generic and inclusive nature of the term *caregiver*, it serves as *in loco parentis*. Please read into the term *parent* all those individuals who care for the children we engage with as play therapists. Schottelkorb et al. (2015) also support the use of parents "as any adult serving as a child's guardian. Therefore, parent consultation can be provided for biological parents, adoptive or foster parents, grandparents or other family members serving as guardians" (p. 222). Certainly, there are caregivers, such as after-school caregivers, extended family providing childcare services, and others such as nannies. However, these caregivers rarely fill the role of parent in case consultations.

Play therapy was initially developed to provide children a way to express themselves. When psychotherapy for children was an emerging field, Margaret Lowenfeld began providing play therapy and training play therapists in London in the 1920s (Homeyer & Lyles, 2022; Lowenfeld & Dukes, 1938). Melanie Klein and Anna Freud also were developing play techniques for use with children during this same time. Soon after, play therapy began being used with clients of all ages. This broad usage is reflected in the definition of play therapy by the Association for Play Therapy (APT), which does not delimit the term *clients*. For this guide, we use the Association for Play Therapy's definition of play therapy:

> the systematic use of a theoretical model to establish an interpersonal process wherein trained play therapists use the therapeutic powers of play to help clients prevent or resolve psychosocial difficulties and achieve optimal growth and development. (Association for Play Therapy, 2022)

Appropriate and useful for all ages, play therapy is seen as the developmentally appropriate therapeutic approach for use with children. Here are the general, neurotypical applications of play therapy:

- ◆ Ages 3–8 or so are most commonly seen in a traditional play therapy playroom.
- ◆ Ages 8–12 begin to use sandtray therapy, therapeutic board games, expressive arts and puppets, and other forms of activity therapy.
- ◆ Ages 11 and 12 through adulthood use sandtray therapy, clay, collages, drawing, drama, writing, movement, music, and more.

Several of these activities were part of Lowenfeld's original play therapy process, including a sand tray (the World Technique), art, music, water, and movement (Lowenfeld, 1979). A garden was accessible, just outside her playroom (Lowenfeld, 1979). Today many of these activities have developed into unique therapies of their own. They would include but are not limited to sandtray therapy, Sandplay therapy, art therapy, music therapy, and movement therapy. Even nature play therapy.

This guide will focus on working with children 12 years old and younger; however, the documentation applies to all ages. There are many clinical theories applied to play therapy. Research indicates that Child-Centered Play Therapy (CCPT) is the most commonly taught in graduate school (Ryan et al., 2002). Also used are Adlerian Play Therapy (AdPT), Gestalt Play Therapy (GPT), Cognitive-Behavioral Play Therapy (CBPT), and others. See Figure 1.1

Figure 1.1 Play therapy theories

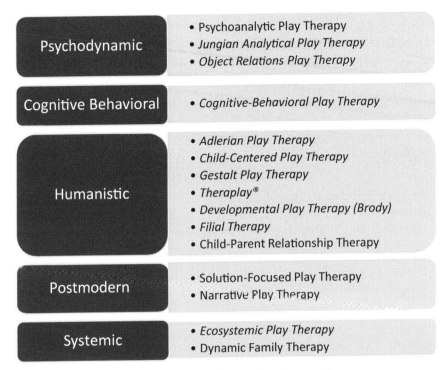

Psychodynamic	• Psychoanalytic Play Therapy • *Jungian Analytical Play Therapy* • *Object Relations Play Therapy*
Cognitive Behavioral	• *Cognitive-Behavioral Play Therapy*
Humanistic	• *Adlerian Play Therapy* • *Child-Centered Play Therapy* • *Gestalt Play Therapy* • *Theraplay®* • *Developmental Play Therapy (Brody)* • *Filial Therapy* • Child-Parent Relationship Therapy
Postmodern	• Solution-Focused Play Therapy • Narrative Play Therapy
Systemic	• *Ecosystemic Play Therapy* • Dynamic Family Therapy

Italicized items are APT's Seminal & Historically Significant Play Therapy Theories

*Terry Kottman stated using a Venn Diagram, AdPT would be in the overlap of psychodynamic, cognitive behavioral, and humanistic. Personal communication, February 21, 2022.

for play therapy theories organized by the movements in the development of psychotherapy. APT's seminal and historically significant theories are identified with italics.

Charles Schaefer and colleagues developed Prescriptive Play Therapy and Integrative Play Therapy. Prescriptive Play Therapy is based on the premise that different theories of play therapy are more effective to treat specific disorders (Schaefer & Peabody, 2016). The Prescriptive Play Therapist selects the play therapy theory based in research for the given diagnosed disorder and uses it with a specific child. Integrative Play Therapy involves using two or more elements from different play therapy theories to create a unique treatment approach for a particular child (Schaefer & Peabody, 2016). Both of these approaches require the play therapist to be competent in several play therapy theories and well-read in play therapy research.

As a growing field, newer approaches and models are being developed. Some of these are Storyplay® by Joyce Mills, TraumaPlay™ by Paris Goodyear-Brown, Attachment Centered Play Therapy by Clair Mellenthin, AutPlay® by Robert Jason Grant, and FirstPlay® by Janet Courtney.

Working from a clinical theory, approach, or model will assist the play therapist in understanding their work with the play therapy client and parents. Examples of session notes for various clinical theories are provided. Suggestions for tailor-making session forms (and many additional forms described throughout this book) and reproducible samples are provided in the appendices. These assist in streamlining the documentation process. It will also help the play therapist focus their work and understanding of the play therapy process.

Some of these elements of the overall case and subsequent documentation are shorter in duration than others. Some are lengthy and will go on for months, such as the actual play therapy treatment. Parent consultations vary in frequency and duration, depending on the case. A treatment plan is a fluid, organic document, while also specific and measurable. Written at the beginning of the therapeutic process, treatment plans may change as time and treatment move along. Session notes are a written record of what occurred in the play therapy session, including play themes and movement toward goals. Parent consultations describe contact with parents to update them on the progress of the treatment of their child. Importantly, consultations also detail the collaboration to implement changes to maximize the prognosis. Finally, at the end of the process is a termination summary. There are also contacts with parents, results of any testing and assessments, possible reports, collateral contacts with appropriate release of information documents, medication records, correspondence, and more.

This guide provides detailed information about each component. There are forms, worksheets, and tip sheets to assist you in developing your own unique guidelines for your practice. These are general enough to apply, hopefully, to each of you who read this book. We hope you feel free to adapt any of the worksheets and forms to fit your unique approach to play therapy and your work setting. Several of these forms are available on the Routledge website. You can download from there and reformat and edit for your specific professional use.

The Golden Thread

The concept of the *golden thread* is used in many settings. The golden thread is a metaphor for linking various parts together to keep each informed of the other for a consistent overall focus. In business, it refers to ensuring all activity is aligned with the mission plan, goals, and vision. It is also referred to as *organizational alignment*. In academic writing, the golden thread pulls the reader through the author's overall argument. The author's posited idea or research hypothesis runs through the professional article from the opening to the closing. In mental health, the golden thread has been used in the field of addiction treatment to bring together and guide all the clinicians, therapists, social workers, medical assistants, and others involved in various aspects of the treatment protocol. More generally, the golden thread of mental health documentation provides anyone reviewing a case file to see the consistent logic of all the components of the client treatment and the subsequent record. Mental health treatment, in most settings, needs to be identified as a medical necessity. In such cases, all the details of the clinical records support the treatment of that medical necessity. In these and other settings, the *standard of care* and *best practices* are easily substantiated through the observance of the golden thread. It weaves its way throughout and ties together all the various parts of the documentation. This guide will follow the golden thread of documentation (Figure 1.2).

Using This Guide

This guide aims to provide basic information about constructing a complete case file from beginning to end. What is offered here is best practices. It protects you as the therapist and provides the provision of an optimal level of care for the client. Having a consistent protocol for your case

Figure 1.2 Golden thread of documentation

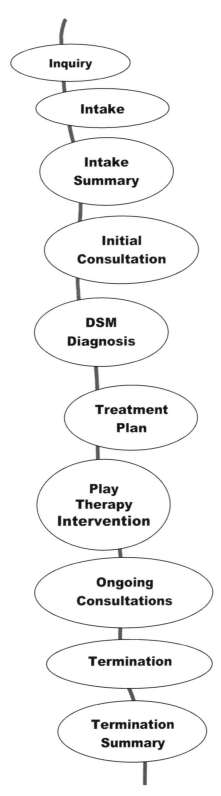

files establishes your level of professionalism. Treating all clients with the same level of care, appropriately and consistently documented, provides legal safety. As equally, or more importantly, it gives the play therapist freedom to do the work. An established routine facilitates our thinking and writing. Reducing the time needed to write documentation frees us up. The golden thread assists us in staying focused on the client's therapeutic needs and aligns our work to meet those needs. It frees us in casework and planning. We become more effective and congruent. More about how to do this will be detailed in each chapter that focuses on each component.

There is a *Resources* section at the end of each chapter to extend the information covered. Readers may be interested in specific areas discussed in the chapter, and we provide additional options for exploring their interests. While not all-inclusive, we hope these resources are helpful. These resources may be ones we use, recommend to our clients or supervisees, or know about. Of course, you may know of others and have especially trusted resources. The play therapy field has grown (and continues to expand), and with it, an abundant number of books, trainings, and conferences to broaden our knowledge base.

There are limits to what this guide offers. Play therapists reading this guide represent various mental health disciplines and practice in different geographic areas and jurisdictions. It is beyond the scope of this guide to cover discipline-specific ethical guidelines. We always defer to your designated code of ethics. Not only do codes of ethics vary from discipline to discipline, but they also change over time. Reviewing the codes of ethics periodically keeps them fresh. Also, our professional associations and licensing entities often alert us of changes. The Association for Play Therapy has a *Play Therapy Best Practices* and a *Paper on Touch* documents. Other play therapy associations worldwide also have codes and guidelines specific to play therapy.

The same limits are true for legal requirements. Licensure and certification laws and rules vary by state and country. Administrative and statute laws change, and new case law is frequently added. These impact both our clients and our clinical work. For example, while in private practice, I (Linda) kept up with the changes in the Texas Family Code. I wanted to be aware of significant changes in the law. My caseload consisted primarily of children in legal situations, and I found an *Annotated Texas Family Code* very useful to easily identify such changes. Although I was very careful not to give legal advice and frequently referred parents to seek the advice of their attorneys, I felt more confident in my work when I kept up with family law. State professional conferences may provide continuing education opportunities regarding new case law that impacts mental health practice.

A final limitation to this guide: It is not meant to inform the reader how to do play therapy. There are many other books, training, and graduate courses that do that. This is about how to document the entire process of the client's work of play therapy and the importance of parent consultations.

Importance of Professional Liability Insurance

Professional liability insurance protects us. We may be diligent in our ethical practice. We may be well trained and competent. We may seek consultation when needed. We may do all the "right" things yet still find ourselves in need of legal counsel. Regardless of how well we do our jobs, disgruntled clients or parents can take legal action or file complaints with our licensure boards or certification bodies. Parents may be in court for divorce, custody, or modification of custody. Subpoenas are served; parents request copies of records. Situations will arise in our clinical practices for which we need a legal consultation or opinion.

Play therapists in private practice know the importance of having professional liability insurance. Those working in other settings like agencies, schools, doing volunteer work, and such should also have their own liability insurance and not depend on the insurance of the organization for which they work or volunteer (Wheeler & Bertram, 2019). Having one's own insurance is an added layer of protection, as the organization's insurance protects the organization. While some of that coverage may extend to you, in some circumstances, it may not.

Most play therapists begin their relationship with a professional liability company while in graduate school. Most programs require student coverage when one begins seeing their first clients. Upon graduation and segueing to postgraduate work, it is easy to simply upgrade that insurance. However, one may benefit from reviewing various companies and their plans. Some plans have a sponsorship relationship with professional associations. Some plans provide free legal consultations before any legal filings are made against the play therapist. The ability to access a legal consultation amid an ethical dilemma or legal concern before a case is filed is reassuring. Some companies will handle responses and give guidance when a subpoena is served, or a request for client files is received. Knowing you have legal counsel when needed is comforting. Some play therapists have their own independent counsel who is a member of their community and do not rely upon the liability insurance company. Of course, this comes at an additional cost.

Also, there are two types of coverage:

♦ *Claims-made coverage:* This type covers claims actually made while the policy is in force. Under this form, coverage stops at the end of the policy year. Therefore, to retain coverage one must continually renew the policy or obtain tail coverage. [Tail coverage extends coverage post-termination of the policy.]

♦ *Occurrence coverage:* This type covers claims for alleged acts that occurred while the policy was in effect, even if the claim is made several years later, after the policy is no longer in force (Wheeler & Bertram, 2019, p. 241).

Further exploration of the details and considerations of the selection of a professional liability insurance company is essential. As with all mental health professionals, play therapists have invested a great deal of time and resources to obtain their license, certification, or registration. Professional liability insurance protects us and our investment in ourselves and our practices.

Importance of Supervision and Consultation

As play therapists, we all need input from another play therapist from time to time. We will discuss this in more detail in Chapter 12: Professional Growth Considerations. For now, give thought to those situations where we can benefit from, and even *need*, another's wisdom, knowledge, experience, and expertise. It is a matter of having a valued colleague with whom to talk through a perplexing situation. These discussions are valued for not only the care of our clients but also for our own self-care. The play therapist working toward their mental health licensure or certification will likely be required to be in supervision for a specific length of time or while logging a specified number of clinical hours. Once licensed for independent practice, participating in a regular play therapy consultation group can be a wise choice. The ongoing support of other play therapists can be gratifying. Having a few colleagues with whom to connect for consultations on an as-needed basis is essential.

In many countries, participation in ongoing consultation is a requirement to practice. They cannot imagine providing ethical services without doing so. Although this is not a *requirement* to practice in the United States, certainly engaging in consultation is an enriching and enlightening activity.

Resources

- ◆ *Play Therapy Best Practices* and *Paper on Touch*, Association for Play Therapy, www.a4pt.org/page/Research
- ◆ Books, play therapy theory specific:
  - Adlerian Play Therapy
    - *Partners in Play* (3rd ed.), Terry Kottman & Kristin Meany-Walen, American Counseling Association, 2016.
    - *Doing Play Therapy*, Terry Kottman & Kristin Meany-Walen, Guilford Press, 2018.
  - Child-Centered Play Therapy
    - *Play Therapy: The Art of the Relationship* (4th ed.), Garry Landreth, Routledge, in press.
    - *Advanced Play Therapy*, Dee Ray, Routledge, 2011.
  - Cognitive-Behavioral Play Therapy
    - *Cognitive-Behavioral Play Therapy*, Susan Knell, Aronson, 1993.
  - Family Dynamic Play Therapy
    - *Dynamic Play Therapy*. Steve Harvey. In C. E. Schaefer & H. G. Kaduson (Eds.), *Contemporary play therapy: Theory, research, and practice*, Guilford Press, 2006.
  - Gestalt Play Therapy
    - *Windows to Our Children*, Violet Oaklander, The Center for Gestalt Development, 1988.
  - Narrative Play Therapy
    - *Narrative Play Therapy*, Aideen Taylor de Faoite (Ed.), Jessica Kingsley, 2011.
  - Prescriptive Play Therapy
    - *Prescriptive Play Therapy*, Heidi Kaduson, Donna Cangelosi, & Charles Schaefer, Guilford Press, 2020.
  - Solution-Focused Play Therapy
    - *Solution-Focused Play Therapy*, Elizabeth Kjellstrand Hartwig, Routledge, 2021.
  - Integrative Play Therapy
    - *Integrative Play Therapy*, Athena Drewes, Sue Bratton, & Charles Schaefer, Wiley, 2011.

- ♦ Books, other:
  - *Advance Sandtray Therapy: Digging Deeper into Clinical Practice*, Linda E. Homeyer & Marshall Lyles, Routledge, 2022.
  - *Attachment Centered Play Therapy*, Claire Mellenthin, Routledge, 2019.
  - *AutPlay Therapy for Children and Adolescents on the Autism Spectrum* (3rd ed.), Robert Jason Grant, Routledge, 2017.
  - *The AutPlay Therapy Handbook: Integrative Family Play Therapy for Neurodivergent Children*, Robert Jason Grant, Routledge, 2022.
  - *Game Play: Therapeutic Use of Games With Children and Adolescents* (3rd ed.), Jessica Stone & Charles Schaefer (Eds.), Wiley Press, 2020.
  - *Nature-based Play and Expressive Therapies: Interventions for Children, Teens, and Families*, Janet Courtney, Jamie Lynn Langley, Louise Wonders, Rosalind Heiko, & Rose Lapiere (Eds.), Routledge, 2022.
  - *Play Therapy for Preschool Children*, Charles Schaefer (Ed.), American Psychological Association, 2010.
  - *Play Therapy with Adults*, Charles Schaefer (Ed.), Wiley, 2003.
  - *Puppet Play Therapy: A Practical Guidebook,* Athena Drewes & Charles Schaefer (Eds.), Routledge, 2018.
  - *Sandtray Therapy: A Practical Manual* (4th ed.), Linda E. Homeyer & Daniel Sweeney, Routledge, 2023.
  - *Therapeutic Metaphors for Children and the Child Within*, Joyce Mills & Richard J. Crowley, Routledge, 2014.
  - *Trauma Play Therapy*, Paris Goodyear-Brown, Routledge, 2019.
- ♦ Other therapy modalities:
  - American Association for Art Therapy, https://arttherapy.org/
  - American Music Therapy Association, www.musictherapy.org/
  - American Dance Therapy Association (includes movement), www.adta.org/
  - International Society for Sandplay Therapy, www.isst-society.com/
  - World Association for Sand Therapy Professionals, www.worldsandtherapy.com/

References

Association for Play Therapy. (2022, January 12). *Definition of play therapy.* www.a4pt.org/page/AboutAPT

Homeyer, L., & Lyles, M. (2022). *Advanced sandtray therapy: Digging deeper into clinical practice.* Routledge.

Lowenfeld, M. (1979). *Understanding children's sandplay: Lowenfeld's world technique.* George Allen & Unwin.

Lowenfeld, M., & Dukes, E. (1938). Play therapy and child guidance. *The British Medical Journal, 2,* 4067.

Ryan, S. D., Gomory, T., & Lacasse, J. R. (2002). Who are we? Examining the results of the Association for Play Therapy membership survey. *International Journal of Play Therapy, 11*(2), 11–41. https://doi.org/10.1037/h0088863

Schaefer, C., & Peabody, M. A. (2016). Towards semantic clarity in play therapy. *International Journal of Play Therapy, 25*(6), 197–202. https://doi.org/10.1037/pla0000025

Schottelkorb, A., Swan, K., & Ogawa, Y. (2015). Parent consultation in child-centered play therapy: A model for research and practice. *International Journal of Play Therapy, 24*(4), 221–233. https://doi.org/10.1037/a0039609

Wheeler, A. M., & Bertram, B. (2019). *The counselor and the law* (8th ed.). American Counseling Association.

Chapter 2

Inquiry Through Intake Summary

Welcome to the initial pre-treatment phase. This preliminary process establishes the standard of care and begins initial documentation. For most play therapists, this phase is before face-to-face contact with the parents or client. This begins with receiving an inquiry and sorting through that initial decision-making process. Issues surrounding screening an inquiry are reviewed using the *Inquiry Decision-Making Worksheet*. Once the inquiry is assessed as within your scope of practice, the initial parent consultation appointment is made, and intake documents are sent. Guidelines for the initial parent conversation are covered, including essential topics and parameters to be set. The chapter examines important intake documents, including the *Intake Form, Informed Consent for Treatment, Child Background Form*, and court orders as needed. Finally, the intake summary is written to synthesize this initial information together and look at it through a clinical theory lens. The use of an *Intake Form* provides the play therapist a place to collect all the current case information and a checklist to verify all information and forms are provided to the parent before the initial parent consultation. In preparation for that first appointment, the play therapist reviews all the information and writes an intake summary. Sample forms are available in Appendix A.

> Inquiry
> Intake Documents
> Intake Summary

The Inquiry

The phone call comes . . . the email arrives:

Can you see my son in play therapy? Noah is 3-years-old and is constantly in trouble at day care. He is also fighting all the time with his older sister. Please let me know if you are taking new clients. The day-care director said he'd be kicked out if he's not getting play therapy. This is the last day care in town that will take him, and we cannot lose it.

My name is Alicia Rodriguez. Please call me back as soon as you can at 555–222–1010.

This is an inquiry. The play therapist might have set up an automatic response to emails or as part of their telephone message system that indicates the time frame for a response. This

DOI: 10.4324/9781003258766-3

Figure 2.1 Inquiry decision-making worksheet

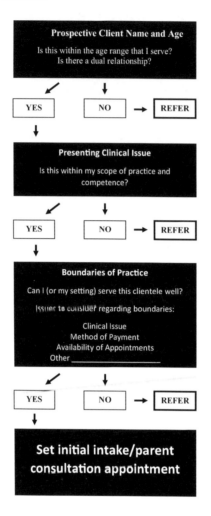

might be 24 or 72 hours. The play therapist can always respond earlier but should respect the maximum time. Remember, the parent is anxiously awaiting your returned call.

Using the *Inquiry Decision-Making Worksheet* (Figure 2.1), the play therapist's first task is to ensure that the inquiry is within their boundaries of practice.

- ♦ *Is the prospective client within the age range I serve?* If this is affirmative, then it's on to the next question. Many play therapists, of course, see clients of all ages, so this would be a non-question needing consideration. Other play therapists may only see specific age ranges. If outside your age range, then refer. Next,
- ♦ *Do I have a dual relationship with this family?* The dual relationship issue can become more complex. If the play therapist has children of their own, it is very common to receive inquiries from your child's peer group. You may not want to complicate your own child's play dates and birthday party invitations with seeing one of their peers as a client. Or, if you have been seeing an adult client who later wants you to see their child in play therapy. How would you handle that? Or, if you are seeing one child and then the parent wants you to see a younger sibling? Some of these may or may not imply a dual relationship. If you practice in a small town or other community setting, you need to decide how to manage the inevitable dual relationship. For

example, there may not be another play therapist to whom to refer to if you practice in a small town. Knowing how to manage all these possible scenarios is critical. We discuss dual relationship in more detail in Chapter 3: Initial Parent Consultation.

Once these are decided, and you continue to move forward, be sure the presenting clinical issue is within your scope of practice and an area of competence. You need to already have clarified these for yourself.

Is this presenting clinical issue within my:

♦ Scope of practice?
♦ Competence?
♦ Ability to provide standard of care?

Having clear answers to these questions is essential to remain ethical (and legal) in your practice and provide efficacious care to clients. A review of these terms may be helpful.

♦ *Scope of practice* is generally defined as the professional activities one may provide within a specific profession. Wheeler and Bertram (2019) remind us that this will be legally defined differently by each mental health discipline and by statutes in each state. Each play therapist can also further set their own boundaries of practice of the clients and issues they choose to serve and not serve. For example, I (Linda) decided only to see young children, not adolescents. I know another play therapist who also sees adolescents and adults. However, she chooses not to see those seeking treatment for eating disorders.
♦ *Competence* begins with education, training, and supervision. It continues as a life-long endeavor (Corey et al., 2019). It includes continuing education, supervision, and consultation as needed, and recognizing any impairment that may occur along life's journey (Wheeler & Bertram, 2019). All the ethical codes of mental health disciplines define competence. This particularly applies to mental health professionals who promote themselves as having a specialty, such as play therapy. If promoting yourself as a play therapist, ethically you need play therapy-specific training, experience, and supervision or consultation in the area of play therapy. Part of competence is the public expectation to receive a *standard of care*.
♦ *Standard of care* is defined as the degree of competence that the public expects to be provided to the community, setting, or role in which the professionals work (Merriam-Webster.com). A question to ask yourself is: *Would another play therapist, reviewing my client files, be able to verify that I provided what is typically expected of a play therapist practicing in my setting?* If so, then you have met the expectation of standard of care.

Other questions occur in response to the inquiry. Does this inquiry fit the boundaries of my practice setting? Play therapists practice in many different settings: schools, agencies, community centers, hospitals, private practices, and so on. Some settings will have specific parameters for clients they accept and those they do not. This might include the payment method for services: Is there a family income criteria, is insurance required (and if so, do I take that insurance), private pay, meeting any funding grant criteria, and so on. Other agencies may require specific presenting issues, such as if the child is a victim of abuse or family violence. Awareness of one's service boundaries is essential, so appropriate referrals can be made.

The No Surprises Act is a federal law that went into effect in January 2022. At the writing of this book, this law is new and there are unanswered questions regarding the obligations of mental health professionals to implement this specific law. Legal professionals recommend disclosing your fee on your website, on the appointment confirmation email, and in your professional disclosure statement. A good faith estimate of the cost of services is required in writing once the client comes for the initial intake. Given the early nature of this law, we recommend seeking legal advice from an attorney knowledgeable in mental health law in your area.

Having referrals readily available when responding to an inquiry is part of best practices. This allows the play therapist to provide options at the moment of interacting with the person making the inquiry, rather than responding later (adding to your workload) or leaving the person without viable alternatives (ethically questionable). Many communities have referral lists available through their community mental health agency. Play therapists also develop their own list of other professionals they know and trust or meet the inquiring person's specific needs.

A common situation for play therapists is the limited availability of after-school appointments. Learning how to manage a waiting list is a must. Also, thinking creatively, perhaps by offering group play therapy. Group play therapy can be very therapeutic for children experiencing social anxiety and peer relationship issues. Also, group play therapy is often used with children experiencing similar

> Initial conversation checklist:
>
> * Reconfirm scope of practice
> * Set appointment
> * Inform re: paperwork
> * Get permission to contact and what means to use (phone, text, email)
>
> MANAGE TIME & CONTENT

presenting issues, such as divorce, family violence, and grief. Heterogeneous groups are also effective. A group that includes children with various issues can expand understanding and provide vicarious learning. A play therapist might begin children in individual sessions and then segue them into groups. Remember, if adding *group* play therapy to your practice, then competence is again an issue. So, seek training and supervision.

Scheduling Initial Parent Consultation

This first interactive contact begins the therapeutic relationship. This might typically be the play therapist making a phone call, especially if additional screening information is needed. Sometimes, the parent's inquiry email will provide sufficient information to set up the intake appointment, also by email. This is a judgment call by the play therapist. What we don't want to happen is have a parent come in for the initial consultation, only to find out that their need is not within your scope of practice.

The first contact is handled with professionalism and care. It is the play therapist's responsibility to manage the time and content of the conversation. Setting healthy boundaries beginning with this first contact establishes parameters for the relationship. One way to stay on track is to use an *Intake Form*. See Table 2.1. It can also be found in Appendix A.

Ethical and legal obligations are embedded in the therapeutic relationship. While seeking to obtain sufficient information to screen for appropriateness, the play therapist must also be aware of time management. This is *not* an initial session. Staying in control of the conversation is a necessary skill. Parents frequently start to disclose too much information, sharing their situation, their child's problems, and more. The play therapist needs to manage the conversation with sensitivity while obtaining any additional information necessary to continue completing the decision-making process to confirm the appropriateness for your practice.

Begin the conversation by reviewing the intake details again to ensure the case meets your scope of practice. Occasionally parents withhold information in this conversation, intentionally or unintentionally. The play therapist's questions may reveal new information pertinent to their scope of practice. Asking the parent, *"can you tell me in two to three sentences what you are looking for?"* is one way to provide some boundaries on the length and amount of details of information for which the play therapist is looking. It also may reveal that they are looking for a speech therapist or occupational therapist. Making an appropriate referral at this juncture saves time for both parties.

Once confirmed as appropriate for your practice, setting an initial parent consultation appointment follows. Some play therapists schedule the initial parent consultation for a longer time than a typical appointment to allow additional time for necessary information gathering, and relationship building. Others may schedule two regular-length sessions. The play therapist's discipline may also impact this initial consultation experience. Marriage and family therapists may desire two or more sessions to explore family of origin issues and work through genograms. School counselors may not have any parent contact, depending on the school district policies. The classroom teacher serves as the source of information. Clearly, how these decisions are made needs to be a part of your regular, standard practice. *Establish your procedure*. If you need to change your typical procedure because of the dynamics of a particular case, document the rationale in your client's file.

Encourage the parent making the inquiry to have all parents attend this initial parent consultation. This is particularly helpful if the parents are divorced, but co-parenting. Developing a collaborative relationship with all those who are parenting the child client is the most effective working model. This might also include other adults in the home, like grandparents or stepparents. In such situations, refer to the legal custody documents to be sure who can be present. For example, a *Consent for Release of Information* (ROI) form might be required for the stepparent to participate in parent consultations. (See sample in Appendix A.) In which case, you may need that signed ROI before the beginning of the initial parent consultation. I (Linda) have had many cases where it is the stepmother who transports the child to play therapy and is the one who provides ongoing information and updates on the child and their behavior. This may also pertain to a nanny or other family member who transports the child to and from sessions. Inevitably, they also provide information about the child's behavior or pass along a message from the parent. Having an ROI in place easily covers all such situations. Chapter 8: Parents Who Challenge Us and Chapter 9: Difficult Parenting Issues offer a deeper discussion of co-parenting and surrounding issues.

Finally, the parents attend this initial consultation without children, either the client child, or siblings. The adults need to have this time to discuss issues without the distraction of caring for and attending to children. We acknowledge some disciplines (like Marriage and Family Therapists) or other approaches may desire all family numbers attend this initial session.

Also, consider the possible legal and ethical implications. What happens if the parent discloses possible child abuse during that appointment-making phone call? You don't yet have a signed informed consent. The parent may know you are mandated to report child abuse, but they may not. There are also other such limitations to confidentiality of which the parent has not yet consented. They may assume that their conversation with a therapist is privileged communication, like with an attorney or physician. Most mental health professionals do not have privileged communication, but rules of confidentiality. It is our responsibility to manage this. Play therapists place themselves and the parent in jeopardy if too much information about the case is given and discussed during this first conversation.

During this initial conversation, also advise the parent of the paperwork to be completed before attending the initial consultation session. Electronic health record (EHR) platforms provide client portals through which all necessary paperwork can be sent, completed by the parent, and confidentially returned before the initial parent consultation. The play therapist might work in an agency or other setting where the administrative staff takes care of this. The play therapist may email paperwork to the parent and ask it be returned before the initial parent consultation session or ask the parent to arrive early to the session to complete the paperwork. There is the advantage of having paperwork completed before the first session. The play therapist has time to review it and further focus the questions and topics for the initial parent consultation.

Table 2.1 Intake form

Intake Form
Date of Inquiry: _____Date of Follow-up: _____ _____
Inquiring Parent:
_____   _____
Name   Contact preferred: phone/text/email
_____ Permission to leave messages
Client Information:
___ Age of Client
___ Dual Relationship
___ Presenting Issue
_____
_____
_____
_____
___ Within Scope of Practice & Competence
___ Method of Payment: Insurance/Private Pay/Other _____
Initial Intake Parent Appointment:_____
People attending (and role): _____
___ Forms sent; Date: _____
___ Informed Consent for Treatment
___ Child Background Form
___ Professional Disclosure
___ Release of Information as needed for stepparent, etc.
___ Other: such as HIPAA, Privacy Policies, etc. _____
___ Confirmed who is authorized to consent for treatment (circle status below)
Married/Divorced/Never married/Widowed/Other: _____
___ Requested divorce decree, custody orders

Determining the legal guardians of the prospective child client is paramount. This is the reason to address it in this initial conversation. In most jurisdictions, it is the responsibility of the play therapist to verify who is authorized to consent for treatment. If the parents are divorced, the play therapist needs a copy of the legal documentation. Unmarried parents may also have legal documentation regarding their rights pertaining to the child. In some jurisdictions, the play therapist must obtain and review a copy of the divorce decree and custody orders to confirm who is authorized to consent for treatment and payment for mental health services. Some disciplines, like psychologists, may not be required to maintain copies in the case file. Other disciplines are required to do so. Regardless, keeping a copy would fall under best practices.

Custody orders and divorce decrees can be confusing and complicated. These are legal documents drafted by attorneys, approved by a judge, or in a court of law, using legal language confusing to many play therapists. Here are some, but not all, of the terms to be aware of. Each of these terms has complex definitions and specifically unique details:

- Managing conservator: the person given legal rights to make specific, designated decisions about the child; usually the person with whom the child resides.
- Possessory conservator: the parent or person who is granted visitation and other stated rights, not the person with whom the child primarily resides.
- Joint managing conservator: typically when both parents are given equal legal rights to make specific, designated decisions about the child; sometimes this means the child resides at the home of each parent, rotating for a specified length of time, such as weekly. This varies, so read the orders in detail.
- Sole managing conservator: the only parent or person with the legal rights to make specific, designated decisions about the child.
- Permanent managing conservator: a legally designated person responsible for a child without adoption. Sometimes this is an extended family member like a grandparent, aunt or uncle, or a previous foster parent.

Even though legal documents may be lengthy, the play therapist needs to read through the entire document. Further details regarding the responsibilities and limitations granted to the conservator may be located later in the document. The play therapist is seeking to identify who is given the legal authority to consent to psychological services or counseling. Orders may only mention *medical services*, which, unless expressly excluded, include counseling and psychological services. Some orders indicate if these decisions can be made individually, require consultation with the other parent, or consent of the other parent. These are detailed requirements. Also, your licensing board may have additional conditions regarding the extent to which the play therapist must be sure the orders are complied with. Consult with a more experienced play therapist in your area, or contact an attorney when in doubt. Having this information before the signing of the *Informed Consent for Treatment* is understandably required. This also impacts who has access to the child's ongoing therapy information or the client file. More on that later in Chapter 8, Parents Who Challenge Us.

Also, be aware that the original orders can be modified, so ask for the most current order. The orders should be signed by all parties. Parties may negotiate changes during the signing process, indicating agreement only once all parties have signed. The order must have an official stamp or seal on the front of the document indicating it has been filed with the appropriate office. In the United States, it typically means the District Clerk's Office for the applicable District Court. The document is not official without this stamp. This is the one needed for the client file as part of the documentation.

A special note here. In most jurisdictions, the parents are *legally* the client. Minors do not have these legal rights. However, in this book, unless specifically stated, we will refer to the child as our client. In these references, we are speaking of the child as our *clinical* client. Of course, family systems therapists would consider the entire family unit as the *clinical* client. We hope this clarifies our usage of the term *client*.

Intake Documents

In preparation for the initial parent consultation, specific paperwork is legally required. As mentioned earlier, paperwork can be sent to the parent before the appointment through the EHR client portal or secure or encrypted email. Suggestions will be made for each item, but the reader should have all forms reviewed for their specific practice. See Figure 2.1; also, a sample *Intake Form* can be found in Appendix A.

Documentation
Intake Form
Informed Consent for Treatment
Child Background Form

Informed Consent for Treatment

The *Informed Consent for Treatment* form is required. From our very first encounter with clients, we are taught to have it signed before beginning any counseling process. Often, the *informed* part of this can get lost along the way. We know the informed consent form must be signed to ethically and legally provide play therapy (and all other counseling). Too often, we rush to get the signature and then move on to what we consider the more important part of the intake session. This is particularly easy when a parent signs it through an EHR client portal. However, the parent (and any client) deserves to be fully informed about several issues concerning the play therapy experience. The signed form is the documentation that the parents understand, and thus *informed*, of the contents. Here are the primary issues our parents should know about to be genuinely informed and most effectively accomplished through a discussion:

♦ The play therapist's name, credentials, and contact information
♦ Limits of confidentiality (mandatory reporting of abuse; danger to self or others; agency or insurance company access to files, subpoenas, etc.)
♦ Definition of play therapy and explain clinical approach or theory in user-friendly terms
♦ Possible impact of the process of play therapy, including risks and limitations
♦ Role of parents and parent consultations
♦ Appointments (scheduling, cancellation, and no-show policy)
♦ Fees and charges (session fees, special charges for writing reports, providing a copy of files, testifying in court, etc.)
♦ How to communicate (through messaging option of the EHR, limitation of electronic communication)

- Use of consultation or notification of supervision relationship
- File retention policy, how to access files if play therapist is incapacitated or dies
- Any required licensure statements on how to handle client complaints

These components are typical. Based on the play therapist's discipline and licensure or certification rules, additional content may be required.

A review of these areas provides the parent the chance to discuss and explore them, to be truly informed about what they are signing or have signed electronically before the session. This time is part of developing the therapeutic relationship. Hearing concerns, expressing respect, developing the give-and-take of questions and answers all work together to build a working relationship.

Professional Disclosure Statement

A *Professional Disclosure Statement* is information specifically about you. In some instances, this information may be included in the *Informed Consent*. However, in many agencies, there is a standard, generic *Informed Consent* used by everyone. The *Professional Disclosure Statement* provides you an opportunity to detail information unique to you. The content includes:

- Qualifications: your education and certifications, if any
- Experience: licensure, length of time practicing
- Nature of counseling: explain play therapy and your theoretical approach

See Appendix A for both a template and a completed sample.

Child Background Form

A *Child Background Form* is an efficient way to collect information from the parent. It includes basic demographic information, including family members and residence; information specific to the child's developmental history, any neurodivergent characteristics; educational and health status; current or previous medical and psychological diagnosis with current medication. Including a checklist about current behavior provides the parent with various options. During the initial consultation, a parent may overlook or fail to recall all helpful information or concerning behavior. This can occur because they are overwhelmed or not fully aware of additional behaviors that may be important and useful for the play therapist to know. The background form offers the structure to assist a parent in providing the information needed regarding the client, their family, and the presenting issue. It also provides a place for the parent to identify the child's areas of strength and resilience giving a more a complete picture of the child and not focus only on the problem. See sample form in Appendix A.

Reviewing this information before the initial parent consultation session informs the play therapist about the client and provides more details regarding the presenting issue. Also, the form documents the parent verifying their legal guardian status and other demographic information.

Court Documents

What is needed in this section will vary by the specific case. Some child clients and their families have no court involvement and, therefore, will not have such documents.

Other children may have divorced parents, a remarried parent, a stepparent, or a court-assigned attorney ad litem. The most common documents are divorce decrees and custody orders. Custody orders were discussed earlier in the chapter regarding identifying the person authorized to consent for treatment. Being aware of what is required by the play therapist's licensing board is critical. All obtained copies of legal documents, such as a divorce decree or custody orders, become a part of the intake packet and the clinical file.

Intake Summary

The intake summary synthesizes the information pertinent to the presenting issue at this point in the new case. Many details may be significant and used in the treatment process, but this summary is only a few sentences, providing the essence of the intake information. Completing the summary assists the play therapist in focusing their attention as they prepare for the initial parent consultation. It might read something like this:

Noah, 3 years old, and his 5-year-old sister are experiencing intense sibling rivalry based on a change of family dynamics. This is demonstrated by attacking and bullying his sister, noncompliance with family rules, alternately pouting with being aggressive. Noah also lacks a desire to connect with others, as shown in similar behavioral difficulties at day care: apparent inability to manage self-control, displayed by his aggressive, noncompliant, controlling behavior.

The intake summary may also reflect the clinical theory of the play therapist:

Noah, 3 years old, and his 5-year-old sister are experiencing intense sibling rivalry based on a change of their family constellation. This is demonstrated by attacking and bullying his sister, noncompliance with family rules, alternately pouting and being aggressive. Noah also lacks social interest and does not connect well with peers, as shown in similar behavioral difficulties at day care: apparent inability to manage self-control, displayed by his aggressive, noncompliant, controlling behavior.

As the reader will note, there are a few Adlerian Play Therapy terms: family constellation, social interest, and connect (one of the Crucial Cs). Introducing clinical theory in this summary documents the beginning of the golden thread of the reasoning for the therapeutic interventions, which continue with the case formulation, diagnosis, treatment plan, and play therapy sessions.

At this point in the case, the play therapist meets with the parent for the initial parent consultation. If all these steps are taken, the play therapist has the beginning of a case conceptualization in their mind. This informs the play therapist of specific information they will be seeking in the parent consultation. The play therapist is ready!

Resources

- *Ethical, Legal, and Professional Issues in the Practice of Marriage and Family Therapy* (5th ed.), S. Allen Wilcoxon, Theodore P. Remeley, Jr., & Samuel Gladding, Prentice-Hall, 2013.
- *Group Play Therapy*, Daniel Sweeney, Jennifer Baggerly, & Dee Ray, Routledge, 2014.
- *The Counselor and The Law: A Guide to Legal and Ethical Practice*, Anne Marie Wheeler & Burt Bertram, American Counseling Association, 2019.
- *Handbook of Group Play Therapy*, Daniel Sweeney & Linda E. Homeyer, Routledge, 1999.
- *Implementing Play Therapy With Groups: Contemporary Issues in Practice*, Clair Mellenthin, Jessica Stone, & Robert Jason Grant, Routledge, 2022.

References

Corey, G., Corey, M. S., & Corey, C. (2019). *Issues and ethics in the helping professions* (10th ed.). Cengage Learning.

Merriam-Webster. (2016). *Merriam-Webster dictionary*. Merriam-Webster, Inc.

Wheeler, A. M., & Bertram, B. (2019). *The counselor and the law: A guide to legal and ethical practice*. American Counseling Association.

Chapter 3

Initial Parent Consultation

A critical piece along the golden thread of the therapeutic process is the initial parent consultation. Without this step, children cannot be seen in ongoing counseling. (There are obvious exceptions to this, such in school settings where parents may not be available, in residential care where parental rights may have been terminated, and so on. However, for the vast majority of settings, parent consultations are an expected part of the treatment process.) During this initial parent consultation, there is information to gather and information to give, all while managing time and building a relationship with the parents. It is easy to understand why many therapists do longer sessions or double sessions for this initial consultation. Parents should have already read and completed your *Informed Consent, Professional Disclosure, Child Background Form, and any other required documents* (see Appendix A). Play therapists need to be prepared for their initial parent consultation, confirm parents signed the necessary paperwork, and create a list of aspects of the informed consent and professional disclosure that are covered orally during the consultation. This includes limits of confidentiality, parental rights, therapist qualifications, cancellation policy, payment options, and any other aspects required by law or ethics. This information must be covered during the first consultation. Reading through their answers to the *Child Background Form* and creating follow-up questions will facilitate the session. Utilizing the *Initial Parent Consultation Preparation Form* (Table 3.1 and Appendix B) will be helpful to prepare for this initial parent consultation. The goal of this form is to help provide structure and reminders for information to give and information to gather from parents. There is also space in this form to create questions the play therapist has after reading the *Child Background Form*. Think of this as a map for the initial parent consultation. In this first consultation, a primary goal is to avoid parents feeling rushed or repeating information already provided (which may result in them feeling unheard and misunderstood).

Play therapy is often not understood by parents and it is confused with speech therapy, occupational therapy, or behavioral therapy. It is worth the investment of the play therapist's time to clarify the type of therapy the parent is looking for before the first consultation. However, as more information is gathered in this initial parent consultation, keep in mind the possibility of the need to clarify. It is important to have an awareness of one's own scope of practice and limits of expertise. If the presenting issue is something with which the play therapist has no experience or training, refer the family to another therapist. Refer back to Chapter 1: Introduction where the ethical boundaries of competence are discussed.

DOI: 10.4324/9781003258766-4

Table 3.1 Initial parent consultation preparation form

Initial Parent Consultation Preparation Form

Parent Names_____   Intake Appointment Date _____

Child's Name/Age_____

Review Informed Consent/Professional Disclosure:

- Introduce self, education, licensure, certifications or additional trainings
- Explain supervision (if applicable)
- Limits of confidentiality
- Reporting of abuse
- If I run into you in public—I will wait for you to say hello
- How records are kept (length, parent records vs. child records if applicable)
- Required statement on complaints
- Both parents included in all email (all communication is part of the record)
- Explain play therapy
- Structure and frequency of parent consultations
- Payment/Good Faith Estimate
- Best way to contact me between sessions
- Appointments/cancellations
- Impact of play therapy including risks and limits

Information to Gather:

- ROI for previous counseling or other services if necessary
- Request assessment reports from parents (if applicable)
- Parents' concerns
- Establish treatment plan goals
- Gather information to make a diagnosis
- Follow-up questions from *Child Background Form*
- Follow-up questions regarding trauma or significant events in the child's life
- Status of client's current relationships (parents, siblings, friends, teachers, other significant adults)
- How is the child functioning at school?
- What are some things your family values most?
- Walk me through your family's typical weekly schedule
- Habits, routines at home/school/after school/bedtime
- Screen time and safety
- Emotional regulation (what makes them afraid, angry, sad, joyful, hurt?)
- Frequency and intensity of behaviors
- Family time (what do you do together?)
- Responsibilities/chores for the child, do they differ from other children in the home
- What does discipline look like in your home?
- Pandemic's impact on the family, child's education, peer relationships
- Significant childhood events (loss, moves, pets, illness, trauma)
- Parental roles/style (who/how handles discipline, how do you show love, how do you handle arguments or challenges?)
- Medication

- Sleep patterns
- Strengths of child
- What do you want your child to get out of counseling? What will it look like when things are better? What are you hoping to get out of counseling?
- Broach the family's cultural identity and how it might impact your relationship with family given your cultural identity.

Information to Give:

- Explaining play therapy to the child
- What parents say to the child after sessions
- Child development
- Information on their specific situation (e.g., children's books on divorce, etc.)
- Therapist's expectations of parents at sessions (stay in waiting room/involved in sessions, length/frequency of sessions)
- Explain *Weekly Parent Feedback Form*

Treatment goal ideas:

Follow-up questions to determine diagnosis:

Questions parents may ask—what are they really asking, what are they feeling?

ASK: Is there anything you haven't shared yet? Do you feel like I understand your child and family?

As stated in the previous chapter, parents are instructed to come to this initial parent consultation without their children. This is sometimes a surprise to parents, so it is important to clarify that all children will be at school or with an appropriate caregiver during the appointment. It is best if all parents with legal rights to the child's mental health care can attend the first parent consultation. If a parent is unable to attend, it is recommended the play therapist reach out to hear this parent's perspective and to form a relationship to involve this parent in the therapeutic process moving forward.

Building the Relationship

Alicia Rodriguez does not know what to do. She never thought her child would need therapy, what has she done wrong? What does the day care think of her parenting? Alicia often finds herself leaving early from family gatherings because of Noah's behavior. Alicia's mother told her she needs to punish him more. Alicia and her husband have tried everything, including time out and reward charts, and Noah's behavior just keeps getting worse. Alicia and Raul sit down in your office. Alicia begins to cry, and Raul holds her hand.

Parents have talked with friends, family, pediatricians, caseworkers, teachers, school counselors, and behavioral specialists, long before they call a mental health provider, a play therapist. Few parents begin their parenting journey thinking their child will need counseling at a young age. The initial contact with parents is critical. If they do not feel heard, understood, and confident in their child's play therapist, they will not likely bring their child in for an appointment. Play therapists keep in mind that they are treating the human-of-the-parent, who has their own struggles, history, and possible traumas, all of which impact how that parent is in relationship with their child and the play therapist. Parents may be struggling, feel terrified, angry, hopeless, and at a loss. Putting in the initial time upfront in the relationship is important, this will enable things to go more smoothly in your work with the child in the long run.

Parents have a lot of feelings when it comes to their child and some of these may be conflicting or even unknown to the parent. Contacting a therapist puts the parent in a vulnerable position. It is the play therapist's honor to hold that vulnerability carefully. It is critical to listen, empathize, and give the parent space and time to fully discuss their concerns. Many play therapists love children but struggle with adults and have trouble remembering that while working with children, *the child is not our only client*. The child may clinically be our client, but without engaged parents, the child will not consistently attend sessions. Many parents have been hurt and criticized by other professionals; you may be the first professional who communicates *"I'm here to help you"* rather than *"This is your fault."* This initial investment of building rapport with the parents and being sensitive and responding to their feelings will help them feel a part of the therapeutic process. The parent's perception of the play therapist is one of the most important aspects of the therapeutic process.

The risk of offending the parent is high. Therefore, parents may not be open or ready for parenting recommendations in the initial parent consultation. Which is challenging, as many parents directly ask for recommendations. Play therapists can delay this feedback by saying,

Let me get to know your child more first and then we will work together to come up with a plan at home that might work better for your family.

By the end of the consultation, the intention is that the parent feels that contacting the play therapist was a good idea; they are feeling confident in the play therapy process and are hopeful for their family. The goal is for parents to feel encouraged and supported in their initiative to request therapy. Parents feeling heard, understood, and that the therapist is invested in their family is the focus.

One caveat here. There are some cases where the play therapist may not see a clear course of action, there may be several complicating factors, more information is needed, or it is unclear how their child will respond to the play therapist. It may be appropriate for the play therapist to say,

Your family's situation is complex. I assure you I will work with you to figure out how to best help your child. Let me get to know your child and we will meet again to decide how to move forward.

While focusing on developing the relationship with the parents is key, gathering information is also a goal of the first session. In a perfect setting, an 80-minute session allows time for both rapport building as well as information gathering. Rarely does a parent have a professional invest that much time talking with them about their child. To prepare for this consultation, the intake paperwork is reviewed: signed *Informed Consent* and *Professional Disclosure*, a completed *Child Background Form*, (see Appendix A) and any appropriate legal documents (see Chapter 2: Inquiry Through Intake Summary). The play therapist reviews the *Child Background Form* and completes the *Initial Parent Consultation Form* to prepare for the parent consultation. Play therapists invite parents to share their reasons for bringing their child to play therapy. As parents share their stories, play therapists are mindful of building the relationship and reflect feelings and content.

Information to Gather

The important information to gather during this session includes goals of therapy, expectations of therapy, understanding of play therapy, information on the family's culture, parent-child relationship, school concerns, and trauma history. Asking what parents love about their child, how they delight in them, as well as behaviors

Information To Gather

- Goals of therapy
- Expectations of therapy
- Family culture
- Parent-child relationship
- School concerns
- Trauma history (Intergenerational trauma)
- Family experiences during COVID-19

that are a struggle in their relationship is a good way to begin the conversation. It is essential to collect enough information to make a diagnosis using the *Diagnostic and Statistical Manual of Mental Disorders 5-TR* (DSM-5-TR; American Psychiatric Association, 2022) at the conclusion of this session. Remember all information is from the parent's perspective, so as you learn more about the child during the play therapy sessions and ongoing parent consultations this diagnosis may change. A posture of curiosity is important; follow-up and clarifying questions help the therapist maintain this posture.

Follow-up Questions for Diagnosis

It can be surprising what parents neglect to share with the play therapist. Remember that parents are not therapists and do not know what information is helpful. Therefore, do not rely solely on *The Child Background Form* for information about the family. Reflecting content and feelings, asking follow-up questions throughout the consultation keeps parents on track and helps them feel heard. Clarifying what parents mean by various expressions they use is critical for diagnosis. What one parent means by, "he's aggressive" or "she is so intense" needs clarification. Gaining clarity regarding the intensity and frequency of the child's behaviors is also important in treatment planning and diagnosis. Asking questions like,

- *What does a meltdown look like?*
- *Does your child hit or kick?*
- *Throw things?*
- *How long do these last?*
- *How often do they occur?*
- *Is there a particular time of day they usually occur?*
- *What happens before and after the meltdown?*
- *Does he struggle with emotional regulation anywhere else?*

In determining parents' goals and expectations of therapy, ask,

- *Describe what you would like it to look like when your child is angry, how would you like him to express his emotion?*

Answers to these questions can help provide information for diagnosis and treatment planning as well as help set parental expectations for therapy.

Gathering Information for Treatment Planning

Garry Landreth (2012, p. 210) uses the four healing messages, "I'm here, I hear you, I understand, and I care" in building the therapeutic relationship with children. Parents need these same attitudinal responses from the play therapist. Phrases that are helpful in responding to parents include:

> *I'm here,*
> *I hear you,*
> *I understand,*
> *and I care.*

- *That sounds exhausting, you are worn out.*
- *It is so hard when children struggle in this way.*

- *You are scared.*
- *I'm sorry that happened.*
- *You all are really struggling.*
- *I'm so glad you have come for help.*
- *Any parent would struggle in your situation.*
- *This is a lot for you to manage and for your child to manage.*

Work to accept parents where they are and believe that, generally, parents do the best they can with the information that they have, and skills they possess. Most parents do not know how to see the world through their child's eyes, have forgotten how hard it is to be a child, may not know about basic child development, or are unaware of the impact trauma can have on all areas of their child's life. They do not know that their child cannot calmly and coherently verbally express their feelings. Therefore, it is the play therapist's job to support their efforts, ease stress when possible, and provide additional tools, skills, and resources when they are ready. In listening to parents describe behaviors, the play therapist is curious about:

- Is this behavior developmentally appropriate?
- What role is development playing in this situation?
- How is this challenging for the family?
- What is the child's behavior communicating?
- What relational or material needs are not being met for the parent or child?
- What are the parents' perceptions of the child's difficulties?
- What are the requirements of the environment?
- Are these requirements reasonable?
- Does the parent have a support system in place?
- Does the parent see the world through the child's eyes?
- How frequent and intense are these behaviors?
- Is the parent regulated in these situations?
- What trauma could have occurred?
- What childhood or adult traumas have parents experienced, how are those playing a role in their parent-child relationship?
- Are there sensory seeking/avoiding behaviors?
- Does the child experience felt safety, does the parent experience felt safety?
- What techniques have the parents tried?
- Have any been successful?

These questions may or may not be asked, but they are all pieces that are used to formulate the diagnosis and theoretical conceptualization of this child.

As parents feel heard and understood they are likely to feel accepted by the play therapist, which then results in their sharing additional information more easily. This feeling of felt safety is needed for building relationships. Felt safety is critical for parents to share their heart for their child with you. Parents are the most vulnerable when bringing their child to therapy; on some level they likely believe they have failed as a parent, and therefore failed their child. Perhaps they believe it's their fault their child was abused, that their parenting is causing the aggressive behavior at home or school, that their choices are "messing up" their child. The play therapist must hold these fears and hurts and provide a space for the parent to talk about them.

As the relationship develops, useful questions for the parents are:

- *What are your strengths as a parent?*
- *What aspects of parenting are you happy with?*
- *In what areas of parenting do you need support?*
- *Are there parenting resources you have used that have been helpful or not?*
- *Is there a parenting tool you rely on in your home to make change happen?*
- *What goals do you have for your child in therapy?*
- *What will things look like in your home when there is improvement?*
- *How would you characterize your relationship with your child?*
- *What do you want your relationship to look like in 20 years?*

Do not ask every parent all of the questions noted here, but these are facilitative to develop an atmosphere of open dialogue with the parents, so they feel heard and understood. These also demonstrate the play therapist knows how difficult parenting is and this is a safe space to discuss challenges.

Robyn Gobbel (personal communication, July 13, 2021), suggests therapists ask parents questions like,

- *Am I getting this?*
- *Do you feel like I have a good understanding of what is going on at home?*

Be sure to look for nonverbal responses that indicate hesitancy; not all parents are willing to say, *"No you don't get it!"* Many parents feel misunderstood, so reflect this, and ask again,

- *What else do you need to tell me, what have I missed?*
- *How will you know I understand?*

Be mindful of the nonverbal communication of the parent. Watching and confronting their hesitancy may be necessary. Parents who do not feel understood are unlikely to return to therapy. Therefore, the main goal of this session is for parents to feel supported and glad they have contacted you.

Culture

Gathering information about the client's family culture is important to understand the full picture of the family. Learning directly from the parent rather than making assumptions regarding culture is critical in building the therapeutic relationship. Broaching (Day-Vines et al., 2007; King, 2021) is a consistent attitude of the counselor that invites clients to explore issues of diversity. King and Borders (2019) found that the clients of counselors who prioritized broaching early in the relationship had more favorable perceptions of the counseling process. Counselors may ask the parent to share about their culture, to talk about what aspects of the family's culture may be different from the therapist's culture. The therapist has an attitude of looking for differences between their culture and the families' culture rather than commonalities. King et al. (2022) recommend the following questions to learn more about the family's culture.

- *What does discipline look like in your home?*
- *What are some things your family values most?*

- ◆ *Are there any responsibilities or expectations that the child has or that differ from the other children in your home?*
- ◆ *What are you wanting your child to get out of counseling? What are you hoping to get out of this experience?*
- ◆ *I am aware that each family has their own culture, experiences, and needs. Throughout our time together you have mentioned the importance of your identity as _____ and what means for you and your family. I am wondering how this might impact our relationship given that I am _____?*

These questions help the therapist broach the topic of culture, which further facilitates the therapeutic relationship as well as the therapist's understanding of the client. As therapists gather this information, it is important to keep in mind that this is very personal information and that the attitude of broaching should continue throughout the therapeutic relationship as parents may feel more comfortable sharing as the relationship deepens.

Family Experiences During COVID-19

COVID-19 hit the United States in early 2020 and lasted beyond the printing of this book. The implications for families and children vary greatly. For some families, the COVID shutdown meant less running around and more family time; for some, it created extreme anxiety, loss, grief, isolation, poverty, homelessness, and a great degree of uncertainty. Families of all socioeconomic levels and ethnicities were impacted in both negative and positive ways. Never before have we had such a significant interruption in schooling and our general social interactions. And honestly, we don't know how this is impacting children, emotionally, socially, and even physically. Therefore, play therapists must ask each family what COVID has been like for them.

- ◆ *How was the parents' work impacted, were they working from home? Did that alleviate or increase stress? Did they lose their job altogether?*
- ◆ *How much school have children missed or completed online?*
- ◆ *Were there services that were suspended due to COVID (speech, PT/OT, etc.)?*
- ◆ *What was their social life like during that time?*
- ◆ *What were the significant changes in your child's activities during COVID? How did that impact them?*
- ◆ *How much screen time were your children getting during COVID?*
- ◆ *How often were children isolated due to exposures to COVID?*
- ◆ *Were there significant losses of people close to the family due to COVID?*
- ◆ *Was there a change in visitation with significant family members?*
- ◆ *Were there aspects of your family that were permanently changed as a result of COVID? These could be positive or negative.*

Information to Give

Parents are eager to hear from the play therapist. A seasoned play therapist will find opportunities to cover these topics throughout the consultation so that the parents do not feel overwhelmed with information. Closing the consultation with a summary of this information can also be helpful to parents. Play therapists should be careful to share with parents an understandable definition of play therapy. Information regarding typical development for their child's age helps to put in context some of their child's behaviors. Discussing the frequency of play therapy and the content of parent consultation sessions is important so the parent knows what to expect. Review the treatment goals established during the parent consultation so the parent is clear on the focus of therapy. Finally, play therapists discuss with parents how to talk with their child about coming to play therapy and prepare their child for the session.

Play Therapy: Explaining It to the Parent

Parents may be appalled by the idea of paying someone to play with their child. Therefore, explaining the clinical aspects of play therapy in a parent friendly way is imperative to one's play therapy practice. Explanations of play therapy will vary depending on your theoretical approach to counseling. Counseling theories provide a guide to explaining why play is valuable and the purpose of using play, the focus of the therapeutic relationship, how change occurs, conditions necessary for change,

> **Information to Give**
>
> - What is play therapy?
> - Treatment options
> - Typical developmental milestones
> - Frequency of play therapy sessions and parent consultations
> - Treatment plan goals
> - How parents can prepare their child for the session

and theories of how maladjustment occurs in clients. As a reminder, the Association for Play Therapy (APT) defines play therapy as, "the systematic use of a theoretical model to establish an interpersonal process wherein trained play therapists use the therapeutic powers of play to help clients prevent or resolve psychosocial difficulties and achieve optimal growth and development" (Association for Play Therapy, 2022).

Terry Kottman defines Adlerian Play Therapy (AdPT) as,

> AdPT is a therapeutic modality in which the therapist uses a plethora of strategies (including adventure therapy techniques, storytelling and therapeutic metaphors, movement/dance/movement experiences, sand tray activities, art techniques, structured and unstructured play experiences) to communicate with clients while conceptualizing and treatment planning based on the principles of Individual Psychology. (Personal Communication, January 22, 2022)

Dee Ray defines Child-Centered Play Therapy as,

> a counseling approach in which the relationship between therapist and child is the foundation for therapeutic change. The therapist provides attitudinal conditions and developmentally appropriate materials to facilitate free expression and self-directed play of the child. Play serves as the child's language. In a safe environment, the child moves toward self-enhancing behaviors and ways of being. (Ray, 2011, p. 54)

Angela Cavett describes Cognitive-Behavioral Play Therapy (CBPT) as it,

> extends the model of cognitive-behavioral therapy (CBT) to young children by allowing for communication through play within the therapy. CBPT is a developmentally appropriate treatment that is sensitive to emotional, cognitive, and linguistic development. (Cavett, 2015, p. 83)

It is important for therapists to use a definition of play therapy that is clear and makes sense to the population of parents with whom they work and is theoretically consistent with how they work. An initial explanation is in the *Informed Consent for Treatment* (Appendix A). In the parent consultation, however, the play therapist can expand on that statement and respond to their questions. Phrases such as, *"Children communicate through play"* and *"toys are used like words by children, and play is their language"* (Landreth, 2012, pp. 9, 12) are helpful in parents understanding their child. A concrete example that relates to their child such as,

Noah is not able to verbally communicate why or what he is feeling or explain his behaviors. He can't explain why he is having such a hard time, which is why you see these challenging behaviors at home. In play therapy I can provide an environment that facilitates his expression and I watch for play patterns, how he plays, what he plays, and what and how he communicates with me to better understand his perspective of his world. In conjunction with the information from you regarding his behavior we can put all these pieces together to help make sense of his struggles and ultimately help him make behavior change.

Sometimes parents respond with, *"I don't get it, he's just playing."* The play therapist reflects the parents' feeling *"You are worried play therapy may not work."* Then make the parallel connection to adult therapy where adults "just talk." And reframe that when children are with a trained professional, they are not "just playing" but communicating and working through challenges in their life. Play therapists are trained to translate play-language to understand the child's concerns and help the child work it through. Encouraging parents to trust the play therapist can be necessary, and together parents and play therapists work to make life more manageable for the client and family.

Presenting Treatment Options

Once information and history is gathered on the child and family, it is time to present treatment options; this might be individual play therapy, group play therapy, parent coaching, a therapeutic parenting modality, or family therapy. The play therapist presents their professional recommendations for treatment, explaining the benefits and limitations of each option and what different treatment options entail for the parents to be fully informed of their decision. It is critical that clients have full informed consent in the type of therapy recommended for their child.

Parent Coaching/Therapeutic Parenting Modalities

In some cases, parents may only need parent coaching. In other cases, some parents may need a more comprehensive therapeutic approach to make changes in their family system. Either way, these may be necessary to support change at home, in addition to or in place of individual play therapy.

In parent coaching sessions, the play therapist helps the parents in making minor adjustments in their relationship with their children. Coaching can help with discipline approaches at home, teaching parents therapeutic skills such as reflection of feeling and other skills that can enhance the parent-child relationship and ultimately create a more peaceful home. There may be parenting classes within the community to which the play therapist may refer parents. Some nonprofit community agencies may provide these at no cost.

Therapeutic parenting modalities such as *Child Parent Relationship Therapy* (Landreth & Bratton, 2020), *Circle of Security Intervention* (Powell et al., 2014), and *Theraplay* (Booth & Jernberg, 2009) among others focus on training parents in therapeutic skills to use at home and sometimes in session with their child. Generally, the focus of these modalities is to enhance the parent-child relationship, by increasing attachment, which ultimately leads to change in both the parent and child. Play therapists must be specifically trained in these different approaches and therefore have a comprehensive explanation for parents. Therapeutic parenting modalities can be the primary method of treatment for children rather than an adjunct therapeutic approach. It is valuable for all play therapists to have a therapeutic parenting modality they are comfortable with and competent in to offer when working with parents.

Family Play Therapy

Many therapists find family play therapy a successful treatment modality while working with the entire family system. In family play therapy, the play therapist uses play as the modality of communication and expression to facilitate connection, attachment, and communication between family members. Gil (1994) discusses the importance of including young children in family play therapy. Gil states that play can engage all family members in meaningful exchanges in therapy. Play is a universal language for children; play lowers defenses and unlocks a deeper level of interaction through fantasy, metaphor, and symbol for all ages of the family. Family play therapy increases a family's ability to identify and express their emotions with one another in a safe, approachable way (Cornett, 2020). Play provides opportunities for joy among family members while also providing the play therapist with the underlying feelings and experiences of the family members that ultimately impact how the play therapist works with the family. Family play therapy may be utilized with families who struggle in understanding each other's perspective or families who have suffered a trauma or loss together. Creating deeper connections within the family can facilitate healing within the family dynamics. Family play therapy may be the primary modality of treatment for a young child when the system is struggling as a whole.

Group Play Therapy

Group play therapy can be valuable for children with a variety of presenting issues. Each theory has a different goal, size limits, and rationale for utilizing group play therapy. Child-Centered Play Therapists structure groups to be heterogeneous, in that children are selected based on their strengths and how they can influence and help the other children grow. A child who is shy may be placed with a child who struggles with boundaries in friendships. Together through play, these children learn to work together and both become more balanced in their approach to friendships. A Cognitive-Behavioral Play Therapist may place children with similar struggles in the same group and focus more on psychoeducation around the shared topic. Different theories have different rationale for how groups are formed; the age differences between children; length and structure of sessions (Sweeney & Homeyer, 1999; Sweeney et al., 2014). Play therapists also see siblings in group play therapy when there is a relationship struggle between the siblings. It is important that play therapists are clinically sound in their decision to see children in a group setting. It is not a decision that is driven by scheduling or space limitations. Meeting the needs of each child in a play therapy group requires additional skills of the play therapist. As with any subspecialty in play therapy, competency needs to be pursued with education and supervision.

Child Development

Growing up is hard to do; typical development brings challenges to life, and frequently parents have no idea of the challenges of normal development in children. Play therapists must be knowledgeable in development and be able to share this information with parents. It is important to emphasize that normal development is challenging and often requires additional support for families. Or in situations of trauma or common life struggles the child's response may be developmentally appropriate but at an extreme end of the continuum. Information on development can help adjust the parent's expectations of their child. Dee Ray's book, *A Therapist's Guide to Child Development* (2016), provides development information for therapists, and in the back of the book, there are very helpful handouts intended for parents of children ages 3–12 years. I (Mary) give these handouts as part of my Initial Parent Consultation. Parents find this information comforting to know that their child is responding just as they should, even if it is hard to manage in the family. There are a variety of resources on development that therapists can utilize in their practice to provide to parents. See the Resources section of this chapter for recommendations.

The play therapist's knowledge of development is also an important piece to conceptualizing clients. Given that our clients may have experienced trauma, neglect, or attachment disruptions that impact their development, therapists should be aware that children come to therapy and may be in different stages of development in different areas of life. A child's development can impact their play and therefore the play therapists' interpretation and understanding of the child's play. See Chapter 10: A Deeper Look at Play for more information on child development and its impact on play in therapy.

Neurodiverse, Neurotypical, and Neurodivergent

The term *neurodiversity* was first used in an article in the *Atlantic* by Harvey Blume in 1998, while Judy Singer (1998) is often given credit for the term. There is evidence that Blume and Singer corresponded about the term and, subsequently, Singer used it in her thesis in 1998 (Grant, 2022). Singer used the term *neurodiverse* as a replacement for the pathological, medical model view of deficits, disorders, or impairments. *Neurodiverse, neurotypical,* and *neurodivergent* are being used more frequently by professionals, including play therapists. Therefore, we should be comfortable with these terms. *Neurodiversity* is a trait possessed by a group, rather than a trait of an individual person. *Neurodivergent* and *neurodivergence* indicate one's brain functions in ways that are not what the dominant social standards consider typical. Neurodivergence could be genetic, produced by brain-altering experiences (e.g., trauma, long-term medication use), or a combination of the two (Walker, 2014, 2021). Diagnoses and differences we might see in play therapy that fall under neurodivergent include obsessive-compulsive disorder, attention deficit disorder, sensory differences, dyslexia, intellectual disability, Tourette syndrome, autism, and twice-exceptional (Grant, 2021). See Figure 3.1. *Neurotypical* indicates one has a style of neurocognitive functioning that falls within the dominant social standards (Walker, 2014, 2021). Play therapists will likely encounter clients who fall into these categories and may find defining neurodiversity helpful to parents to understand their child at a deeper level. As with any population, we recommend some specialized training and supervision to be a competent clinician if specializing with any of these populations.

Frequency of Play Therapy Sessions and Parent Consultations

In the initial consultation with parents, it is important to clarify their expectations of session length and treatment duration. Generally speaking, weekly individual sessions for

Figure 3.1 Neurodivergence
Source: Copyright, 2021, Robert Jason Grant, AutPlay Therapy Resources. Used with Permission.

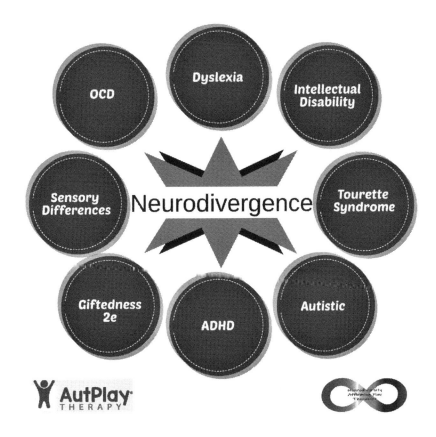

children over 3 years of age are 45–50 minutes. Forty-five minutes give children enough time to start and finish play; shorter sessions do not allow the child time to explore and settle into the relationship. For children younger than 3, depending on the presenting issue, a therapeutic parenting approach may be the most effective. If parents are not available for therapy, 30-minute sessions are developmentally appropriate for very young children. In working with younger children, the play therapist is mindful of the parent-child attachment and its role in the therapeutic process. Weekly sessions are important for the therapeutic relationship to develop and momentum of the therapy to continue. Adults have the ability to think about therapy, to choose their own therapist, and begin the therapeutic process of change when they are ready. Therefore, they are usually ready to begin therapy at the start of the first session. Children, however, do not have the same experience, in that an adult decides on their behalf that therapy is appropriate. Therefore, it takes longer to build the therapeutic relationship and the play therapist may not have significant information to share with parents until after several sessions. Helping parents understand this experience can be helpful in managing their expectations of what the play therapist will be able to report.

Parents like to know how many sessions it will take to resolve their child's problems. Bratton and Lin (2015) completed a meta-analysis of play therapy outcome research and determined that the optimal number of sessions for play therapy is 35 sessions. The Bratton and Lin (2015) meta-analysis of Child-Centered Play Therapy research revealed 10–12 sessions were optimal for CCPT. It is challenging to give parents a precise number of sessions it will take for their child to make progress for several reasons. First, often what parents report is the issue is actually not the problem and may or may not be as significant as the actual problem. Second, parents typically focus on the problem behavior and do not understand the underlying heart issue or experience that may result in challenging behaviors. For example, aggressive behavior at home might be in reaction to being bullied at school. Giving parents a possible number of sessions for play therapy can set them up for unrealistic expectations. Rather, setting expectations that we will meet after every third session (or however often is consistent with your theory) to evaluate treatment plans and make adjustments is helpful for parents to know what to expect in the therapeutic process.

Providing parents with information so they know how often they can expect feedback and inviting them into the evaluation process helps reduce their anxiety. The play therapist is also quick to say,

If I ever think your child has been hurt or is in danger, I will let you know immediately. And I trust you will quickly inform me of any major life changes.

Play therapists do not want parents to think information about their child is being withheld.

Explaining to parents the structure and level of involvement of future parent consultations is helpful. Providing helpful and meaningful feedback such as explaining play themes rather than only reporting play behaviors is more meaningful and useful to parents. Reporting that Noah painted and then played in the sand is not helpful. Instead, explaining what these play behaviors mean and how that relates to the treatment goals is helpful. That may sound like,

Noah's play is full of mastery; he is working to feel more competent and capable and take more risks. This is good news as he works to feel more secure and have less need to control his life.

Helping parents set appropriate expectations of the therapeutic process will help parents feel more satisfied and a part of the process. Reassure parents that they are a part of the treatment team and will participate in ongoing consultations. For details of these consultations, see Chapter 6: Ongoing Parent Consultations; but for now, these include asking for their insight on progress, addressing parenting questions, teaching therapeutic parenting skills, and other resources as needed. Play therapists do this every day, and this is perhaps a parent's first time in therapy, and they have no idea what to expect, or they have created expectations that the play therapist might not be able to meet. Giving brief but informative details helps parents know what to expect.

Preparing the Child for the Playroom

Coaching parents on what to tell their child will empower the parent in how to prepare the child and reduce anxiety for the child to know what to expect. Play therapists encourage parents to be positive and optimistic in talking with their child. It is important to ask parents what they have told their child about play therapy. This will give direction if any misconceptions regarding play therapy need to be clarified. Play therapists will coach parents differently based on their theory, the child's age, and presenting issues. In general, parents should be genuine and optimistic with their child.

We are going to go see a play therapist. Sometimes when kids are having a hard time (or have experienced something hard), it is helpful to go to the playroom to play and talk about your feelings. I met with a friendly play therapist today, and they have a playroom with lots of interesting toys for you to play with. We will start going tomorrow.

It is essential to clarify with parents if they think their child will easily separate and go to the playroom. Creating a plan with the parent on how to respond if the child has trouble separating will allow this potential challenge to go more smoothly. It is easy for both parents and play therapists to feel anxious when this happens. Reminding parents that their child is not doing anything wrong if they have trouble separating. Typically, this is one of the reasons the child is coming to therapy, so the treatment begins the moment the play therapist meets the child. The play therapist wants to avoid the child having a negative experience in the first session, making subsequent sessions challenging. Creating a relationship with the child facilitates security, even if that occurs only in the waiting room for that session. Encourage parents to follow your lead, not pressure, guilt, manipulate, or try to force the child into the playroom. Play therapists provide the core conditions the first moment they see the child. Accepting the child right where they are will help the therapist relax and focus on the relationship. Getting down on the child's level and speaking to the child first will communicate that play therapists are different. Connecting with the child may sound like,

It is hard meeting someone new.
   I bet you've never known a grown-up to have a playroom; that sounds so silly.
   I see you've got that thing on your shirt right there.

The play therapist determines if the child might be willing to come on their own with a simple choice of,

It's time to go to the playroom. Do you choose to race me down the hall or choose to walk next to me?

Or if it is evident this child is not likely to separate today, a choice of,

Do you choose for dad to come with us to the playroom or choose for him to stay in the waiting room until we come back?

If the child chooses for the parent to come to the playroom, invite them in, and reflect the child's feeling,

You feel safe with mom coming to the playroom. I am new, and the playroom is new, so it feels good for mom to come.

Once in the room, if the child begins to feel comfortable and starts playing, giving the child a choice gives the child some control.

Do you choose for mom to stay five more minutes or ten more minutes?

It is critical the play therapist does not rush this. If the parent needs to stay in the room the whole session and gradually work up to the parent leaving, this is essential clinical work. I (Mary) once had a parent that would sit outside the playroom door in our clinic; the child felt safe and was able to work in the playroom. Building the relationship and accepting the child are the most important goals: whether in the playroom or the waiting room, work is being done in either place.

Parents need to stay in the waiting room and not leave while their child is in session. This will need to be explained to parents, as they may be comfortable dropping their child at sports or play dates. Parents are unlikely to realize how scary it is for children when parents are not in the waiting room if they come out to go to the bathroom or if the ultimate limit is set and the session ends early. Not to mention, occasionally, parents are late picking up their child, and play therapists usually have another client and are not able to sit in the waiting room for the parent to arrive. Therefore, the best practice is for parents to wait for their child to finish the play therapy session.

Coaching parents on what to say at the end of the session is also important. Play therapists encourage parents to say,

Ok, it's time to go, or, *It looks like you are finished. See you next week.*

Discourage parents from asking a lot of questions, especially,

Did you have fun? What did you play with?

For many children, play therapy is not fun, as the feelings and experiences they play out may be complex or intense. Remind parents you will share important information at the parent consultation, so there is no need to question their child.

Managing Dual Relationships

Dual relationships are important to identify immediately. Remember, the play therapist does an initial screening for this at the point of the inquiry (see Chapter 2: Inquiry Through Intake Summary). However, as the intake conversation provides more information, details that reveal a dual relationship may occur. The play therapist may have their own children, making dual relationships occur more frequently and be a little more complex. Children deserve privacy, and it is our responsibility to hold that carefully and know how it may impact a child to have a dual relationship with the therapist. Parents want what is best for their child and trust their child with a play therapist they know feels good to them. They are unaware of the repercussions of a dual relationship for themselves or their child. Parents do not understand the depth of vulnerability they will likely face while their child is in counseling, let alone the vulnerability their child may experience. Therefore, it is our responsibility to know this and refer out when necessary. There are a variety of different boundaries one may set to avoid dual relationships, for example, not seeing any children your own children's age or grade, seeing other children who attend your child's school or are on your child's sports team, and children who have siblings that are in the same grade as your children. It would be unfortunate for our children's friend group to be dictated by our dual relationships. Having a work life balance includes having friendships with other parents in our social circle. This is one of the ways we provide self-care, to have our own friends with whom we can talk about our personal struggles in life. It is not uncommon for your friends, who are parents, to call you for help with their child. This is a slippery slope for a play therapist. Having other therapists you can refer to in town is critical to your personal boundaries. Explaining to friends that it is unethical for you to see their child in therapy and that you would prefer to remain friends can help in the discussion and maintain that boundary.

Setting boundaries in dual relationships for play therapists who live in rural areas, small towns, or school settings is more challenging. It may not occur to clients that they may not want to share with their neighbors that you are their therapist. Therefore, if you talk through it before it happens, they have a narrative they can feel confident about. For example,

If I see you in public, I will let you say hello first. You may not want to say hello, because you may not want to explain how you know me to other people. It will not hurt my feelings if you choose not to say "hello."

There are also essential boundaries to set to protect yourself as well, for example,

When you see me at school, it may be tempting to chat in the hall about the tantrum Noah threw last night. It will be best for us if you write that down and save it for our next parent consultation, so we have the time to devote to talking about that issue.

Alerting your child client that they may run into you at school is also part of protecting the therapeutic relationship. Young children may be excited to see you, while older children may feel embarrassed or unsure. Letting these children know you might see them could sound like,

My kids also go to your school. You might see me one day in the cafeteria or at pick up. It is up to you if you want to say hello. Some kids like seeing me outside of the playroom at school, and some kids like seeing me only in the playroom, so you can decide to say hello or not.

Other Considerations

Play therapists may want to use assessments to learn more about the child. Some play therapists have parents or teachers complete assessments before or after the initial parent consultation. Consider providing assessment results at a follow-up parent consultation. The parent will likely be overloaded with information in this initial consultation; therefore, saving assessment results for the subsequent parent consultation may be more helpful. Many therapists have parents complete the Adverse Childhood Experiences Questionnaire (Felitti et al., 1998) for themselves and their child. There are several different versions. Each can provide play therapists with additional insight into the family. Keep in mind that as more information is revealed about the child. Other assessments may be useful and helpful to the therapy process.

Referrals for other services or release of information forms may be necessary to speak to other professionals in the child's life. Teachers, school counselors, speech therapists, court-appointed special advocates (CASA), pediatricians, and a host of other professionals create the therapeutic web (Perry & Szalavitz, 2006) that facilitates healing for a child. Asking parents if they need referrals for legal services or other community support agencies and groups can be helpful, as some families may not know how to navigate these services. Broaching these topics takes the support we offer clients to the social justice level (King et al., 2022). Thinking on your feet is helpful and keep in mind that you can always go back and obtain more information from the parent. This is an ongoing relationship.

Closing the Session

At this point in the parent consultation, the hope is that parents feel encouraged and optimistic about how play therapy will be able to help their child. It is also highly possible that parents feel overloaded and may not honestly remember everything discussed. Providing a quick summary of treatment goals, the date of the first session, and the date of the first parent consultation is a constructive way to end a session. Providing a summary of these important points helps parents feel grounded regarding the immediate action items.

Final Summary

- Treatment goals
- First session date and time
- First parent consultation date and time

People to Paper: Documentation

After every human interaction, play therapists document. This weaves the golden thread of best practices. The initial parent consultation continues this process. *The Child Background Form* is very helpful because much of what the parents reported in this consultation is

Initial Parent Consultation Documentation

- Overall concerns
- Referrals, if any
- Treatment plan goals
- Recommended frequency of play therapy sessions and parent consultations

Table 3.2 Initial parent consultation session note

Initial Parent Consultation Session Note

Child's Name_____ Date of Parent Consultation_____

Child's Date of Birth _____

Parent(s) Attending:

Name & Role _____

Name & Role _____

Ethical and Legal Documentation covered:

___ Informed Consent and Professional Disclosure Statement

___ Limits of Confidentiality

___ Custody Agreements/Orders (if necessary)

___ Explanation of Treatment Approach

___ Development Information

Parent Reported Concerns:

Treatment Focus:

Treatment Approach (individual, group, family play therapy, etc.) and frequency of sessions:

Referrals/Recommendations Made:

_____   _____

Play Therapist Signature with Credentials   Date

already documented here. Therefore, referencing this form on the *Initial Parent Consultation Session Note* (Appendix B) makes note writing easy. Play therapists should document parents' overall concerns, any referrals made, treatment plan goals, and frequency of play therapy sessions and parent consultations. See the example of the *Initial Parent Consultation Session Note* in Table 3.2. This note is relatively straightforward, a reflection of the session's content and those attending. In this note, play therapists report verbally addressing essential aspects of informed consent. Stating the parent's concerns, which may read like, "*parent reported, Noah is having a difficult time with emotional regulation.*" The section titled Treatment Focus provides a space to make notes to create treatment goals. The wording of this section may read more like a list of behaviors, experiences, and emotions to keep in mind. If subsequent recommendations are made, such as parenting resources or referrals to other professionals, note it on this session note. Then, sign and date, and your documentation is complete.

In Closing

The most crucial goal of the initial parent consultation is for the parent to feel safe and understood to ensure they follow through and bring their child for play therapy. It is critical for play therapists to hold ethical standards high, review legal documents, and keep all parties informed of their work with the child. Establishing a relationship of trust and openness is critical for the parent to feel a part of the play therapy process and be committed to being a part of the therapeutic process for their child. In the next chapter, we will discuss treatment planning and diagnosis.

Resources

♦ Association for Play Therapy. (February 17, 2016). *Introducing Andrew* [Video]. YouTube.www.youtube.com/watch?v=reJpo-GaopM
♦ Ray, D. C. [deeray8]. (January 12, 2010). *Introduction to Play Therapy for Parents* [Video]. YouTube. www.youtube.com/watch?v=Onn_qF4pZ9Q
♦ Ray, D. C. [deeray8]. (January 12, 2010,). *Introduction to Play Therapy for Children* [Video]. YouTube. www.youtube.com/watch?v=fmKxvTtSWoc
♦ *My Book About Play Therapy*, Sandra L. Wilson, 2018.
♦ APT Play Therapy Brochure can be ordered from www.a4pt.org
♦ *A Therapist's Guide to Child Development*, Dee Ray, Routledge, 2016.
♦ *Association for Play Therapy Parents Corner*, Association for Play Therapy. www.a4pt.org/general/custom.asp?page=ParentsCornerHomePag

References

American Psychiatric Association. (2022). *Diagnostic and statistical manual of mental disorders* (5th ed.—TR). American Psychiatric Association. https://doi.org/10.1176/appi.books.9780890425596

Association for Play Therapy. (2022, January 12). *Definition of play therapy*. www.a4pt.org/page/AboutAPT

Booth, P., & Jernberg, A. (2009). *Theraplay: Helping parents and children build better relationships through attachment-based play* (3rd ed.). Wiley.

Bratton, S. C., & Lin, D. (2015). A meta-analytic review of child-centered play therapy approaches. *Journal of Counseling and Development, 93*(1), 45–58. https://doi.org/10.1002/j.1556-6676.2015.00180.x

Cavett, A. (2015). Cognitive-behavioral Play Therapy. In D. A. Crenshaw & A. L. Stewart (Eds.), *Play Therapy: A comprehensive guide to theory and practice* (pp. 83–98). Guilford Press.

Cornett, N. (2020). Family play therapy: Why and how. *PlayTherapy, 15*(2), 8–11.

Day-Vines, N. L., Wood, S. M., Grothaus, T., Craigen, L., Holman, A., Dotson-Blake, K., & Douglass, M. J. (2007). Broaching the subjects of race, ethnicity, and culture during the counseling process. *Journal of Counseling and Development, 85*, 401–409.

Felitti, V. J., Anda, R. F., Nordenberg, D., Williamson, D. F., Spitz, A. M., Edwards, V., & Marks, J. S. (1998). Relationship of childhood abuse and household dysfunction to many of the leading causes of death in adults: The Adverse Childhood Experiences (ACE) study. *American Journal of Preventive Medicine, 14*(4), 245–258.

Gil, E. (1994). *Play in family therapy*. Guilford.

Grant, R. J. (2021). *Neurodivergence*. AutPlay Therapy Resources.

Grant, R. J. (2022). *The AutPlay therapy handbook: Integrative family play therapy for neurodivergent children*. Routledge.

King, K. J., Chen, H. L., & Walker, M. (2022). *Providing a culturally competent parent intake*. Texas Association for Play Therapy Annual Conference, Austin, TX.

King, K. M. (2021). "I want to, but how?" Defining counselor broaching in core tenets and departed components. *Journal of Multicultural Counseling and Development, 49*, 87–100. http:/doi.org/10.1002/jmcd.12208

King, K. M., & Borders, I. D. (2019). An experimental investigation of what counselors broaching race and racism. *Journal of Counseling and Development, 97*, 341–351. http:/doi.org/10.1002/jcad.12283

Landreth, G. L. (2012). *The art of the relationship* (3rd ed.). Routledge.

Landreth, G. L., & Bratton, S. (2020). *Child-parent relationship therapy: An evidenced based 10-session filial therapy model* (2nd ed.). Routledge.

Perry, B. C., & Szalavitz, M. (2006). *The boy who was raised as a dog*. Basic.

Powell, B., Cooper, G., Hoffman, K., & Marvin, B. (2014). *The circle of security intervention*. Guilford.

Ray, D. C. (2011). *Advanced play therapy*. Routledge.

Ray, D. C. (2016). *A therapist's guide to child development*. Routledge.

Sweeney, D. S., Baggerly, J. N., & Ray, D. C. (2014). *Group play therapy*. Routledge.

Sweeney, D. S., & Homeyer, L. E. (1999). *Handbook of group play therapy*. Wiley.

Walker, N. (2014, September 27). *Neurodiversity: Some basic terms & definitions*. Neuroqueer. https://neuroqueer.com/neurodiversity-terms-and-definitions/

Walker, N. (2021, May 21). Neurodiversity: Some basic terms & definitions. *Planet Neurodivergent*. www.planetneurodivergent.com/neurodiversity-and-neurodivergent-basic-terminology/

Chapter 4

Diagnosis and Treatment Plan

Back to the paperwork! This is the professional life of the play therapist—the movement back and forth between interacting with play therapy clients and their families and then completing the paperwork to put those interactions into words: documentation. At this point in the case, the play therapist has met with the parent for the initial parent consultation session. More details were learned, which provide a more complete picture of the child, their environment, and life experiences. A case conceptualization is the written statement that provides the play therapist the opportunity to concisely discuss the client from their clinical therapy or approach. Having this concisely in mind is the grounding statement from which the treatment plan is framed. Experienced play therapists tend to do this automatically as they think through the case. We are suggesting writing it down, especially for the new play therapist, to provide a structured step to mentalize the client and the case.

Important, specific, measurable details about the child's behavior obtained during the initial parent consultation provide the play therapist with sufficient information to use the *Diagnostic and Statistical Manual of Mental Disorders* (DSM-5-TR; American Psychiatric Association, 2022) to make a diagnosis. Then, based on the diagnosis and the change the parents seek, a treatment plan can be written and agreed upon. The diagnosis of a disorder is mandatory to document *medical necessity*. A determination of medical necessity is required for payment of services by a third party, typically a health insurance company.

Some, but not all, practice settings require a DSM diagnosis to provide services. Some mental health disciplines obligate us to make a diagnosis. Others do not. Each play therapist should know what is required of them in their jurisdiction. For example, in Texas, Licensed Professional Counselors (LPCs) are required by law to have a treatment plan but not required to make a diagnosis. However, best practices would include one, as it documents the continuity of the golden thread.

Case Conceptualization Statement

As a starting point, the intake statement can be the basis for expanding, elaborating, and identifying the case dynamics from the play therapist's clinical theoretical perspective. It continues to weave the golden thread into the case.

DOI: 10.4324/9781003258766-5

Let's take a look again at the case of Noah. Here is his intake summary:

Noah, 3 years old, and his 5-year-old sister are experiencing intense sibling rivalry based on a change of their family constellation. This is demonstrated by attacking and bullying his sister, noncompliance with family rules, alternately pouting and being aggressive. Noah also lacks social interest and does not connect well with peers, as shown in similar behavioral difficulties at day care: apparent inability to manage self-control, displayed by his aggressive, noncompliant, controlling behavior.

With the additional information from the initial parent consultation, this can be further expanded:

Noah, 3 years old, lives in the home of his intact family. The family constellation includes his parents, Alicia and Juan, and his 5-year-old sister. His parents appear to be functioning from superiority personality priorities. The parenting style appears to be authoritarian. Noah and his sister are experiencing intense sibling rivalry based on a change in their family constellation. His mother has become the primary caregiver because his father is now traveling for work several days a week. Previously, also based on work schedules, when Noah was born, Alicia was his primary caregiver, and Juan became primary caregiver for the daughter.

- ◆ *Noah's Goal of Misbehavior is: Revenge.*
- ◆ *His Private Logic is:*
  - • *I AM lost, I don't matter anymore in my family, I have lost my place, no one cares about me.*
  - • *OTHERS ARE dismissive of me. If they reject me, I will reject them. Especially my sister who has taken my place.*
  - • *THE WORLD IS not worth connecting to; who knows if they will treat me the same, so I'll be sure that cannot happen.*
  - • *THEREFORE, I will be sure that I won't let others get close enough so I might come to count on them. And being mean will keep them away.*

Noah's private logic energizes his behavior of attacking and bullying his sister, noncompliance with family rules, alternately pouting and being aggressive. Noah also lacks social interest and does not connect well with peers, as shown in similar behavioral difficulties at day care: apparent inability to manage self-control, displayed by his aggressive, noncompliant, controlling behavior.

A Child-Centered Play Therapist might write:

Noah is experiencing incongruence between his sense of self and his environment.

- ◆ *His internal message is: I am unimportant, I must strike out at others to prove I am important. No one cares for me and I have been abandoned. I must take power over others to prove my worth.*
- ◆ *Noah's conditions of worth: I am only loved when I behave; I must be nice to be noticed and cared for.*
- ◆ *Noah's real self and ideal self are incongruent: The real self uses aggression to be in control and have predictable experiences; the ideal self is quickly heard, and powerful.*

These case conceptualizations were written by Linda, an Adlerian Play Therapist, and Mary, a Child-Centered Play Therapist. Others of the same clinical theories may write these differently, but still use similar theory terms and concepts. We encourage each play therapist to develop their own style and focus, while also thinking through and implementing their theory of choice.

Developing the DSM Diagnosis

While students in mental health graduate programs, most play therapists learn to make a diagnosis in a psychopathology class. Experience and practice in creating and using a diagnosis occur in internships and continue throughout our professional lives. We learn a process, which facilitates and expedites the time taken to do so. Here is just such a process that can be used.

Early in the intake process, we begin to develop clinical hunches regarding a possible diagnosis. We often work with similar diagnoses as play therapists; consequently, several become familiar. We begin obtaining detailed, specific information during the initial parent consultation. This is helpful as we build on that information to ask specific questions needed in the final decision-making process. For example, as Noah's parents share his reactions to the change in the family dynamics and their roles, adjustment disorder is a possible diagnosis. Being familiar with this diagnosis, I know that the onset of symptoms must occur within three months of the stressor. So I am sure to clarify that information. As discussed in the previous chapter on the initial intake consultation, the play therapist needs the following details about problem behavior, which are all required for diagnosis and the subsequent treatment plan:

♦ Duration
♦ Frequency
♦ Intensity

There can be so much information and storytelling in the initial intake consultation that, sometimes, asking for such detailed diagnostic information is overlooked. However, a diagnosis cannot be made without it.

After listing the problematic behavior gathered from the parent, reframe the behavior into diagnostic criteria. This requires relabeling a child's behavior with the appropriate clinical term, then a corresponding diagnostic criterion. See Table 4.1. This process also provides us with words and concepts to use when talking with the parent.

Table 4.1 Identifying diagnostic criteria

Child's Behavior	= Symptoms	= Diagnostic Criteria
kicking others at day care	= impulsivity & aggression	= significant impairment in social functioning
angry at sister	= emotional outbursts	= marked distress

Once the diagnostic criteria are identified and you have initial thoughts regarding a possible disorder, look specifically at the disorder in the DSM. Each disorder has a specified number of criteria to be met to confirm that diagnosis. Review each of the criteria to determine if the child meets the requirements of that disorder. Document the diagnosis, the criteria used, and the child's specific behavior. Here is an example for Noah:

F43.24, *Adjustment Disorder With Disturbance of Emotions and Conduct, Persistent*
DSM 5-TR Criteria:

- ♦ A. Behavior symptoms within three months of an identifiable stressor
  - • Noah's behavior began two months ago after his father began traveling out of town for work and his mother started a new job.
- ♦ B.1. Marked distress
  - • Noah exhibits angry outbursts aimed at his mother and sister, and noncompliance with family and day-care rules and directives indicate his inability to understand and manage his emotions.
- ♦ B.2. Significant impairment in social functioning
  - • Noah impulsively kicks his peers at day care resulting in the threat of expulsion and possible injury to his peers.

Noah's stressor, his change in family functioning, did not cease within the six-month time frame. However, the disorder guidelines also provide for that possibility; it becomes identified as a *persistent form.*

Writing this in the file clearly documents the basis for the diagnosis and the accompanying medical necessity. It also established a routine process in the play therapist's practice to sustain the standard of practice.

Creating the Treatment Plan

Once again, the play therapist's discipline and clinical theory or approach will impact the development of a treatment plan. Various mental health disciplines label parts of treatment plans with their own unique terms. Regardless of the terms used, the plan should

Treatment Plan Core Components

- • Identify problematic behavior
- • Identify desired behavior
- • Interventions

be user-friendly and easily understood by parents and nonprofessionals. Sometimes play therapists, and mental health professionals, in general, can use clinical terms and concepts that have little meaning to those outside of the mental health field.

The treatment plan is a living document. That is to say, it is written at a point in time but may change over time. Throughout the play therapy process, more information becomes known, the child and family's situation may change, and new life experiences may impact the initial problem. Therefore, the treatment plan, and even the diagnosis, may be updated. Long-term goals may change. Over time some of the long-term goals are met, and new ones are added. The treatment plan is a living, fluid document that reflects the client's needs and those of their family. And it guides the play therapist in the treatment process. Finally, it meets legal and ethical requirements.

The core components of the treatment plan are (1) identifying the child's presenting problematic behavior; (2) identifying the parent's desired behavior; and (3) the interventions the play therapist, parents, school, and possible others, will use to facilitate those changes. Many mental health professionals use the SMART guidelines (Doran, 1981) when writing these. Hartwig (2021) identifies this model for play therapists as:

♦ Specific: Target a specific behavior that will change.
♦ Measurable: Quantify, or at least suggest, an indicator of progress.
♦ Achievable: Ensure that the goal is doable for the child.
♦ Realistic: Confirm that the goal can realistically be achieved given the child's abilities and available resources.
♦ Timely: Specify when the goal can be achieved. (Hartwig, 2021, p. 92)

This ensures that goals and objectives are clear and concise. As you read through this SMART model, you can see the detailed information needed to write these. For example, a parent might say, "*I want my son to be the happy little boy he used to be.*" While we hope it will be Achievable, it is not Specific or Measurable. The Time needed to meet that goal is not identified, nor is it yet known if it is Realistic. Exploring this more fully, as discussed in the previous chapter on the initial parent consultation, is needed. This reflects why the initial parent consultation is critical to obtaining sufficient detailed information to write a treatment plan.

Steps to Developing a Treatment Plan

Let's begin by looking at the first two core components. First, identifying the child's presenting problematic behavior or the issue that motivates the parent to bring their child in for play therapy at this point in time. Second, identify the parent's desired behavior or what the child's behavior will look like to consider that play therapy has been successful.

Let's look at Noah's case as a working example. From the diagnosis, we have two areas of concern. To continue the golden thread, we need these to be in his treatment plan as well.

♦ Noah exhibits angry outbursts aimed at his mother and sister, and noncompliance with family and day-care rules and directives indicate his inability to understand and manage his emotions.
♦ Noah impulsively kicks his peers at day care resulting in the threat of expulsion.

This is the time to restructure these into no more than three long-term goals and include the SMART guidelines while crafting them.

#1 Concern:
Aggressive behavior between siblings as demonstrated by arguing, pouting, and dysregulation (six times daily); attempts to hurt his sister by throwing toys and other items at her (three times daily).

#2 Concern:

    Noncompliance with parental requests and family rules, tantrums when responding to parental requests and family rules. This includes arguing, pouting, and dysregulation (four to six times a day).

#3 Concern:

    Aggression toward peers at day care; the possibility of being expelled; attacks (kicks) other children at nap time (daily), resulting in no friends and possibly harming them.

These are the behaviors causing the parents the most distress and the most difficulty for family functioning.

While writing the long-term goals, other dynamics need to be considered. There are a wide variety of dynamics that impact the functioning of the child, the parents, and the family. Any one of these may inform the ability to achieve long-term goals. These may also require a referral for adjunctive services.

- Child Development (neurotypical, neurodivergent)
- Neurobiology (ability to regulate, manage Window of Tolerance)
- Attachment (disruptions, style of child and parents)
- Trauma (age when trauma was experienced, type of trauma, chronic or acute)
- Medical Issues (current or previous diagnosis impacting presenting issue; medication and possible side effects; chronic medical issues of parents or siblings)
- Cultural Considerations (resources, resiliency, inherent strengths and risks)
- Educational Considerations (repeated grades, scholastic issues, special education, gifted/talented)

While reviewing the information received from the parents regarding Noah, the following notations are made with each of these:

- Child Development: Noah is neurotypical; he met developmental milestones within neurotypical ranges.
- Neurobiology: Noah cannot self-regulate and is often hyperaroused. His mother may also need assistance to regulate when experiencing increased annoyance with him and learn skills to co-regulate with him.
- Attachment: Noah's parents adjusted their parenting tasks to manage their busy schedules when he was born. Noah's mother was his primary caregiver, while his father focused on his older sister. Now he is old enough to go to day care, his father is traveling more for his job, and his mother has gone back to work. Noah is experiencing a rupture in his relationships, and is having difficulty adjusting. Parents may need to learn reparative skills.
- Trauma: There is no reported trauma.
- Medical Issues: There are no medical issues.
- Cultural Considerations: Noah lives in a multicultural, multiracial home. His father's Hispanic culture highly values respecting elders and, in his home, purposefully reduced machismo; his mother's Anglo culture values academic and social achievement. The family's strong conservative Christian commitment imbues obedience, importance of being "nice" to others, and the father being the "spiritual leader head of the home."

◆ Educational Considerations: At 3 years old, his behavior may impact his readiness for kindergarten and ability to make and maintain peer relationships.

Based on this additional information, and the change of behavior requested by the parents, we are ready to write the long-term goals, keeping in mind the SMART guidelines.

#1 Long-term goal:
Noah and his sister will develop a typical sibling relationship with appropriate levels of regulation, evidenced by one to two arguments a day.
#2 Long-term goal:
Noah complies with family rules and parental requests with only one tantrum a week. He can self-regulate 60% of the time and responds to parents' co-regulating.
#3 Long-term goal:
Noah will interact age-appropriately with peers at day care, with typical disagreements but no attacks; Noah will develop peer relationships, evidenced by two or three friends.

Now that the long-term goals are written, it's time to work on how we will get there: the interventions specific to play therapy, parents, and any other pivotal people in the child's life. The play therapist's clinical theory or approach will influence the interventions selected. For example, interventions designated by a Child-Centered Play Therapist will differ from a Solution-Focused Play Therapist, Adlerian Play Therapist, or Integrative Play Therapist. Another play therapist reading the treatment plan could readily identify the theory or approach being used. At the same time, the words and terms used are understood by the parents and other nonprofessionals. Remember, part of the *Informed Consent for Treatment* is that the parent can decline to participate, or for their child to participate, in any experience during the treatment process. They will also be asked to review and sign the treatment plan. Even if not required by licensure and certification codes, parent signatures would be considered best practice.

Here is an example of interventions for Noah from an Adlerian Play Therapy perspective:

#1 Interventions/Objectives:
Sibling play therapy: Strengthen the sibling relationship through increased self/ sibling awareness; increase courage to connect; increase feeling vocabulary; increase relationship skills.
Parents: Improve family atmosphere: increase all-family-member activities while decreasing parent-child dyads; increase skills to reflect children's feelings and intent; increase Noah's perception that he counts. Teach regulation skills through the Window of Tolerance.
#2 Interventions/Objectives:
Individual play therapy: Increase Noah's courage to develop relationships outside of the family: Expand the ability to participate in co-regulation beginning with the play therapist and expand to self-regulation; expand creativity and increase problem-solving skills.

#3 Interventions/Objectives:

Individual play therapy: Expand types and complexity of play to increase frustration tolerance; expand social interest through experiencing joy within the therapeutic relationship. Increase ability to label and use a feeling vocabulary.

Parents: Teach parents to use limit setting; learn and purposefully implement co-regulation skills; begin Family Meetings.

Day-care staff: Provide consultation to encourage the use of limit-setting and reflecting feelings. This expands similar encouragement across Noah's environment.

A play therapist using Child-Centered Play Therapy might write the following:

#1 Interventions/Objectives:

Sibling play therapy: Reflect feelings to identify and validate sibling's experience. Relationship reflections to facilitate sibling relationship and connection.

Parents: Refer or schedule separate sessions for Child Parent Relationship Therapy (CPRT).

#2 Interventions/Objectives:

Individual play therapy: Reflect feelings to identify and validate his feelings and increase his feeling vocabulary. Reflect themes of power and control to facilitate feelings of control. Set limits and use choices to help Noah learn to manage behavior. Co-regulate Noah in session so he can learn to self-regulate.

Parents: Highlight the parents using limit setting and choice giving from CPRT to assist in helping Noah manage his need for control. CPRT also implements the "Be-With" attitudes and how to use them in interactions with Noah during special playtimes.

#3 Interventions/Objectives:

Individual play therapy: Provide the six basic core conditions for Noah to facilitate his expression of emotion and perception of his world. Provide acceptance to Noah to establish a sense of worth without needing to use aggression. Facilitate decision-making and return responsibility for Noah to increase his self-esteem. Utilize relational responses to facilitate Noah's understanding of his role in relationships.

A play therapist using Solution-Focused Play Therapy (SFPT) might write the following.

#1 Interventions/Objectives:

Sibling play therapy: Use a nondirective approach to provide opportunities for Noah and his sister to express emotions and behaviors. Use SFPT skills of complimenting and amplifying solution talk to acknowledge strengths of each child and times when they are playing collaboratively and communicating. Use skills of reflecting behavior, content, and feeling to affirm the childrens' perceptions and listen for who and what are important to each child.

Parents: Schedule a parent consultation to discuss the goal and what progress toward the goal would look like at home. Ask parents to describe times when Noah and his sister play together in adaptive ways at home. Give parents a mission to notice times when the siblings are communicating and playing collaboratively. Ask parents to compliment children when they notice these times.

Schedule another parent consultation in a few weeks to check in on progress toward the goals.

#2 Interventions/Objectives:

Individual play therapy: Use a nondirective approach to provide opportunities for Noah to express anger. Reflect content, feelings, and behavior when Noah expresses anger or frustration. Use directive activities to share regulation skills with Noah. These activities can include music, dance, belly breathing, sand tray, expressive arts, and puppets. Use SFPT skills of complimenting and amplifying solution talk to identify Noah's strengths and capabilities of being able to regulate his body.

Family play therapy: Bring family together to practice regulation skills. Allow Noah to demonstrate belly breathing and have family members practice this with music. Ask family members to choose puppet characters and then role play with the puppets. The puppets will practice taking turns getting frustrated and then reminding each other to use the belly breathing skill. Give all family members a mission of practicing this regulation skill at home and reminding each other to use regulation during times when they feel frustrated.

#3 Interventions/Objectives:

Individual play therapy: Use empathy and practitioner's nonverbal behavior to acknowledge that Noah is capable of managing his anger and impulsivity in play therapy. Reflect content, feelings, and behavior when Noah expresses anger or frustration. Use limit setting as needed to give Noah opportunities to make choices to manage his behavior. Use complimenting and amplifying solution talk to highlight Noah's strengths and capabilities of being able to manage his anger and impulsivity.

Day care: Consult with Noah's day-care teachers. Identify Noah's goal of reducing anger outbursts and developing peer relationships. Ask teachers to describe times when Noah does not have anger outbursts and also times when he chooses to play with peers. Ask teachers to compliment Noah at times when he is playing collaboratively with peers and chooses to express anger in maladaptive ways. Schedule a time to check in with teachers on Noah's progress within one to two weeks (E. Kjellstrand Hartwig, personal communication, January 21, 2022).

Gestalt Play Therapy

#1 Interventions/Objectives:

Individual play therapy: Use nondirective play to provide new beliefs-of-self through the therapeutic relationship. Use directive play to express emotions and increase connection with self and others. Example: Use Feeling Words Handout and use instruments for full-body expression of feelings.

Parents: Teach to reflect feelings and the use of games, including body movement to integrate body-emotion awareness.

#2 Interventions/Objectives:

Individual play therapy: Provide directive activities to strengthen Noah's knowledge of himself and his own uniqueness—artwork, clay, sand tray.

Parents: Raise parents' awareness of the child's perspective through therapeutic limit setting.

#3 Interventions/Objectives:

Sibling play therapy: Begin once Goal #1 has been met. Nondirective play and directive activities to assist in learning one's own and others' boundaries and connections. Example: joint creating in the sand tray and collaborative drawings.

These examples provide samples of what interventions or objectives might be. They would vary, of course, by the play therapist. For those play therapists whose clinical theories are more directive, then there will be familiar and favorite techniques. We suggest these play therapists develop their own list of such techniques from which to select for a particular client. It simply makes it easier when writing treatment plans. There are also treatment planning books, such as *The Child Psychotherapy Treatment Planner, Fifth Edition* (Jongsma et al., 2014). These are not written from a play therapy perspective but can give ideas to be reframed in play therapy terms.

Now that the core of the treatment plan is written, other data are also required:

♦ Name and age (or date of birth) of the client
♦ Parents' names
♦ Play therapist name
♦ Date written
♦ Diagnosis
♦ Other professionals or agencies involved, for example, school personnel (classroom teacher and school counselor), pediatrician, psychiatrist, other (remember an ROI is needed)
♦ Estimated completion dates, noting when achieved
♦ Dated signatures of play therapist and parents

A sample treatment plan form is located in Appendix B. The reader is encouraged to alter and adapt the layout to meet their specific needs. Change the terms as appropriate.

Sharing the Treatment Plan With the Parents

All the EHRs have a built-in treatment plan. These will have the aforementioned components. It will also provide a confidential method to send the completed plan to the parents, electronically sign it, and return it. It will automatically be part of the client's electronic record. We suggest that the treatment plan be shared with the parents in a consultation session to ensure they agree. Any modifications can then be made before sending it to them for their signature. Be transparent during the presentation of the treatment plan to the parents that this is the plan at the moment. Discuss the situations that might result in a change of the plan.

Most often change happens when the initial long-term goals are met, and new ones are added. The initial treatment plan should focus on the more immediate change needed and desired by the parent. This does imply there may be desired secondary changes. However, a plan is most effective when focusing on one to three long-range goals. A life experience might occur that propels a new, more urgent goal that must be addressed. This might be something like the sudden death of a parent. Or, for example, I (Linda) had several play therapy clients when we experienced a severe storm resulting in a devastating flash flood in our part of Texas. We all watched the television news coverage of houses floating down swollen rivers. Some clients experienced water damage in their homes. All the children on my caseload needed to address this life event before moving back to their previous treatment plan long-term goals. This change of treatment focus should be noted in some way in the client file. If the event significantly impacted the child (and family) and is anticipated to take several sessions to work with, then a new goal should be added to the treatment plan. If it seems to be of short duration, then noting it on a session form may be sufficient. Or noted in the communication log with the parent or both.

Now we are set to go! The diagnosis and treatment plan are complete and the play therapy treatment phase commences. In reality, however, play therapy sessions are likely already occurring. The diagnosis may change based on information we continue to gather during the initial play therapy sessions and parent consultations. How the child is described in the initial paperwork and initial parent consultation may actually be different from the child we see in our playroom. Our professional assessment during our interaction with the child informs our understanding of the problematic behavior. While changing the diagnosis is not typical, it may need to be done. Document the rationale for the changes and move forward.

As treatment continues, we continually assess progress, and hence the treatment plan. We might meet some long-term goals sooner than anticipated. There are so many variables we don't know at the beginning, such as child adaptability and resilience, parent compliance and implementation of our (and often, jointly developed) recommendations, and other life events (over which no one may have any control). This is a primary reason for ongoing parent consultations. These are critical to keeping the parents engaged as part of the treatment team, receive their continued input, and for us to adapt to the shifting and unfolding needs of the case.

Resources

- ♦ *A Therapist's Guide to Child Development: The Extraordinarily Normal Years*, Dee Ray, (Ed.), Routledge, 2016.
- ♦ *The Child Psychotherapy Treatment Planner* (5th ed.), A. E. Jongsma, L. Mark Peterson, William P. McInnis, & Timothy J. Bruce, Wiley, 2014.
- ♦ *Clinician's Thesaurus: The Guide to Conducting Interviews and Writing Psychological Reports*, (8th ed.), Edward Zuckerman, Guilford Press, 2019.

References

American Psychiatric Association. (2022). *Diagnostic and statistical manual of mental disorders* (5th ed.—TR.). American Psychiatric Association.

Doran, G. T. (1981). There's a S.M.A.R.T. way to write management's goals and objectives. *Management Review, 70*(11), 35–36.

Hartwig, E. K. (2021). *Solution-focused play therapy: A strength-based clinical approach to play therapy*. Routledge.

Jongsma, A. E., Peterson, L. M., McInnis, W. P., & Bruce, T. J. (2014). *The child psychotherapy treatment planner* (5th ed.). Wiley.

Chapter 5

Treatment Phase: Session Notes

Welcome back to the paperwork. You've had a play therapy session, and now you need to transfer that experience to paper—in words. Play to words! The playroom is where play therapists spend most of their time. And where we do what we love to do: being in the playroom with our client! The playroom is where the play, healing, and therapeutic change occur. Then, it is back to documentation. Not so much fun, not so gratifying.

Consequently, note writing gets delayed, partially completed, and ignored as much as possible. Unique to the play therapist is also the task of translating play-language from the playroom into written words on the session notes. The ability to translate often mystifies the play therapist. Resulting in more delay and procrastination. Let's reframe that perspective! Writing session notes provides the play therapist the moment needed to stop, recall, contemplate, reflect, and make clinical sense of what happened in the playroom. A time to mentalize our client. To celebrate the wonder of the child's engagement in the play process and the play therapist's interactions. This time, in words.

The play therapist's clinical theory or approach to play therapy will be most helpful and noticeable when writing session notes. Also helpful are concepts regarding understanding the underlying meaning of play, the role of the play therapist, and understanding playroom dynamics. These will be explored later in the chapter.

Let's begin with looking at a generic session note and the parts that need to be included. All session notes begin with core elements to meet standards of practice. The case's golden thread is also evident through the completed session note. Session notes also provide the ability to see the progress of treatment over time and serve as documentation of that ongoing assessment.

Session Notes

The Play Therapy Session Note—Nondirective (Table 5.1) is in the classic SOAP outline: subjective, objective, assessment, and plan. It also includes information needed:

- ♦ Client name
- ♦ Session number and date

DOI: 10.4324/9781003258766-6

 ♦ Other's present, as needed (parent, sibling, etc.)
 ♦ Length of session
 ♦ Date of next session
 ♦ DSM diagnosis
 ♦ Play therapist signature with credentials and date written

Some settings will also require documentation of suicidality risk, medication check, and a mini mental status exam (MMSE). A play therapy session form can be created using most EHR platforms' custom form options. With the use of drop-down options and short text answers it can be quickly completed. The example form, Table 5.1, contains these categories and other possible options. It is created so the play therapist can quickly check or circle words and details immediately after the session. If need be, the play therapist can return at the end of the day or when time allows to complete the form. For those who have several back-to-back sessions during the day, the quickly notated form serves as the basis as a quick reminder of what occurred in a session. From personal experience, we know that it is easy for sessions to blend together at the end of a busy day. Ann Mehan (personal communication, February 9, 2022) recommends having an "appointment with yourself" to write notes. As with other appointments, it should not be canceled!

This generic play therapy session template aligns with nondirective play therapies. A reproducible form is available in Appendix D. Later in the chapter will be another template (also reproducible and found in Appendix D) for more directive play therapists. Of course, many play therapists are both directive and nondirective. This is the point of this guide. The reader is encouraged to adapt and develop effective forms for their settings, clinical theory, and approach to play therapy. The examples throughout this chapter provide several options and suggestions for the reader to create a tailor-made way of documenting one's work.

SOAP sections are adapted for the *Play Therapy Session Note—Nondirective* (Table 5.1). The four sections are:

1. **Subjective**
   This section records the subjective perspective of the child, the emotions and feelings expressed during the session. A child communicates feelings and emotions within their play (i.e., the play express the feelings), through nonverbal body language, and sometimes, verbally. Listed on the form are primary feeling categories: happy, sad, angry, afraid, confident, confused, curious, and anxious. These are further differentiated with a range of related emotions. Each play therapist can establish their own method of identifying the various emotions displayed and noting the primary one on the form. Also note if there is a shift during the session, such as the child begins the session by expressing anger then moves to confident-strong-play. Also identify the quality and intensity of the emotion.

2. **Objective Information**
   This section records the child's play, noting the toys used and play behaviors. There is no clinical interpretation or assessment at this point; simply document the primary and meaningful play. The list of toys, of course, can be adapted to coincide with those toys in your playroom. Toys and materials may vary by available space, setting, and clinical theory. Alter the session form template to meet your specific needs. Begin by checking the primary toys used in the session.

Describe the Play

The blank space in this section provides room to document a short description of the play behavior and play sequences. This description might be something like:

Noah entered and began playing the drums as he has for several sessions. He then did a long sequence of play with the snakes in the sandbox and ended drawing at the art table.

Table 5.1 Play therapy session note

Play Therapy Session Note—Nondirective

Child's Name _____ Session #_____ Date: _____

Other's Present: _____ Length of Session ____minutes DSM _____

SUBJECTIVE

HAPPY: pleased, satisfied, delighted, excited, silly, elated, surprised, relieved

CONFIDENT: proud, strong, determined, comfortable, relaxed

SAD: disappointed, hopeless, pessimistic, discouraged, lonely, worthless, guilty

CONFUSED: ambivalent, hesitant, uncertain, timid, nervous, embarrassed

ANGRY: impatient, irritated, annoyed, frustrated, mad, mean, jealous, bored

CURIOUS: interested, focused

AFRAID: vulnerable, helpless, distrustful, fearful, fearful, terrified

ANXIOUS: nervous, worried, tentative, tense

QUALITY/INTENSITY: flat, broad, restricted, contained, ambiguous

OBJECTIVE INFORMATION

__sandbox/water	__cash register/money/telephone/camera/flashlight
__puppets	__medical kit/bandages
__kitchen/cooking/food	__musical instruments
__easel/painting	__games/bowling/ring toss/balls/ball & target
__bop bag	__building blocks/materials, boxes
__dress up/jewelry/hats/masks/wand	__vehicles/planes
__crafts table/clay/markers/etc.	__animals: domestic/zoo/alligator/dinosaurs/shark/snake
__doll house/doll family	__soldiers/guns/knife/sword/handcuffs/rope
__baby dolls/bottle/pacifier	__blocks

TOYS/PLAY BEHAVIOR

PLAY TYPE: solitary, parallel, onlooker, associative, cooperative, collaborative, competitive, combative

RELATING STYLE: egocentric, identifies w/other, helpless, seeks, rejects, confrontative, rescues

ASSESSMENT

_____

_____

PLAY THEMES

Exploratory/Mastery	Safety/Security/Protection
Relationship Building & Interpersonal	Family/Nurturance
Power/Aggression/Helpless/Inadequate	Sexualized
Control/Safety Death-Loss-Grieving	Abandonment

Other:

CASE CONCEPTUALIZATION

_____

_____

PLANS/RECOMMENDATIONS/HOMEWORK

_____

_____

Next Appointment ____/_____/20__

_____   _____

Signature & Credentials   Date

As needed, this might also include,

Noah had a play disruption when having the snakes fight in the sand. He left the sandbox, quickly filled and began drinking from a baby bottle. After a couple of minutes, holding the bottle in his teeth, he returned to the sandbox.

Note there is no interpretation. Noah is displaying the ability to self-regulate, but that assessment of the meaning of the play is documented later. This description is short and notates the session's highlights; it is not meant to be a full-session narrative. Keep it brief, salient, and meaningful.

There are two additional optional elements to assist in documenting a specific session and, therefore, change over time. First is the overall *play type*. This identifies the child's play in the playroom and inclusion, if any, of the play therapist in the play. These are based on the developmental stages of play. The second is documenting the *relating style* with the play therapist or with characters within the play sequence (Table 5.3). Movement and change in these two elements across sessions again is a way to document the treatment progress.

The play therapist may desire to identify and document additional incidents during the session that match their clinical theory and approach of working with children.

Significant Verbalizations

Children use a spontaneous verbal narrative during the session. Sometimes the child provides a running narrative of the story during their play sequence. Other times the child might carry on a dialogue with the play therapist. Sometimes they sing to themselves, speak

Table 5.2 Play types

Solitary	Plays by self, away from play therapist; birth to 2 years of age
Onlooker	Watches, may ask questions, no effort to join in play (if play therapist is co-playing in the playroom); 2 years of age
Parallel	Plays along with the play therapist but in a different activity; 2 years of age and older
Associative	Plays the same activity as the play therapist, but no give-and-take or interaction; 3–4 years of age
Cooperative	Plays jointly with play therapist, sharing, compromising, helping, develops interdependence; 4 years of age and older
Collaboration	Plays in an organized, structured way with rules, procedures, role plays, may work independently from the play therapist but toward a common goal; 4 years of age and older
Constructive	Building, putting things together, problem solving; 4 years of age and older
Competitive	Plays to win, works to beat others (may be with the play therapist, or using toys within a play sequence), winning is the goal, dominating, controlling; 4 years of age and older
Combative	Uses intimidation or aggression to control the play therapist, fights, snatches, hits, throws, may also be toys within a play sequence; 4 years of age and older

Table 5.3 Relating styles

Egocentric	Relates primarily to self, unable to see other perspectives
Identifies with others	Supportive, validating
Helpless	Solicits others to help without first trying
Seeks/rejects	Seeks/rejects support from others to help self
Empathic	Extends self to support and understand others
Able to confront	Direct but not attacking
Rescues others	Rescues others to avoid emotions or to caretake

their negative self-talk out loud. There may be lots of verbalization. All of this need not be written into the session notes. However, occasionally, there is a statement that is *significant*. When writing these in the session notes, use quotation marks to denote what the child actually said. An example might be, "*this is my dad hitting my mom*" as they narrate their play, or spontaneous verbalization seemingly unattached to their play, such as "*I hit Molly at school today.*" Take care, however, to be sure that when using quotes it is *actually* what the child said. Specific quotes are often helpful if the play therapist needs to make a report to Child Protective Services or Child Welfare. Otherwise write, *the child talked about how her parents argued and sometimes physically fought as she played at the dollhouse.* If the play therapist is directive, notate if the child's statement was in response to a specific question or directive of the play therapist.

Physical and Behavioral Aspects

Noting the quality of the child's physical and behavioral interaction in the session may also be helpful (Table 5.4). These relate more to the child's interaction, or lack thereof, with the play therapist.

Play Therapist Interventions Used

In many settings, play therapists are required to notate in the session notes what interventions they used in each session. Table 5.5 provides several possible interventions. Most play therapists use some type of limit setting. It may be helpful to indicate the reason the limit needed to be set. Also, theoretical viewpoints may use other terms or conceptual perspectives for the term *intervention*. For example, CCPT uses *skills*, and Gestalt Play Therapists use *engagement*. For our purposes, we will use the general term, *intervention*. Table 5.5 is not an all-inclusive list. However, it provides a beginning point for the reader to identify what they are implementing in the session. We encourage the reader to add to and adapt this list to their own way of working. Tables 5.2 through 5.5 are also in Appendix D, Play Therapy Cues & Clues: Objective Information.

3. **Assessment**

    The assessment section of the session notes is where the play therapist documents their clinical understanding of what happened during the session. Table 5.1, the *Play Therapy Session Notes* again provides the option of identifying the themes and space to identify that theme to specific play sequences, if desired. That space also is where the play therapist writes a short case conceptualization. Each of these is described more later in the chapter.

Table 5.4 Physical and behavioral aspects

Eye contact	Consistent, appropriate; purpose: checking on therapist's attention/cautionary/relational; culturally aware
Engaged with play	Strong, weak, sporadic
Engaged with therapist	Strong, weak, sporadic
Working	Systemically/trial and error; persistent/gives up easily; authentic effort/looks for direction
Cooperation	Resistant/cooperative; secretive/open; deceptive/inclusive; exclusive/competitive

Table 5.5 Play therapist interventions

Limit setting (reason for limit)	Protect child Protect therapist Protect property Structuring (end of session, staying in session, etc.) Socially unacceptable behavior
Nondirective interventions (CCPT refers to these as "skills")	Tracking behavior Reflecting content Reflecting feeling Facilitating decision making Returning responsibility Facilitating creativity Esteem building, encouraging
Directive interventions (Gestalt play therapists refer to these as "engagements")	Complete feelings check-in Provide alternatives Problem solving Verbal redirection Encourage participation Provide simple directives Solicit feedback Credit the effort Physical restraint Reinforcement Validation Encourage listening Exploration of thoughts/feelings Cognitive reframe Initiated time out Recognition Therapeutic cradling/holding Confrontation Choice giving

Themes

This is all about developing the clinical understanding of the therapeutic process. Begin with identifying the child's play themes throughout the session. Most play therapists find high-lighting primary themes helpful when assessing change over time and for use in parent consultations.

> *A child is never playing nothing!*

Already noted in the Objective Information section are play behaviors and play sequences. These generally become thematic play. See Table 5.6 for how play behaviors build the play sequences which embody themes. Some play is just that, play. The child is taking delight in interacting with a toy they may not have at home. Or it's a favorite toy that provides a feeling of comfort and mastery. That play is usually short in duration and low in intensity as it helps

Table 5.6 Creating play themes

Play Behaviors	=	Play Sequences	=	Play Themes
In the kitchen using pots and pans		Cooking several kinds of foods		Mastery
Putting out plates Placing food on plates		Feeding self and play therapist		Nurturing Relationship building

the child regulate. This is often used as a ritual to begin each session as the child segues from the real-world to the playroom-world. The play might also be a moment of child development. I (Linda) had a 3-year-old child in the playroom who, when being messy with the paint at the easel, discovered by happenstance being able to make handprints. It was sheer delight. And a child development moment. In subsequent sessions, she used that play to display competency, purposely painting her hands and making handprints. Working with a child over time, we may frequently have the joy of witnessing a moment of such discovery and maturation.

Dee Ray defines a "play theme as a coherent metaphor from which the child communicates the meaning he or she attributes to an experience. The theme informs the therapist of the internal meaning-making system" (2011, p. 106). Play metaphors are contained within a play sequence. Themes occur more than once, within and across sessions. Children may express themes using different play sequences with various toys. For example, the theme

> Play themes have:
> • Repetition
> • Intensity
> • Context

of nurturing may be embedded in the child cooking for and sharing the meal with the play therapist. The same child, in the same or another session, may show nurturing by inviting the alligators to play, or the child changing the baby doll's diaper. It's also important to remember that the child's play "can reveal (a) what the child has experienced; (b) reactions to what was experienced; (c) feelings about what was experienced; (d) what the child wishes, wants, or needs; and (e) the child's perception of self" (Landreth, 2012, p. 14). So this child may be sharing that she is experiencing nurturing in her environment, likes feeling nurtured, or wishes she could get more nurturing. Knowing the context of a child's specific situation is crucial in making sense of the theme and assessing which of the three possibilities most correctly apply.

Observing play sequences for themes is assisted in awareness of repetition, intensity, and context of the play (Ray, 2011). Thematic play does *feel* different. The play therapist resonates with the importance of the play for the child. Having entered the child's world, we see the play through the child's eyes and join in the emotional meaning of the play. Already mentioned is that thematic play is *repetitive*. The repetition reflects the importance to the child as they work at making meaning and developing resolution and mastery. *Intensity* is also an indicator of an embedded theme.

> Intensity is marked by the energy and focus applied to play behaviors within sessions. For the self-aware play therapist, one way to determine intensity is by how the therapist is feeling. Intense play often has a reverential quality in which the therapist may feel a need to be respectful and quiet in the moment. There might be a hesitancy to interrupt the intensity for fear of disrupting the importance of the child's play. (Ray, 2011, p. 107)

Context is the one characteristic of thematic play that occurs outside the playroom. This consists of the child's developmental history, personality characteristics, life experiences, and presenting issues (Ray, 2011). Context also includes all the areas discussed in the initial parent consultation and developing the case conceptualization and treatment plan. Suppose we continue to follow the child's nurturing thematic play mentioned earlier. In this case, the wishful-meaning is evident if she comes from a neglectful home where she also experiences family violence. If she is well attached and her parents provide ample nurturing, her thematic play shows her lived experience to the play therapist.

Table 5.1 provides a list of major, typical themes:

- ♦ Exploratory
- ♦ Mastery
- ♦ Relationship building and interpersonal relationships
- ♦ Power, aggression, helplessness, inadequate
- ♦ Control, safety (by being in control of self or environment)
- ♦ Safety, security, protection
- ♦ Family, nurturance (self or others)
- ♦ Sexualized (could also be labeled victimization, re-enactment, re-empowerment)
- ♦ Death, loss, grieving, abandonment
- ♦ Meta themes

An expansive list of additional play therapy behaviors for each of these themes is in Appendix D, Play Therapy Session Cues & Clues, Major Themes and Play Behaviors.

Conceptualization

Here you take all of the information documented thus far on the form and develop a case conceptualization statement of the session. As you complete the form, be attentive to your own reflective functioning of being in the session and thinking about the child's play and interaction with you. What was it like to be in the play, in the child's world? What were you resonating with? What feelings were being activated? Integrate all of this in-the-moment information with your understanding of the child's presenting issues, the context of the child as identified by Dee Ray. When arriving at the conceptualization section, ideas are likely already coalescing in your mind. This is the mentalization of the child and the session.

The play therapist's clinical theory will continue to be integral to developing this statement. This is the play therapist's meaning-making of what happened clinically in the session. This statement also includes what the child could do and perhaps what the child still cannot manage. This ties into the treatment plan goals, weaving in the golden thread. An example, using Noah, might be:

> *Noah consistently displays his increased ability to connect as he uses his initial play* [drums] *to reconnect to the playroom, toys, and the therapist. He continues to engage in self-initiated self-care and self-regulation after a play disruption* [using baby bottle]. *Noah continues to develop insight into his need for revenge and the struggle to maintain control of 'good behavior'* [snake battles in the sandbox]. *Noah connects easily with me and involves me in his play through his dialogue and ability to maintain limits indicating growth in social interest.*

Using the *Cues & Clues* reference list of concepts and terms by clinical theory, developed for writing case conceptualizations is also helpful here. Examples are in Appendix C.

Additionally, should the play therapist need to provide a summary of treatment, these conceptualization statements will be instrumental and incredibly valuable to pulling that report together.

4. **Plans & Recommendations & Homework**
    Yes! Finally! We are at the final, quickest section of the session notes. This section transfers the parent's assessment of how the treatment is going from the *Parent Feedback Form*. There is space allotted to enter the three ratings. Next is the reminder to include the date of the next appointment. Also noted might be:

    - Any homework given to the child and/or parents
    - A reminder to schedule any collateral contacts, such as with a teacher or school counselor
    - Request a *Consent for Release of Information* for these contacts

    Of course, in the next session's note, document the completed items and the status of those not yet finished. For example, if parents fail to comply with recommendations or the agreed-upon homework, this is the place to document it as the case progresses. This documents the level of engagement of parents and others noted in the treatment plan. You can also mention what circumstances may have precluded their ability to follow through. Such as, *the parent had to work extra shifts at work and was not available to contact the school counselor during school hours.* Or, *the child was ill and unable to keep the appointment with the psychologist for testing.* Should the play therapist need to refer because the parents are uncooperative with the play therapy process, it will be essential to have documented this over time.

Lastly, the play therapist signs the note, complete with credentials and the document's date. We are done!

While this seems lengthy, writing notes is more easily completed once you have a form that fits your practice and you become very familiar with using it.

Let's look now at a *Play Therapy Session Notes—Directive* (see Appendix D). Table 5.7 contains all the standard components for session note documentation as identified earlier. The reader will note it is also similar to the nondirective form. Most directive play therapists use both nondirective and directive play. Adlerian Play Therapists for example will use both within a single session. Cognitive-Behavioral Play Therapists (CBPT) and Solution-Focused Play Therapy (SFPT) use an even more theory-specific form. See examples in Appendix D.

Let's take a look at the directive-specific elements of a session note.

In the *Objective Information* section, add the directive intervention used and any needed materials. This might be using bibliotherapy and noting the name of the book. It might be a specific experiential activity, like making slime.

In the *Assessment* section, add the result of the directive intervention, and tie it to the treatment plan.

Sally was able to remain engaged while making slime. She tolerated the messiness and delighted in the nonstructured play. This works on her treatment goal of reducing perfectionistic behavior.

Or, it might be a different response to the directed play:

Sally was unable to engage in the messy slime activity. She still maintains the stance of having to be in control of all aspects of her play (perfectionism).

In the *Plans—Recommendations—Homework* section, add the goals for the next week and the interventions that you will use. Some directive play therapists use different terms, homework, engagements, plans, action, and so on. So edit the form to meet your specific theory or approach terminology.

Additional Dynamics to Document

The work of the play therapist is complicated. Cases are complicated. Understanding the theory of change and how it is manifested in the child's play is complicated. In addition to the in-depth competence in clinical theory and play therapy, play therapists frequently augment their work with specialized education, training, and supervision/consultation to work with specific populations. The desire of play therapists to be competent is seen, in part, in the proliferation of the special certifications that can be earned. Other play therapists may take advanced courses and consultations in a specific area. This might include areas such as attachment, abuse, trauma, neurobiology, neurodivergence, addictions, grief and loss, CPRT, Eye Movement Desensitization and Reprocessing (EMDR), and many more.

Table 5.7 Play therapy session note—directive

Play Therapy Session Note—Directive

Child's Name _____ Session #_____ Date: _____

Other's Present: _____ Length of Session ____minutes DSM _____

SUBJECTIVE

HAPPY: pleased, satisfied, delighted, excited, silly, elated, surprised, relieved

CONFIDENT: proud, strong, determined, comfortable, relaxed

SAD: disappointed, hopeless, pessimistic, discouraged, lonely, worthless, guilty

CONFUSED: ambivalent, hesitant, uncertain, timid, nervous, embarrassed

ANGRY: impatient, irritated, annoyed, frustrated, mad, mean, jealous, bored

CURIOUS: interested, focused

AFRAID: vulnerable, helpless, distrustful, fearful, fearful, terrified

ANXIOUS: nervous, worried, tentative, tense

QUALITY/INTENSITY: flat, broad, restricted, contained, ambiguous

OBJECTIVE INFORMATION

__sandbox/water

__puppets

__kitchen/cooking/food

__easel/painting

__bop bag

__dress up/jewelry/hats/masks/wand

__crafts table/clay/markers/etc.

__doll house/doll family

__baby dolls/bottle/pacifier

__cash register/money/telephone/camera/flashlight

__medical kit/bandages

__musical instruments

__games/bowling/ring toss/balls/ball & target

__building blocks/materials, boxes

__vehicles/planes

__animals: domestic/zoo/alligator/dinosaurs/shark/snake

__soldiers/guns/knife/sword/handcuffs/rope

__blocks

TOYS/PLAY BEHAVIOR

Directive Intervention Name: _____

Materials Used: _____   _____

PLAY TYPE: solitary, parallel, onlooker, associative, cooperative, collaborative, competitive, combative

RELATING STYLE: egocentric, identifies w/other, helpless, seeks, rejects, confrontative, rescues

ASSESSMENT

_____

_____

_____

PLAY THEMES

Exploratory/Mastery

Relationship Building & Interpersonal

Power/Aggression/Helpless/Inadequate

Control/Safety Death-Loss-Grieving

Other:

Safety/Security/Protection

Family/Nurturance

Sexualized

Abandonment

CASE CONCEPTUALIZATION

_____

_____

_____

PLANS/RECOMMENDATIONS/HOMEWORK

_____

_____

_____

Next Appointment ____/_____/20__

Goals for next week: Intervention for next week:

_____   _____

Signature & Credentials   Date

Trauma Work

Many, if not most, of the children seen in play therapy have experienced trauma. There are several sources of trauma. Play therapists may further specialize in one or more of these areas: natural disasters (hurricanes, tornadoes, earthquakes, floods), human-made (war, terrorism, forced migration, food deprivation), interpersonal (bullying, sexual assault, domestic violence), medical (chronic illness, results of accidents), witnessing death, complicated grief, and vicarious trauma. Any of these can be acute, chronic, or complex. As a play therapist working in one of these areas, understanding the dynamics of the experience, the resulting effect on the child (and entire family system, peers, and community), and resolving clinical issues is critical.

Trauma concepts and dynamics play therapists may want to include in their session notes:

♦ Hyperarousal, intrusion, terror, constriction; change in body movement, breathing, etc.
♦ Fragmentation; moving quickly from one play activity to another
♦ Integration; ability to blend types of play, sequences of play into an extended play narrative
♦ Activators, triggers; sound, touch, sight, smell, movement; may result in play disruption
♦ Making meaning; linking sequential events narrative with embodied limbic memories
♦ Containment; through limit setting; closure activity at the end of session

Eliana Gil (2017) discusses in depth posttraumatic play, in her book *Posttraumatic Play in Children*. For those reading this book who work extensively with traumatized children, Gil's work would be invaluable for your play therapy work. Gil differentiates between *dynamic* posttraumatic play and *toxic* posttraumatic play. Dynamic play is productive, and the child moves toward resolution and health. Toxic posttraumatic play is "stuck through its repetition and rigidity," and does not result in relief or meet the goal of mastery and "keeps children feeling retraumatized" (Gil, 2017, p. 24). Toxic play requires "direct and well-designed clinical interventions . . . if left unattended, toxic posttraumatic play is potentially retraumatizing and halts all therapeutic progress" (Gil, 2017, p. 44). Examples of toxic posttraumatic play are:

♦ Constricted/flat affect
♦ Unavailable for emotional connection
♦ Breath is shallow and held
♦ Physical tension
♦ No evidence of release after the play
♦ Story is repetitive, without change
♦ No new characters enter the play sequence
♦ Rigid interaction with play (Gil, 2017, p. 197)

See the complete list of dynamic and toxic posttraumatic play and full discussion of working with posttraumatic play in Eliana Gil's book, mentioned earlier. As you work with traumatized children, a significant level of self-awareness is needed to differentiate between toxic and dynamic play. This play therapist may need a consultation to help in maintaining self-awareness.

Jenny Findling et al. (2006) developed a Trauma Play Scale for use by play therapists in the playroom. The scale has subscales: (1) Intense Play, (2) Repetitive Play, (3) Play Disruptions, (4) Avoidant Play Behavior, and (5) Expression of Negative Affect. The research team rated play noting,

- ◆ Control
- ◆ Helpless
- ◆ Exploratory
- ◆ Loss/death
- ◆ Constructive mastery
- ◆ Deconstructive mastery
- ◆ Nurturing
- ◆ Power
- ◆ Approval seeking
- ◆ Relational ambivalence
- ◆ Relational connecting
- ◆ Relational distancing/rejecting
- ◆ Relational manipulative
- ◆ Relational reparative
- ◆ Relational testing
- ◆ Revenge/retaliate
- ◆ Safety/protection
- ◆ Sexualized

The researchers also took note of any physiological changes occurring within the child during the play segment: rapid breathing, urination, and defecation.

Neurobiology

Neurobiological concepts and dynamics play therapists may want to include in their session notes:

- ◆ Regulated, dysregulated; ability of child to stay in a regulated state, perhaps the length of time; state when entered session, shift from one state to another
- ◆ Play disruption; the abrupt break in play and move to a 'non-play' regulating activity
- ◆ Dissociation; child's heart rate increases, appears to 'zone out'; falling into the dorsal vagal system
- ◆ Hyperaroused, hypoaroused; connect with the play behavior or sequence, especially when shifts in state occurs
- ◆ Window of Tolerance (staying within the optimal zone, the ventral vagal system, and what child and play therapist (if theory appropriate) uses to down/up regulate)

The play therapist closely observes the child's physiological behavior. Also, through attunement and neuroception, resonates with the child to track the child's state. While in co-regulation, the play therapist can assist the child in up and down regulating. Document this in the session note.

Using Scales

The use of scales provides a quick and consistent measurement of dynamics play therapists consider important. These might be more general, as seen in Tables 5.8 and 5.9. The meaning of the ratings on the scales are subjectively interpreted by the play therapist using them. Generally, the rating of 5 and 6 would reflect what would be normal and typical for a child at the same developmental level. The key is for the play therapist to consistently apply the rating values across all cases. The rating scales provide a quick visual; it becomes easy over time to notice the change occurring from session to session during the play therapy intervention process. Scaling is integral to Solution-Focused Play Therapists (SFPT). See the sample SFPT session note in Appendix D. Other dynamics can be placed on a scale to show growth and change. We encourage play therapists to be creative in measuring their own perspective dynamics fundamental to them in their particular approach.

Table 5.8 Child's overall play behavior

Child's Activity Level LOW	1 2	3 4	5 6	7 8	9 10	Child's Activity Level HIGH
Intensity of Play LOW	1 2	3 4	5 6	7 8	9 10	Intensity of Play HIGH
Inclusion of Therapist LOW	1 2	3 4	5 6	7 8	9 10	Inclusion of Therapist HIGH
Destructive	1 2	3 4	5 6	7 8	9 10	Constructive
Messy/Chaotic Disorganized	1 2	3 4	5 6	7 8	9 10	Neat/Orderly

Table 5.9 Child's affect and play

Sad/angry/depressed/fearful	1 2	3 4	5 6	7 8	9 10	Content/satisfied appropriate affect
Anxious/insecure	1 2	3 4	5 6	7 8	9 10	Confident/secure
Low frustration tolerance	1 2	3 4	5 6	7 8	9 10	High frustration tolerance
Dependent/clingy/needy	1 2	3 4	5 6	7 8	9 10	Autonomous/independent
Immature/regressed hypermature	1 2	3 4	5 6	7 8	9 10	Age appropriate
External locus of control	1 2	3 4	5 6	7 8	9 10	Internal locus of control (self-controlled)
Impulsive/easily distracted	1 2	3 4	5 6	7 8	9 10	Purposeful/focused
Inhibited/constricted	1 2	3 4	5 6	7 8	9 10	Creative/expressive/spontaneous/free
Isolated/detached	1 2	3 4	5 6	7 8	9 10	Connected/Sense of belonging

Identifying Stage or Phase

Some theories and approaches have stages or phases of treatment. Noting these may be helpful to those therapists.

- ♦ Adlerian Play Therapy phases:
  - • Phase One: Building Egalitarian Relationship; Phase Two: Exploring Lifestyle; Phase Three: Developing Insight; Phase Four: Reorientation & Reeducation (Kottman, 2011)
- ♦ Cognitive-Behavioral Play Therapy stages:
  - • Assessment, Introduction/Orientation, Middle, Termination (Knell, 2019)
- ♦ Jungian Play Therapy phases:
  - • Entrance, Chaos, Struggle, Reparation & Resolution, Exit (Allen, 1997), or
  - • Acclimation, Exploration, Working, Resolution (Lilly, cited in Kottman, 2011)
- ♦ Theraplay phases:
  - • Introduction/Orientation, Negative Reaction, Working Through (Kottman, 2011)

Other clinical theories and approaches will have their own way of monitoring treatment's progress. This may or may not include phases or stages. However, if this dynamic has meaning for you, do so in your session notes. It might be writing the stage or phase. Or, adding a line at the top of your session form template that you can circle, such as for AdPT:

Phase: 1: Egalitarian Relationship, 2: Exploring Lifestyle, 3: Developing Insight, 4: Reorientation & Reeducation

This same type of insertion can be used to tailor-make the play therapy session note for each play therapist's practice.

New Life Experience, Environmental Stressors, and Changes

Life continues to happen to our clients and their families as we continue the intervention process. If something impacts the child's functioning, notate it in the client file. When and how we learn about the information will indicate where it is documented. It might come to us through a telephone call or email. In that case, it is recorded in the Contact Log in the client's file. It might be information received during a parent consultation. In that case, it's documented on the *Parent Consultation Session Note*. Frequently, we are given the information by the parent when bringing their child to a play therapy session. They let you know that a pet has died, a parent has moved out, there was a fire at their house, or some other change. Notate this information in the "Plan" section in the session form. For example:

Before the session, the mother reported her son's paternal grandmother had died after a long illness. They will miss next week's session as they will be out of town for the funeral.

or,

Before the session, mom reported that the transfer to another school had been approved, and her daughter would be attending the new school beginning Monday.

Remember to follow up on the impact of the new experience during the next parent consultation. Or, if the experience has a significant impact on the child and family, scheduling an immediate conversation with the parent for a more detailed update would be appropriate.

In Closing

The translating of the child's play and the content of the play therapy session to words occurs on the *Play Therapy Session Note*. There are components that are required in a session note, to meet the standard of care. Once those are included, the form can be tailor-made to meet the clinical theoretical perspective of the play therapist to maintain the golden thread. We encourage readers to adapt the forms in the appendix or companion website to meet their unique work and include dynamics important to them.

For those readers who delight in learning more and viewing play from a variety of viewpoints we have included Chapter 10: A Deeper Look at Play. We hope this will engender a deeper look with a curiosity that brings richness to your work.

Resources

♦ *Clinical Applications of the Therapeutic Powers of Play: Case Studies in Child and Adolescent Psychotherapy*, Eileen Prendiville & Judi Parson, Routledge, 2021
♦ *Multicultural Play Therapy: Making the Most of Cultural Opportunities with Children*, edited by Dee Ray, Yumiko Ogawa, & Yi-Ju Cheng, Routledge, 2022.
♦ *The Therapeutic Powers of Play: 20 Core Agents of Change* (2nd ed.). Charles Schaefer & Athena Drewes, Wiley, 2014.

References

Allen, J. (1997). Jungian play therapy. In K. O'Connor & L. M. Braverman (Eds.), *Play therapy theory and practice: A comparative presentation* (pp. 100–130). Wiley Press.

Findling, J. H., Bratton, S. C., & Henson, R. K. (2006). Development of the trauma play scale: An observation-based assessment of the impact of trauma on the play therapy behaviors of young children. *International Journal of Play Therapy*, 15(1), 7–36.

Gil, E. (2017). *Posttraumatic play in children*. Guilford.

Knell, S. (2019). Cognitive-behavioral play therapy. In K. O'Connor, C. Schaefer, & L. Braverman (Eds.), *Handbook of play therapy* (pp. 119–134). Wiley Press.

Kottman, T. (2011). *Play therapy basics and beyond*. American Counseling Association.

Landreth, G. L. (2012). *Play therapy: The art of the relationship* (3rd ed.). Routledge.

Ray, D. (2011). *Advanced play therapy: Essential conditions, knowledge, and skills for child practice*. Routledge.

Chapter 6

Ongoing Parent Consultations

Working with parents is a struggle for many play therapists, as many play therapists make a conscious choice to work with children rather than adults. The very nature of working with children, and therefore their parents, makes the work of play therapists more complex than working with individual adults. Play therapists who feel anxious when thinking about talking with parents, let alone working with them in a therapeutic relationship, should seek supervision, consultation, and perhaps personal work with their own therapist. Self-reflection of one's feelings, beliefs, and perceptions around parents and parenting issues will help develop professional skills in working with parents. Explore expectations one may have of parents and parenting and feelings one experiences when parents are not meeting those expectations. Parents can undoubtedly respond in ways that activate play therapists, and it is the therapist's response to the parent that facilitates success or failure in the parent consultation (Sanders & Burke, 2014). Continually working to identify and address one's feelings regarding parents will add to one's strength as a play therapist. Even for play therapists who are comfortable working with parents, be ready; a parent will likely surprise you, and awareness of how your response impacts the therapeutic process is important. Play therapists cannot expect to be able to psychologically and emotionally hold parents and help co-regulate them without awareness of their own internal regulation.

What Is the Purpose of a Parent Consultation?

Play therapists tend to envision parent consultations as a time to share the child's progress with the parents and facilitate insight into the parent-child relationship. We have the assumption that parents will receive this information with sensitivity, care, and be open and willing to learn new skills to facilitate more growth and change at home. Sometimes parents respond in a way that makes our job easy. But sometimes, the struggle in a parent consultation is when we are challenged by parents who are not responding in ways we thought they would. Play therapists are often surprised and frustrated by how parents react to their children. The play therapist senses hurt at that moment on behalf of the child. Play therapists may feel astonished if parents are not interested in learning new skills and trying a more

DOI: 10.4324/9781003258766-7

therapeutic approach to connecting with their child. Parents who are angry with their child and place blame on their child, taking little to no responsibility in the relationship, stun play therapists.

Play therapists must rethink the parent consultation. Regardless of your theoretical approach to counseling, all theories hold the core conditions as a necessary part of the therapeutic process. Like any other client, parents need the core conditions as part of the therapeutic relationship (Rogers, 1957). First and foremost, they need to be in psychological contact with the play therapist. If the parent does not feel connected to the play therapist, progress cannot be made. The parent must be in a state of incongruence, being vulnerable, or anxious. Parents need a play therapist who can provide congruence. The therapist provides a warm, welcoming, and stable environment for the parents' emotions

> **Core Conditions**
>
> - Two people in psychological contact
> - Client in a state of incongruence
> - Therapist is congruent
> - Therapist provides unconditional positive regard for the client
> - Therapist provides empathy for the client
> - The client receives congruence, unconditional positive regard and empathy from the therapist

Additionally, parents need the play therapist to provide genuineness, empathy, and unconditional positive regard. Parents need to receive and experience these conditions just as much as children do. Parents need a space to talk, process, and understand what is happening with their child and themselves.

Very few parents ever thought their child would have behavior challenges or experience trauma and need the services of a play therapist. It also does not occur to parents that they have their own unresolved childhood struggles that are impacting their current relationship with their child and their child's behavior. This is where a family systems perspective is helpful. Exploring the multigenerational patterns and intergenerational trauma sets the context of the child in our playroom and the parents in our consultation room.

A parent consultation aims to include parents in the therapeutic process. Post et al. (2012) found that including parents in parent consultations increases the likelihood of success in play therapy. Parents are part of the therapy team, even if they do not realize they are. If given a choice to come to a parent consultation, many parents will say no, as they may not think they have things to share. Parents may be worried that they will be blamed or shamed regarding their child's behavior. Or feel so incompetent that they cannot imagine being helpful to the process. Parents who are not included in the therapeutic process are more likely to terminate prematurely than parents who are included (Athanasiou, 2001). Therefore, it is important that the play therapist take the lead, informing parents that parent consultations are part of the therapeutic process.

Scheduling regular parent consultations demonstrates to parents that this is an expected part of the therapeutic process. Play therapists work to help parents see the world through their child's eyes during parent consultations. To see the change and growth in their child. Understanding the child's work in the playroom is connected to how the child functions outside the playroom. Once parents feel safe and seen by the therapist, we also use parent consultation to facilitate change in the parent by teaching therapeutic parenting skills. The play therapist has these goals while providing attitudes of empathy, acceptance, understanding, and curiosity.

Basic Components of a Parent Consultation

Never go into a parent consultation unprepared. Play therapists must provide parents with thoughtful feedback on their child's progress. The *Parent Consultation Preparation Form* is found in Table 6.1 and Appendix E to help you collect your thoughts. It is unwise to enter a parent consultation without some preparation. When you are prepared for a parent consultation, the focus can be on the therapeutic relationship and being present with the parent. Providing thoughtful, cohesive feedback regarding their child's therapeutic process is a primary goal of parent consultations.

Basic Components of Parent Consultation

- Therapeutic relationship with the parent
- Inquiring about progress at home and school
- Sharing clinical information regarding treatment progress
- Treatment plans: monitoring and updating
- Teaching therapeutic parenting skills
- Connecting parents to resources

Table 6.1 Parent consultation preparation form

Parent Consultation Preparation Form
Client Name: _____   Date of Session: _____
Number of Sessions with Child:_____
Goal of Session_____
Conceptualization of Parent(s):_____
Treatment Plan Goals:
1.
2.
3.
Therapeutic Progress of Treatment Plan Goals:
Play Therapy Themes or Theory Concepts to Share:
Follow-Up Questions to Ask:
Parenting Skill to Teach (if parent is ready):
Encouraging Comments About the Child:

Gather the *Parent Feedback Forms* since the last parent consultation and compare them to information from the *Initial Parent Consultation Session Note*, *Treatment Plan*, and the child's diagnosis. Also, review the conceptualizations from the *Play Therapy Session Notes* since your last parent consultation. Note any progress you have seen in therapy on these issues. Make a short note on your conceptualization of the parent and your goal for the consultation. Keep this information in mind as you consider how to provide feedback in ways the parent can best hear. When giving feedback regarding play themes, work to connect this information to behaviors parents have reported outside of the session. Making these connections helps parents understand the play therapy process and provides insight into their child. If the parent is ready to learn a new parenting skill, limit this to one skill at a time. Allowing ample time to teach, demonstrate, and practice the skill with the parent is critical. Providing information on the skill in writing and providing a handout is also helpful for the parent to utilize the skill at home. There are practice worksheets on *Reflection of Feeling* and *Limit Setting* in Appendix F. Closing the session with a verbal summary of progress and a comment about the child's strengths helps the parents leave your office feeling encouraged.

Regardless of your theoretical approach, some foundational aspects of counseling are necessary for successful parent consultations. During ongoing consultations, the foundations include focusing on the therapeutic relationship with the parents, inquiring about progress at home and school, sharing clinical information regarding treatment, monitoring treatment plans, teaching therapeutic parenting skills, and connecting parents to resources. *The Parent Consultation Preparation Form* can help you keep the session focused and effectively manage time.

Therapeutic Relationship With the Parent

The core conditions of empathy, unconditional positive regard, genuineness, and congruence are the attitudes required of therapists toward their clients in a therapeutic relationship. Parents need to feel safe and seen by the therapist before they can be transparent with the struggles they are having or before they will be open to making changes. Parents must feel supported, encouraged, and not criticized during their work with you. There are cases where the parents are very resistant to encouragement, so you may have to begin with the most minor example of positive change. You may also need to adjust your expectations of what you believe the parent is capable of in their relationship with their child. Start small and build on the small but continuing areas of growth. At the minimum, encourage the parent by identifying that they are seeking help for their child, coming to sessions, taking time out of their day, and sacrificing finances to bring their child to play therapy. As the parents continue to feel supported over time, their confidence increases. They are increasingly willing to take relational risks, listen, and try to implement the information you are sharing. In each parent consultation, it is important to remember that the investment in the relationship is a critical component of the process. It is easy to assume your relationship with the parent is more secure than it actually is and therefore think it is time to dive into deeper issues before the parent is ready. Pressing in too soon can be counterproductive to everything you have done thus far with the family. In the worst-case situation, the parent removes the child from therapy. Remember, relationship development is ongoing, and parents are humans who have their own struggles and need substantial support.

Parents' Report of Progress

How are things at home? Inviting parents to report their perception of their child at home and school first is helpful. This provides a lot of information about what the parents perceive at the moment. It is essential to listen carefully to the parent's tone to differentiate between a difficult day (and a frustrated parent) and a child whose overall progress has regressed. Many parents report about the last few days rather than reflect holistically over the previous few weeks. As parents provide information, the play therapist works to connect those behaviors to the play behaviors and themes the child is working through in the playroom. Connecting behaviors in the playroom to those at home and school is an aspect of the parent consultation that parents appreciate; it helps them see the process is working (Lee & Ray, 2020).

Listening, reflecting, and asking follow-up questions comparing what they reported in the last session or in the *Weekly Parent Feedback Form* to what they are reporting now can help parents be more reflective about their child's progress. Managing time and storytelling is also important. Parents have a lot to say; helping them feel heard while keeping them focused is challenging. There is always something to work on, children will always be noncompliant or challenging in some way, and every parent desires an easier, more compliant child. Therefore, therapists must help parents determine if their behavioral struggles continue to require clinical intervention. Here are options of possible questions for Alicia in a parent consultation:

- ◆ *Last month you reported Noah was having fewer meltdowns; do you think he is having them more often now?*
- ◆ *It's really challenging to manage sibling arguments. Noah and his sister continue to argue; are the arguments as intense as they have been? Is he still throwing toys in anger?*
- ◆ *Last month you reported Noah was compliant about three times a day, which was a small improvement. What is it like now?*
- ◆ *On the* Weekly Parent Feedback Form, *it seems things are improving. Do you feel like that today?*

Therapist's Report of Progress

Connecting the clinical happenings in the playroom with the parents' report and with the other specific treatment goals being addressed in the playroom is a primary goal of parent consultation. It is important to give parents helpful information, so explaining the play themes and connecting them to a treatment goal enables the parent to understand how progress is made. It also helps parents connect the dots with behaviors they may be seeing at home. Informing the parent about their child's world, how their child perceives their world, and the beliefs the child has about themselves helps provide meaning to therapy. Increasing the parents' awareness of how their child perceives their world can help the parent empathize and understand their child's behavior. This might sound like,

In the playroom, Noah's play indicates a need for control, predictability, and mastery. This is consistent with his resistance to your requests at home. The changes in your family dynamics, with dad traveling more and mom needing to attend more to your daughter, all of which are necessary, explain why he is feeling so out of control. It might be helpful for us to talk about some age-appropriate ways he can have more control at home.

Often, when behaviors make sense, parents can be more understanding and empathetic with their child, therefore responding with more love and patience. Most parents have never thought about how situations feel for the child. A parent who files for divorce perceives they are making things better for their child, and they would be grateful for the fighting to end. Rather than understanding why their child is angry at the parent who "sent the other parent away." Parents need play therapists to interpret their child's behaviors, which hopefully facilitates more empathy and acceptance in the parent-child relationship.

Treatment Plans: Monitoring and Updating

Many therapists use a *Weekly Parent Feedback Form* (Table 6.2 and Appendix E) to track parents' weekly progress reports. This form also provides a place for parents to share any new information, happenings, or significant events. The *Weekly Parent Feedback Form* states initial problematic behavior and related treatment plan goals. Parents provide feedback on the progress for each treatment goal for their child. Referencing these forms during parent consultations can help you keep parents' evaluations more global rather than focused on today's challenges. Keeping the conversation focused on treatment goals provides structure and gives the play therapist opportunities to update progress on goals. Over time, it may be essential to update the treatment plan; as clients progress, goals are achieved, allowing space to adjust the focus of therapy. It is also possible that new information is revealed or recent trauma or a significant event occurs that requires a shift in treatment plan goals. Therefore, it is helpful for the play therapist to consistently refer back to the treatment plan and make adjustments and updates as necessary to keep therapy focused on the client's most immediate needs.

Therapeutic Parenting Skills

It is easy to overwhelm parents with parenting techniques and concepts. Parents are likely to only retain a portion of what you share with them, so be selective in what you share. Parents can benefit from concepts of Interpersonal Neurobiology and child development to help them understand why their child behaves and responds in particular ways. This can help parents develop more empathy and understanding for their child. We also normalize the child's behavior by providing this type of information. However, it is crucial not to dismiss the parents' struggle, developmentally appropriate behaviors can still be challenging. Applying Interpersonal Neurobiology to parents is part of this. As parents understand their own Window of Tolerance and the impact the size of their window has on their child, we can more

Table 6.2 Weekly parent feedback form

Weekly Parent Feedback Form		
Date: _____ Child Client: _____ Parent/Rater: _____		
Behavior at Intake	**Current Rating**	**Desired Behavior**
Treatment Plan #1	1 2 3 4 5	Treatment Plan #1
Treatment Plan #2	1 2 3 4 5	Treatment Plan #2
Treatment Plan #3	1 2 3 4 5	Treatment Plan #3
Other comments you want to share with your child's counselor:		

directly change the family atmosphere. Their understanding increases in teaching these skills and using Interpersonal Neurobiology to support these skills. As you teach reflection of feeling, think of an adult example, a time someone reflected your feeling recently and how you responded versus when you did not feel understood, as an example to share with parents.

Before parents can be open to new parenting skills, they may need to arrive at the conclusion that what they are doing at home is not effective. Asking questions such as,

♦ *What is the primary parenting tool you rely on to create behavior change in your children?*
♦ *How is that working for you?*

Teaching parents the most basic counseling skills can make a meaningful impact on their interactions with their child. I (Mary) refer to reflection of feeling as the "little black dress" of counseling. It's a basic part of every lady's wardrobe. Reflecting feelings is the most powerful counseling skill we can share, and it can be used in just about any situation, just like the little black dress with flip flops or pearls; it goes anywhere. Most adults question children, which takes the child out of the right side of their brain and into their left side, looking for a correct answer rather than facilitating emotional expression. Reflection of feeling is often an unfamiliar concept for parents. Teaching, demonstrating, and role-playing reflection of feeling with parents is critical for parents to truly learn reflection of feeling. Teaching in isolation without the demonstration and practice is more often overwhelming to parents, and their ability to use this skill with their children decreases. Parents worry that reflection of feeling is coddling or "giving into" the child. Address this directly and explain that it is not giving in. It acknowledges the child's feeling, communicating to the child an understanding of how they are functioning at the moment. It is not condoning the accompanying behavior. I often explain the importance of touching the right, emotional side of the child's brain so that the child can get to the left, more logical side of the brain (Siegel & Bryson, 2012). Bratton and Landreth (2020) created the "Be With Attitudes" which communicates, "I'm here, I hear you, I understand and I care and does not mean, I always agree, I must make you happy or I will solve your problems" (p. 13). I caution parents that dismissing their child's feelings when they are young can ultimately lead to children who don't share experiences with their parents as they get older. Often parents need to be reminded that it is challenging to be a child, that school is hard, navigating friends can be hurtful, and that rolly pollies are exciting!

> *I'm here,*
> *I hear you,*
> *I understand and I care*
> *it does not mean,*
> *I always agree,*
> *I must make you happy or*
> *I will solve your problems.*

When teaching reflection of feeling, making statements short and simple is best. The *Reflection of Feeling Practice Worksheet* (Appendix F) can be used with parents as part of *teach-demonstrate-do model*. Children can get lost in lots of words and not hear the message we are attempting to relay. Reflection of feeling involves as little as three words,

♦ *You are excited.*
♦ *You are disappointed.*

Parents tend to want to make it more complicated. When we keep it short and stop talking, it leaves space for the child to respond and give us even more information about their perception of what is happening in their world. In my own home, I (Mary) am very guilty, in my parenting, of what I refer to as a "drive-by reflection of feeling," which generally means I am saying the words, but my tone of voice lacks genuineness. I warn parents of this possibility, as it is easy to do when parents are busy and distracted by other things rather than truly stepping into their child's world. The brain processes nonverbal behaviors, tone of voice, facial expression, and hand gestures faster than verbal information. Therefore a parent's tone of voice is critical to the child being receptive to the parents' words. When done well and when the child is in a receptive space, a reflection of feeling can increase a child's feelings of happiness and decrease their sad feelings. This results in feeling felt and connected, not misunderstood and alone. Typically behavior changes, and a stronger parent-child connection occurs when children feel seen, heard, and understood. It is important to remember that parents may be good at doing but struggle in being with their child. Teaching parents the importance of sitting with their child and slowly reflecting on their feeling, likely longer than is comfortable, can significantly affect their parent-child relationship, ultimately leading to behavior change.

This idea that a more robust relationship leads to behavior change can be difficult for parents to understand. Most likely, when their children behave in unhelpful ways, parents desire to reject and push the child away rather than press into the relationship. Helping parents see that they are protecting themselves in these moments, just as their child does when they feel hurt by someone. All people deserve a relationship that provides acceptance and love. Helping parents see that in these relationships in their life when they are feeling understood, they are more likely to be compassionate when that friend is hurtful to them. Just like our children are more flexible and more likely to be compliant when they feel seen and understood by their parents.

The definition of discipline is to teach. Teaching children new behaviors to replace unwanted behaviors is an important skill for parents. So often, parents only focus on extinguishing unwanted behaviors and neglect to help the child learn an acceptable alternative. Limit setting is utilized in all play therapy theories. There are nuanced differences among the theories regarding the exact wording. These differences have a theoretical rationale for the specific wording choices. Noting differences is beyond the scope of this chapter; play therapists are encouraged to study their theory text to fully understand the theoretical rationale. Most play therapy theories use an adaptation of either the Child-Centered or Adlerian model for limit setting.

The ACT Limit Setting (Landreth, 2012) is a valuable skill for parents. However, it is often met with resistance. We recommend first teaching reflection of feeling and allowing parents to practice and report how they are using it and how it is working in their home. Without successful use of reflection of feeling, parents are not receptive to limit setting. Connecting Interpersonal Neurobiology concepts to limit setting is also helpful. In ACT, we touch

> **ACT Limit Setting**
> - **A**cknowledge the child's need, wish, or want
> - **C**ommunicate the limit
> - **T**arget an alternative

the right side of the brain before moving to the left, more logical side of the brain. Having engaged both sides of the brain, the child is more likely to comply (Siegel & Bryson, 2012). See the *ACT Limit Setting Practice Worksheet* in Appendix F with examples and opportunities to practice so that parents can refer back to this more advanced skill.

Adlerian Play Therapists (AdPT) use a slightly different limit setting format. The AdPT limit clearly reflects the egalitarian perspective of the play therapist and the child. The Adlerian Play Therapist first states the limit. Secondly, the child's feeling is reflected, or the therapist metacommunicates about an underlying purpose of the behavior. Third, the therapist works with the child to generate alternative options. Finally, if the child is unable to comply with the limit, the child and therapist collaborate in creating logical consequences (Kottman & Meany-Walen, 2016). The *Adlerian Play Therapy Limit Setting Practice Worksheet* is also in Appendix F to use with parents in the teach-demonstrate-do approach.

Spending time in subsequent parent consultations talking through possible limits with parents provides opportunities to help with everyday challenges. Parents feel very supported when therapists take time for this. It is easy to overwhelm and cause parents to feel defensive when introducing parenting skills too early or too many at once. Use your clinical judgment and theory to determine when the timing is right and only teach one skill at a time.

Resources for Parents

Play therapists have abundant resources for parents. We find that parents no longer rely on their pediatrician to help them investigate behavioral problems with their children, and teachers are limited in what they can say or recommend to a parent. This is where play therapists can help. A posture of curiosity can be helpful to families to identify the different pieces of the puzzle to explain their child's behaviors. Understanding how other professionals work with children and what challenges they treat can be helpful. We suggest you know the other professionals in your community to whom you can refer clients who are struggling in ways that are outside your scope of practice. We frequently refer to:

♦ Occupational Therapists—Sensory issues, fine motor, developmental delays, visual-perceptual skills, cognitive skills
♦ Speech Therapists—Articulation, fluency, language disorders, feeding disorders
♦ Couples Counselors—Challenges within the couple relationship of the parents
♦ Family Therapists—To treat the family unit if you are going to continue seeing the child individually
♦ Psychologists—assessments for learning difficulties, ADHD, autism, and other mental health disorders
♦ Pediatric Psychiatrists—For medication

General parenting resources are helpful as well. Play therapists should be well versed in the parenting resources their community relies upon. Knowing your clients and their preferred method of learning will help determine what resources you recommend. If you recommend books, suggest a particular chapter to begin reading. Then discuss it in a parent consultation. For busy parents, the thought of finding time to read and apply an entire book is too much to manage, so they don't read any of it. Even parents who are readers often benefit from listening to the book on audio. Especially if they are auditory learners and spend time commuting in their cars. Many authors read their own books and the author's tone of voice adds to the understanding. There are beneficial podcasts, YouTube videos, blog posts, and other social media feeds that provide parenting support. We suggest you keep a running list with electronic links to the resources you recommend to parents. A few of our favorites are listed in the Resources section of this chapter. Handouts you create yourself with bullet points for parents to put on the refrigerator are helpful. This is useful for visual learners. Parents do the best they can with the information they have, and we can help guide and direct them to more intentional ways of interacting with their child.

Basic Skills in a Parent Consultation

While providing the core conditions for parents, we must also gather information, clarify nonverbal expressions, and ask follow-up questions. We work to see the world through the parent's eyes. As we listen to parents, it is important to ask questions that clarify what the phrase means to the parent. For example,

The parent states, *Noah is aggressive with his sister.*

   The therapist might ask, *What does his aggression look like? How long does it last? How many times a week is there aggressive behavior?*

Then, based on the answer, there could be additional questions to gain more specifics:

When he is aggressive, what else is happening?
   Is he trying to get what he wants?
   Is he walking by and hitting without being provoked? Or is it something else?

Asking more precisely what a particular behavior looks like is critical. We are assessing the parents' tolerance for their children's behaviors and attentiveness to it and more specific information to determine how we can be helpful. When asking parents follow-up questions, alternate with reflecting content so parents feel understood. Therapists may also ask,

Behavior is communication; I wonder what your child is trying to communicate with this behavior?

By wondering with the parent rather than asking direct questions, you have entered into a supportive, problem-solving role, rather than sitting in the expert role and judging parents.

   Play therapists also have to be careful how we ask questions as we do not want to cause further alarm in the parent. For example, asking parents,

Has the teacher ever asked to have an autism assessment? or
   Do you have any reason to think your child has been sexually abused?

may cause alarm. Work to have a posture of curiosity and be aware of your tone of voice, so you sound supportive. When you do ask hard questions, use information you have gathered both in and out of session, for example,

I wonder what information we could get from an assessment. There are a lot of pieces to this puzzle, and an assessment might help us understand some of Noah's challenges better. Has day-care personnel ever asked about assessing him?

Remember, after each answer use a reflection of feeling or content, which will help you pace your questions and allow the parent to feel even more heard. This also reinforces the skills we have asked the parent to use with their children, reflecting feelings and showing understanding.

Parent Blaming

Play therapists must have an underlying belief that parents are doing the best they can with the information and skills they have. It is a slippery slope for a play therapist to fall into the trap of parent blaming. Even the most competent and best parents make a lot of mistakes. Their Window of Tolerance is only so big, and they have hard days; sometimes, even the most straightforward task is simply too much. Parenting is complex and demanding, but it is easy to be critical of parents. As play therapists, we only experience the child for 45 minutes once a week in a playroom. We must have empathy for how hard it might be to get this child to do things she does not want to do, calm her down when your boss just yelled at you, or when two other children are screaming. After all, parenting is challenging and seldom what a parent expects it will be like. Should you find yourself blaming parents, we encourage you to consult with a colleague who may help you gain some empathy for the parent. Parents may sometimes trigger responses and feelings in us, which impact the therapeutic relationship. See Chapter 8: Parents Who Challenge Us and Chapter 9: Difficult Parenting Issues for more awareness of how parents trigger you.

Parent Expectations of Parent Consultations

Lee and Ray (2020) surveyed parents (N=19) to determine what they believe to be the more important and most valuable information they receive from play therapists. Parents reported appreciating a play therapist who collects thorough background information, including medical, educational, and home functioning, and the child's current status. We believe a significant part of our work as play therapists is to help parents problem-solve, sit, and be curious as to why their child is struggling. Play therapists who help bridge an understanding of behaviors in the playroom with those at home and school were reported as helpful by parents. Connecting play behaviors and themes to the parents' experience outside of the session help them develop a deeper understanding of their child's perspective (Lee & Ray, 2020). Often parents have forgotten to consider their child's perception of experiences, which may explain their behavior. This posture is important in developing empathy and understanding for their child. Parents reported appreciating play therapists who teach parenting skills and who have expert knowledge regarding children. Parents report wanting a play therapist who works to understand their families' unique concerns. Finally, one who is qualified to be a play therapist, who has training and supervision specifically in play therapy, was reported as valued (Lee & Ray, 2020). As we conduct ongoing parent consultations, this information was identified as important to keep in mind as we structure our time with parents. Parents are the gateway to their children. If the play therapist cannot provide support and information that is meaningful and helpful to them, they are more likely to stop therapeutic services for their child prematurely (Campbell et al., 2000).

Parent Consultation Models

You are not likely to be surprised to read at this point in the book that how and when you conduct your parent consultation will depend on your theoretical approach and the needs of the particular client and family. While all theories would support the basic rationale for parent consultations, how a therapist may conduct them will depend on the theory and subsequent role of the therapist. So the first question to consider is, are you a guide, a teacher/expert, or one traveling with the client?

Kottman and Meany-Walen (2016) relate the four phases of Adlerian Play Therapy to parent consultations. Adlerian therapists focus Phase 1 on building an egalitarian relationship with the parent. Phase 2 on gathering information about the parents' lifestyles, family constellation, parenting styles, and such. Phase 3 on helping parents gain insight into their lifestyle and how it impacts their new understanding of their child's lifestyle and goals of misbehavior. Phase 4 to reorienting-reeducating the family. These phases are not linear and may flow back and forth depending on the client's struggles. Throughout the treatment process, Adlerian Play Therapists focus on providing insights into the child's lifestyle for parents and facilitating some insight for parents into their own lifestyle and how that impacts the parent-child relationship. The frequency of parent consultations is flexible and depends on the therapist's setting, availability, and client need. Therapists may meet with parents every week, include them in play therapy sessions, or only meet with them every few weeks. Kottman and Meany-Walen (2016) encourage Adlerian therapists to rely heavily on their theory to conceptualize parents' lifestyles to best deliver information and help facilitate insight in the parents so that each parent can hear and understand. In the final phase of treatment, Kottman and Meany-Walen (2016) recommend teaching parents parenting skills to facilitate growth in the parent-child relationship.

Schottelkorb et al. (2015) propose a model for Child-Centered Parent Consultations (CCPC) that includes five components (1) forming and maintenance of relationship through core relationship conditions, (2) demonstrating present awareness to listen and respond, (3) respecting parents as experts on their own children, (4) sharing relevant knowledge, and (5) teaching therapeutic skills. These components happen simultaneously and are focused on the attitudes the therapist conveys within the core conditions. In CCPC sessions, the therapist works to "Be-With" (Bratton & Landreth, 2020) rather than to quickly problem-solve for parents. When sharing relevant knowledge, CCPT therapists focus on sharing play themes to facilitate the parents' understanding of the child's world. Discussing themes also helps assess progress in play therapy (see Chapter 5: Treatment Phase: Session Notes and Chapter 10: A Deeper Look at Play for more information on identifying themes). When teaching parents therapeutic skills, Schottelkorb et al. (2015) recommend using the CONNECT model (Helker et al., 2007) to help adults learn foundational therapeutic skills. CONNECT stands for Convey acceptance, Offer understanding, Notice children's behaviors, Negotiate choices, Encourage self-esteem, Communicate limits, Trust yourself to be genuine. Using Interpersonal Neurobiology to help parents understand how using therapeutic skills impacts their child's brain and their relationship is also encouraged. Parent consultations are recommended every three to four sessions in the CCPT model. Starting sessions by inviting the parent to share how the child is progressing at home and school, followed by the play therapist sharing progress and themes. Play therapists use their clinical judgment to determine if therapeutic skills in the CONNECT model or information regarding child development should be presented first. Parents generally need the skills in the CONNECT model and child development. Therefore, play therapists can use their clinical judgment to know which should be presented first. All information shared by Child-Centered Play Therapists shares the main clinical goal of facilitating deeper relationships between parent and child. Child-Centered Play Therapists believe that a more profound understanding between parent and child will facilitate more acceptance and genuineness in the relationship, which ultimately leads to more positive behavior for both the parent and child.

Similarly, Stulmaker and Jayne (2018) state the goals of parent consultations in a CCPT model are to (1) provide the core conditions, (2) support parents in understanding the child's behavior and internal experience, (3) help parents experience greater empathy and understanding for their child, and (4) to promote change in the child's environment. To achieve these goals, parent consultations are recommended after every third or fourth session for 30 minutes to 50 minutes in length. The goals of the initial parent consultation are to establish a trusting relationship with the parents and gather information regarding the presenting issue as well as the developmental history of the child. In subsequent parent consultations, the play therapist continues to focus on the relationship with the parent and progress or regression in the child's behavior at home. The play therapist takes this information and links it to play behaviors and themes the child exhibits in session. The authors caution play therapists regarding teaching parenting skills too soon, as the parent may perceive this as a threat to their self-structure, which can put the therapeutic relationship in jeopardy (Stulmaker & Jayne, 2018). Clinical judgment regarding the therapeutic relationship is the primary focus of the Child-Centered Parent Consultation.

Susan Knell (2009) explains the importance of parent involvement in Cognitive-Behavioral Play Therapy (CBPT). Depending on the presenting issue, parents might be a part of each play session, a part of the child's homework, such as helping the child journal or keeping their own journal of their child's behaviors. Play therapists provide parents with information regarding the child's progress, child development, and monitor the parents' interactions with the child. These are all considered to be a part of the CBPT therapeutic process.

As described earlier, parent consultations can be structured in several different ways, depending on the play therapist's clinical theory of counseling. Forming a strong therapeutic relationship with parents is the most critical component in each of these models. Campbell et al. (2000) report that a lack of parent involvement is a cause of parents prematurely terminating their child's play therapy. Therefore, this is a critical area that therapists should reflect on and intentionally spend significant time developing in their practice.

People to Paper: Documentation

Welcome back to paperwork. You have had a parent consultation, and now it is time to document all you discussed. Documentation completes the golden thread. Table 6.3 is a copy of the *Parent Consultation Session Note* (Appendix E). In this session note, you will

Table 6.3 Parent consultation session note

Parent Consultation Session Note
Client name _____ Parent/Guardian present_____
Date of session/session number _____
Parent report of client behavior and progress:
Therapist report of session progress: (play or verbal themes, significant insights, etc.)
Therapeutic parenting skills or insights shared:
Recommendations, homework/action plan:
_____   _____ Play Therapist Signature & Credentials   Date

report the information you shared with parents regarding their child's progress, review of treatment plan progress, and any therapeutic parenting techniques you may have shared.

It is also important to document information the parent shares, including progress at home and school, current behavior challenges, and other significant details. When writing these notes, therapists use the same language they would in an adult session summary. For example, phrases such as "parent reported," "parent stated," "therapist observed," and "therapist reported" will be helpful in these session notes.

In Closing

Involving parents in the therapeutic process is a critical component of client care. Play therapists work to develop the therapeutic relationship with both parents and children for the whole family to be open to change. Providing parents with helpful feedback regarding session progress and making connections with parent-reported behaviors and improvement in session helps parents understand the therapeutic process. And finally, teaching parents, when they are ready, therapeutic parenting skills to enhance their connection with their child makes a difference in the therapeutic process. All of these aspects are then documented to continue the golden thread.

Resources

There are a plethora of informative parenting resources. This is by no means an exhaustive list but a few of our favorites.

Books
♦ *How To Talk So Little Kids Will Listen and Listen So Little Kids Will Talk*. Joanna Faber & Julie King, Simon and Schuster, 2017.
♦ *How to Talk So Kids Will Listen and Listen So Kids Will Talk*. Adele Faber & Elaine Mazlish, Scribner Book Publisher, 2012.
♦ *Toddler Discipline at Every Age and Stage*, Aubrey Hargis, Rockridge, 2018.
♦ *A Therapist's Guide to Child Development: The Extraordinarily Normal Years*, Dee Ray, Routledge, 2016.
♦ All parenting books by Dan Siegel and Tina Payne Bryson.

Social Media Resources

Instagram:
♦ Tinapaynebryson
♦ BigLittleFeelings
♦ Curious.Parenting

Podcasts:
♦ Parenting after Trauma Podcast by Robyn Gobbel
♦ Raising Good Humans with Dr. Aliza

Websites:
♦ Tinabryson.com
♦ Julieking.org

References

Athanasiou, M. S. (2001). Using consultation with a grandmother as an adjunct to play therapy. *The Family Journal, 9*(4), 445–449.

Bratton, S. C., & Landreth, G. L. (2020). *Child parent relationship therapy (CPRT) treatment manual*. Routledge.

Campbell, V. A., Baker, D. B., & Bratton, S. (2000). Why do children drop out of play therapy? *Clinical Child Psychology and Psychiatry, 5*, 133–138. https://doi.org/10.1177/1359104500005001013

Helker, W. P., Schottelkorb, A. A., & Ray, D. C. (2007). Helping students and teachers CONNECT: An intervention model for school counselors. *Journal of Professional Counseling: Practice, Theory, & Research, 35*, 31–45.

Knell, S. M. (2009). Cognitive behavioral play therapy. In K. O'Connor & L. Braverman (Eds.), *Play therapy theory and practice: Comparing theories and techniques* (pp. 79–97). Wiley.

Kottman, T., & Meany-Walen, K. (2016). *Partners in play* (2nd ed.). American Counseling Association.

Landreth, G. L. (2012). *Play therapy: The art of the relationship*. Routledge.

Lee, K. R., & Ray, D. C. (2020). Child-centered play therapy parent services: A Q-Methodological investigation. *International Journal of Play Therapy, 29*(3), 131–143. https://doi.org/10.1037/pla0000120

Post, P. B., Ceballos, P. L., & Penn, S. L. (2012). Collaborating with parents to establish behavioral goals in child-centered play therapy. *The Family Journal, 20,* 51–57. http://doi.org/10.1177/1066480711425472

Rogers, C. (1957). The necessary and sufficient conditions of therapeutic personality change. *Journal of Consulting Psychology, 21*(2), 95–103. https://doi.org/10.1037/h0045357

Sanders, M. R., & Burke, K. (2014). The "hidden" technology of effective parent consultation: A guided participation model for promoting change in families. *Journal of Child and Family Studies, 23,* 1289–1297. https://doi.org/10.1007/s10826-013-9827-x

Schottelkorb, A., Swan, K., & Ogawa, Y. (2015). Parent consultation in child-centered play therapy: A model for research and practice. *International Journal of Play Therapy, 24*(4), 221–233. https://doi.org/10.1037/a0039609

Siegel, D. J., & Bryson, T. P. (2012). *The whole-brain child.* Bantam.

Stulmaker, H. L., & Jayne, K. M. (2018). Child-centered play therapy parent consultation model: Clinical implementation and implications. *Journal of Child and Adolescent Counseling, 4*(1), 3–19. https://doi.org/10.1080/23727810.2017.1344795

Chapter 7

Termination

And finally, we are here: Termination.

It's been a journey. Some cases have been an exciting, if complicated, journey. Some took longer than expected. Others were delightful. Some have stretched us and expanded our skills, confidence, and competency. Most have reaffirmed our work and reinforced why we chose this profession. The golden thread has guided us on the journey: ups and downs, necessary expansions, and inclusions, even a few side trips. The golden thread weaving it all together. We now see the importance of this golden thread. It kept us focused and helped clearly connect all of the work with the child and their parents.

Termination Summary

A *Play Therapy Termination Summary* (Table 7.1) assists in pulling all the case data together. The summary provides a template that contains the standard of care information. The *Summary* is short and quick to complete. It is documentation of the most essential data about the case, decisions regarding termination, and any recommendations to the parent for post-termination. A termination summary continues to be helpful as it completes the golden thread. Here, we knot that golden thread as we close the case. Here we have a quick review if needed for any follow-up reason. Most importantly, a termination summary completes the professional documentation recommended as best practices.

The form begins with identifying *Client Information*:

♦ Client name
♦ Age
♦ Address
♦ Parent name

Note if there was a change in the location of the child's residence during your time of treatment. Sometimes this occurs because of a divorce becoming final, moving to another foster home, or moving in with an extended family member. It is also important to note any change

DOI: 10.4324/9781003258766-8

Table 7.1 Play therapy termination summary

Play Therapy Termination Summary
Client Information
Client Name:
Client Age:
Client Address:
Parent Name:
Treatment Data
Intake Date:
First Session Date:
Final Session Date:
Number of Sessions:
Counseling Modalities Implemented:
DSM Diagnosis:
Termination Information
Reason for Termination (check the appropriate option)
☐ Met treatment goals
☐ Parent terminated; treatment goals not met
☐ Referral for relocation of client
☐ Referral for other treatment intervention
☐ Referral for failure to comply
Post-treatment Recommendations:
_____   _____
Play Therapist Signature and Credentials   Date

in primary parent. This might be a change in custody, death of a parent, new foster parent. Include dates of these changes.

The *Treatment Data* section is next. This is very quickly completed.

♦   Intake date
♦   First session date
♦   Final session date
♦   Number of sessions
♦   Counseling modalities implemented
♦   DSM diagnosis

While documenting the total number of sessions, remember to include parent consultations. Some play therapists choose to differentiate this data: separate entries for the number of play therapy sessions, parent consultations, sibling, and family sessions. Others will simply list one total of all therapeutic intervention sessions. You can decide. Just be consistent in all your cases.

The counseling modalities implemented would be the type of play therapy, such as Child-Centered Play Therapy; Cognitive-Behavioral Play Therapy, and so on. If a therapeutic parenting modality was also provided by the play therapist, then include that, so it might read:

Individual Child-Centered Play Therapy and *Child-Parent Relationship Therapy*

Only list the therapeutic interventions you, yourself, provided. Should you want to note interventions that the parent or child received elsewhere, that is fine. However, they should be pertinent to the case. If you desire to do so, then write:

Individual Child-Centered Play Therapy. Parents completed Child-Parent Relationship Therapy with Dr. Bennett.

While writing in the DSM diagnosis, it might be informative to notice the number of sessions. Do you see a trend in your own practice for the length of treatment, that is, number of sessions, for a given diagnosis? This helps inform your future initial parent consultations when parents want to know how long treatment will take.

The third and final section is *Termination Information*. We all hope and plan that the reason for termination is successful treatment. The treatment plan goals were successfully met. The issues that brought the child to therapy are resolved, and the child and family can move forward in their lives. Sadly, that is not always the case. Sometimes, the client moves and can no longer come to your office. Occasionally we find that the child and family's clinical issues are outside our scope of practice and competence, so we refer.

Reason for Termination
♦ Met treatment goals
♦ Parent terminated; treatment goals not met
♦ Referral for relocation of client
♦ Referral for other treatment intervention
♦ Referral for failure to comply

Finally, and rarely, we might need to terminate because the parents do not comply with treatment. This might include frequently missing scheduled sessions making progress extremely difficult. Or not following through on recommendations, such as referral to a psychiatrist for assessment for possible medication. Or adhering to a safety plan for suicidal ideation. Or repeatedly not following through with mutually developed homework or action plan. It is difficult to terminate with a parent who is not engaged in the therapeutic process and whose behavior may be counterproductive. However, it is an ethical imperative. If we cannot be effective with our client, in this case, because the parents will not participate in treatment, then we must refer. It is also a liability issue. If the child has suicidal ideation or attempts that the parent does not take seriously, it may be too high risk for the play therapist to continue the therapeutic relationship. Contemplation of termination for failing to comply would be a situation when consultation is also appropriate. A consultation with another play therapist to explore other ways to engage the parents; with an attorney to verify this is not client abandonment or other liability issues. In cases where we must refer for failure to comply, we often have our own internal struggle with severing the therapeutic relationship with the child. However, if we have been unable to engage the parents then they are not to be part of the treatment team (i.e., repeated failure to comply with recommendations or follow through with co-created changes) then we need to allow another play therapist the opportunity to serve the child and family.

The final area to document is if you have *Post-treatment Recommendations*. You may not have any. In that case, simply write, *"None."* You might suggest continued special playtimes as learned in Child-Parent Relationship Therapy. Or recommend a follow-up reassessment with the occupational therapist. Or if terminating for failure to comply, give at least three referrals.

The *Play Therapy Termination Summary* serves as a concise documentation of the case. It is useful for other professionals who may request records. Believing they will read through every session note and make sense of the work of play therapy may be unreasonable. Completing this form at the end of the case may save you a great deal of time and energy at a later date.

Then sign and date. Done. Done. Done!

Termination Discussion With Parents

The decision for termination is ideally a joint decision, between parent and play therapist and this is a conversation that happens over time. As therapy is progressing and treatment goals are nearing completion, talking with parents about termination is important. Parents know that termination is indeed your goal, keeping their child in therapy forever is not your goal. Phrases such as,

Your child is making great progress in therapy, they have reached some of their treatment goals, we can start talking about termination.

Sometimes, the child displays improved behavior and reduced symptomology in their real world early in the treatment process. When this is reported by parents, however, the play therapist may know that the child is still in the working phase. This is definitely why ongoing parent consultations are needed. And the frequent communication about progress in and out of the playroom. Without this communication we set ourselves and the child up for premature termination. The parent decides that therapy has been successful, and they are ready to terminate treatment. This results, sometimes, with the child coming into the playroom stating, *"Mom said this was the last time I'm coming,"* much to our surprise. If this happens, request a parent consultation and find out what the parent is thinking.

In a perfect setting, the parent is reporting significant improvement outside of session and it is clear treatment goals have been met. Reviewing with parents some of their concerns from your initial intake might be helpful for parents to truly realize how far they have come and how hard their child has worked. It is in these conversations that therapists compliment the parent on how hard they have worked as well, at minimum the parent has brought the child to therapy regularly, which is no small commitment. Once the play therapist and parent agree that the child reached their goal, the therapist will recommend one or more termination sessions so the child and therapist can have closure in their relationship. This is especially essential for children whose presenting issues surround abandonment or attachment issues. Our society does not, generally, do adequate preparation for ending relationships for children through death, divorce, separation, moves, and so on. Modeling how to end-well is also part of the therapeutic process.

Termination is a process, not an event. The number of termination sessions may be impacted by issues outside of the play therapist's control, such as the family's schedule or the requirements of the agency or insurance company. Best practice would be the therapist having two to three termination sessions to end the treatment process. I (Mary) find it rare to have three termination sessions, so I am grateful to get one such session.

While preparing the parent for termination, it's important to alert the parent that once the child is told it is possible that they may initially see a bit of regressed behavior. Inform the parents that this is to be expected and that the child will adjust. Explain to parents that it is just as if you were to take away their enjoyable daily walk or weekly conversation with a friend where they were able to unload all their stress, it's expected that it would take time to adjust to the new rhythm of life and that loss. Remind parents to continue using the new skills they learned in parent consultations; this will be important to help their child to continue their therapeutic growth and change. Encourage parents to be patient during this transition. If the transitional adjustment behavior does not resolve after four to five weeks they should contact you.

Letting parents know that the door to therapy is not permanently closed, is important. We always want parents to know we are always a resource. For parents whose children are very young, it is important to prepare them that it is not unusual for children to return to therapy at different developmental stages. This is especially true for young children who have experienced trauma. As children grow and mature, they process their trauma at new and more complex cognitive developmental levels. Therefore, revisiting therapy is often necessary, and you will work to get them in as soon as possible.

It is not uncommon for a parent to be ready to terminate before the play therapist would recommend it. In these situations, work to consider the parent's motivation. Is the parent struggling to get to appointments, is there a financial situation, or is the parent not seeing progress? Reflect their feelings and respond to their concern, help them feel seen and heard. Once you can establish their real reason for terminating therapy, you speak to that directly. If it is clear that you are unable to convince them to continue, work to maintain the relationship so the parent will feel comfortable calling you after they terminate. If the parent is not interested in bringing the child for the termination process, finding a way to gain closure with the child is recommended. It might be helpful to write a note, make a video, or draw a picture that the parent can give to the child. The intent is that the child knows you care about them and that you remember your time together. In this challenging situation, it is important to do all that you can to leave the door open so the parent feels they can call you again. The therapeutic relationship does not end when clients leave the office, it is an ongoing relationship that is walking with them in all areas of their life.

In many cases, by the time the child has made significant progress and the parents are ready to terminate, the parents are possibly just as attached to you as is their child. In some cases, parents may not be ready to terminate when their child is ready. These parents are worried they cannot do it without you, they worry about who they will call when there is a struggle. They may just miss seeing you. They, like their child, have enjoyed experiencing the core conditions and feeling safe. These are the sweetest of termination conversations! When you find yourself in this situation, celebrate and compliment yourself that you have formed a strong therapeutic relationship with this parent. Encourage this parent that you are always available for them and remind them of the skills they have learned and how capable they are in loving their child. Take time to end this relationship and model the healthy ending of adult relationships.

Termination Closure for the Play Therapist

Another note regarding termination: Don't forget about yourself! Our experience is that play therapists are thoughtful and conscientious about preparing child-clients and their parents for termination. Not so much about themselves. Remember, the therapeutic relationship is just that —*a relationship:* two people. How to experience a healthy ending of a relationship is essential for both the child (and parents) and the play therapist. During the time of preparing the parents and child for termination be aware of the importance for themselves.

After termination, some play therapists will create a reflective scene in the sand tray. Others may sit for a moment in the playroom and reflect on the play sequences that occurred in the playroom. Then, while completing the *Termination Summary*, purposely taking time for reflective functioning and take a moment to be thoughtful of the case. Mentally review the growth and challenges that occurred for *the play therapist*. What was learned, both about play therapy and about self? This is a time of closure. And of moving forward to the next child and the next case.

Resource

Termination Challenges in Children, Eliana Gil & David Crenshaw, Guilford Press, 2016.

Part Two

Looking Further

Chapter 8

Parents Who Challenge Us

Regardless of experience level, we all encounter parents who challenge us in new and different ways. One of the great joys of being a play therapist is that our clients consistently present us with new ways to learn and grow. (Yes, that is a positive reframe!) During these moments of growth, we can continue learning and make our work interesting. All parents need help and support in their parenting; some parents may be resistant. What is that resistance about? Why is this parent such a challenge for me? These are essential questions to ask when encountering challenging parents.

Counseling Theory in Parent Consultations

Theory is our guidebook; theory provides structure and guidance when clients feel chaotic, or therapists feel ineffective. Theory provides a space to rest during our client's struggles and make sense of what they are experiencing and how we can help them. Theory gives us direction as to what to do next. These same truths are applied when working with parents. Theory is often put aside when working with parents, but it can be useful and helpful in understanding parents and thus communicating more inten-

> **Core Conditions**
>
> 1. Client and counselor in psychological contact
> 2. Client experiences incongruence
> 3. Therapist is congruent
> 4. Therapist experiences unconditional positive regard for client
> 5. Therapist has empathy for client
> 6. Client experiences all the above

tionally. Parents are the big humans that bring in the little humans, and they are often just as hurt, lost, confused, and scared as the little ones we see in the playroom. All counseling theories hold Rogers' (1957) necessary and sufficient conditions as an important component in the therapeutic process. Only Child-Centered Play Therapists see these conditions as both necessary and sufficient. Other theories see these conditions as necessary but not sufficient for client change. These are commonly referred to as the "core conditions" of the therapeutic relationship.

DOI: 10.4324/9781003258766-10

There is a misconception among therapists that there are only four core conditions; there are, in fact, six conditions. The first is that the client and counselor are in psychological contact; the client needs to feel connected to the therapist. The second is that the client is experiencing incongruence, feeling anxious or vulnerable; the client needs to acknowledge they are struggling. The third, fourth, and fifth conditions are that the therapist is congruent in providing genuineness, empathy, and unconditional positive regard for the client. And the final condition is that the client receives these conditions (Rogers, 1957). It is important to keep all six conditions in mind when working with parents; if any of these conditions are not met, it is highly possible that both the play therapist and parent will feel frustrated. If the play therapist and parent are not connected, and the parent does not feel supported, the therapeutic relationship is strained. If not attended to, the parent will likely terminate therapy prematurely (Rogers, 1957).

Just as we encourage you to take the time to conceptualize your client from your theoretical perspective in Chapter 5: Treatment Phase: Session Notes, we encourage you to conceptualize the parent from your theoretical perspective as well. A conceptual understanding of who the parent is and how they think, feel, and behave in the world will provide a deeper understanding of how you can facilitate the therapeutic process. Even though you are conceptualizing parents, it is clear that the child is still the focus of the parent consultation. We also note that marriage and family therapists may view the entire family as the client. (See, theory does impact our work!) Theoretical conceptualization provides the therapist with additional tools to connect with the parent.

For example, Adlerian Play Therapy (AdPT) provides the play therapist with the structure to guide parent consultations. Understanding the phase of treatment and the parent's personality priority offer the play therapist a congruent way of working with the parent and the child. Phase 2 focuses on collecting parent lifestyle information, generally focused on Crucial C's and personality priorities. This information enables the play therapist to understand the parent's perspective and assist the play therapist in being empathetic. When we know why the parent responds in a particular way, it is easier to empathize with that parent. For example, a parent with a superiority personality priority would respond well to learning the skill of reflecting feelings. Parents with a personality priority of superiority strive to be more capable, more right, and better than others (Kottman & Meany-Walen, 2016). The play therapist might say,

Reflection of feeling is a therapeutic skill that will allow you to intentionally touch your child's heart more deeply and thus strengthen your relationship.

Using the phrase "therapeutic skill" is meaningful to a parent with a superiority personality priority because they can be better than other parents using this skill. A parent with a pleasing personality priority would be motivated to learn the same skill because they can please the therapist in learning it and avoid conflict with their child when they accurately reflect feeling (Kottman & Meany-Walen, 2016). The play therapist could word it this way to a pleasing parent,

I think reflecting feelings will help your child feel seen and understood and likely reduce the conflict in your home.

So the same skill is presented in slightly different ways, increasing the possibility of the parent being open to this new idea.

In working with parents, there may be a time when the play therapist feels frustrated or even stuck with a parent. Conceptualizing the parent and then looking at the world through the parents' lens may help understand them more deeply. After all, play therapists believe that behavior is communication; what are the parents communicating? Gaining empathy with the parent increases our ability to connect and make clinical recommendations that are truly possible for that particular parent and assist in managing our expectations of the parent.

Juan, Noah's dad, continues to punish Noah for noncompliance with limits by sending him to his room for an extended period of time. Juan stated,

Noah is obstinate and just wants to get his own way all the time and the whole family tiptoes around him to avoid a meltdown.

Juan does not like Noah having so much power. From a Cognitive-Behavioral perspective, Juan has developed the cognitive distortion that 3-year-old Noah has all the power in the house. That all children obey joyfully and immediately when parents set a limit and that Noah has all the responsibility in this situation. Juan recalls he always obeyed his parents. Juan feels trapped in his own home, and his primal mode is activated as he feels threatened by Noah. Reflecting Juan's feeling and confronting a cognitive distortion sounds like,

You are angry with Noah. Parenting is not what you thought it would be and sometimes you feel out of control. You think Noah has too much power at home.

Providing space for Juan to hear his beliefs and the opportunity to dismiss them as unreasonable gives the Cognitive-Behavioral Play Therapist a chance to create a more valid cognition with Juan.

Noah's mom, Alicia, is angry with Noah for his aggressive behaviors related to his dad's current work schedule. Working from a Child-Centered Play Therapy (CCPT) perspective, this parent is experiencing dissonance between her real self, feeling angry, sad, and disappointed in her current season of life, and an ideal self that is strong and capable. These two opposing views create incongruence, and this parent struggles to understand that her child is angry, scared, and confused about why their family has changed. The play therapist might say,

You seem to be feeling disappointed by how your family life has changed. Noah is also hurting and confused, which is why his behavior is challenging. Noah is functioning in the downstairs part of his brain, and fear often looks like anger in young children. Noah's world feels chaotic, as does yours, so he is working to gain some control, which right now looks like noncompliance. This is really challenging to you, as having a peaceful household is important to you.

In this feedback to Alicia, the CCPT play therapist can provide the core conditions and help Alicia feel heard and understood at a deeper level to be in a place to listen to more about Noah's behavior.

Exercises in conceptualizing parents from a theoretical perspective remind the play therapist that parents are human and may not even realize the thoughts or feelings regarding their child and how those impact their child. Providing parents with the core conditions of genuineness, empathy, and unconditional positive regard facilitates the therapeutic relationship. When we do not see the parents as hurting people, it is difficult to provide those conditions, progress is nearly impossible, and the risk of the parent terminating therapy is increased.

Therapist Attitudes

The play therapist's attitudinal responses to the parent facilitate successful parent consultations (Sanders & Burke, 2014). Some specific attitudes play therapists need to maintain as they work with parents: Respect the parent's role in the parent-child relationship as the most critical relationship in the child's life. Honor the parent's knowledge and experiences of their child. Assume the parent has positive intentions and that parents are doing the best they can. "Regulated, connected parents, who feel safe, can be the parent they want to be" (R. Gobbel, personal communication, July 14, 2021).

Most parents with whom we work are parenting more effectively than how they were parented, as evidenced by the fact that they are in our office seeking help. This belief assists the play therapist in providing the core conditions for the parent and ultimately creating a safe relationship where change is possible (Ray, 2012; Sanders & Burke, 2014).

> **Therapist Attitudes**
>
> - Respect the parent-child relationship
> - Honor parent's knowledge and experiences of their child
> - Assume parent has positive intentions

Play therapists love children and work to advocate for them, understand their experiences, and help them navigate life's challenges. Frustration often occurs when other adults are not prioritizing children or empathizing with them. These adults may be parents or even other professionals in the child's life. Play therapists need to remember that not all adults view the world as a play therapist does. They may not understand that behavior is communication or know the importance of seeing the world through the child's eyes. Parents stop being curious about their children at some point in their parenting journey, likely in the preschool years. Often, they have forgotten how to have fun with their children. These are essential truths that play therapists may need to remind themselves frequently.

People are slow to change; it is not uncommon for play therapists to have an unrealistic view of how quickly parents are capable of making changes in their lives. We often have more patience with our child client's change process, but not the same level of patience with their parents. Grace and compassion for the parent and their attempts to institute change should be noticed. Without that encouragement and support from us, how can we expect parents to keep trying? Parents are much more fragile than we often realize. They are often running on fumes, are reactive, unaware of how their own struggles impact their parenting, and few have thought deeply about how they want to parent. *"They rely on instinct, love, and their own childhood experiences"* (J. Zuboy, Personal Communication, May 1, 2016). Most parents would admit that parenting is much more complex than they anticipated. They are not prepared for the physical and emotional energy that is required. In addition, they lack knowledge of helpful information such as child development, trauma, or Interpersonal Neurobiology. Sue Bratton (personal communication, February 12, 2000) frequently says, *"We must believe all parents are doing the best they can with the information that they have."* Play therapists may need to be curious about the parents, is it possible that the parent was also abused? Do they lack skills? Is it possible they are in a violent relationship? Do they have their basic needs met? Where is their hurt coming from? We need to see past the parent's mask and touch their heart so they can experience a therapeutic relationship and get to a place where they can love their child well.

A play therapist's way of being with parents needs to be a balanced approach of both humility and expertise. Parents appreciate the warmth and honesty of a humble therapist as well as the confidence that comes from a therapist with expertise. This is a delicate balance, as parents need to feel confident in your expertise but not intimidated by your knowledge and experience. Therefore, as discussed, relying on counseling skills is critical to convey these two attitudes successfully.

Responding to Parent's Questions

The play therapist's response to the parent's questions will facilitate growth and success in a parent consultation. Play therapists who are defensive, resistant, or judgmental toward parents are unlikely to have a therapeutic connection with the parent and ultimately risk the parent ter-

- What is the parent really asking?
- How is the parent feeling?
- How is the therapist feeling?
- Respond with empathy rather than react with defensiveness.

minating therapy prematurely (Sanders & Burke, 2014). Line and Ray (2022), suggest play therapists look at common parent questions, then ask themselves, what is the parent really asking? What is the parent feeling? And respond to the parent's feelings.

For example, let's look at Noah's case again:

Juan asks,
How do you know this is working? Isn't he really just playing in there?
Perhaps Juan is really asking:
  Did I make the right decision putting Noah in play therapy?
  What if Noah never gets better?
  Did I ruin Noah's life because I travel for work?
  Did I cause his behavior problems?
What is Juan feeling:
  Scared?
  Insecure about his work decision?
  Inadequate because his child has behavior problems?
  Inadequate because he doesn't really understand what play therapy is?

Concurrently, the play therapist may feel defensive, angry, or unheard. It is important to be aware of your cortisol levels increasing to make sure your amygdala does not get control of this session. You maintain control, regulation, and remember your focus, as the play therapist is to respond to the parent's feelings.

Play therapist response:
  I know you are scared. I'm wondering if you are worried that Noah will never get better.

Pause—sit in the feeling with him—think about what he is really afraid of—it would be terrible if Noah never gets better.

The therapist then responds with humility and confidence,

Noah is responding to play therapy just as I would expect for a child his age. I see that he is working to take more risks in session, in regulating his emotions a little bit longer, and asking for help when he needs it.

Now let's imagine a parent consultation with Noah's mother.

Alicia asks:

How long will this take?

Have you seen a child like Noah before?

Perhaps Alicia is asking:

How much will this cost?

When will things be better at home?

If this takes too long, will he get kicked out of day care?

Is he the worst kid?

Is this therapist experienced enough?

Did I make the right decision in choosing this play therapist?

What is Alicia feeling:

Afraid that her child has long-term problems?

Insecure about how she is handling things at home?

Unsure if things will ever get better?

Currently, the play therapist may feel frustrated (having already explained the research to the parent that it will take at least 16 sessions, and we are on session 8), defensive (I am not doing enough), or inadequate (I am not a good enough therapist). Notice the feeling in yourself, so you can take a breath, get centered and regulated, and respond to the parent's feelings rather than react to your own feelings. Your defensiveness will not benefit the parent nor the therapeutic relationship. This moment of self-awareness might result in seeking consultation regarding how this particular parent is activating you. Or, if this is occurring with several parents, perhaps a time for some counseling of your own to explore underlying personal issues.

Play therapist response:

I know you are eager for things to get better, you are worried he won't get better. You are worried about how much this will cost, you are concerned about a lot of things right now (pause and sit in the feeling with her). Noah's behaviors are a challenge and it is impacting your whole family. At this point in therapy, he is making progress in managing his frustration, he is beginning to ask for help. He is able to comply with limits in session. I am feeling good about the progress he is making, we are moving in the right direction. The weekly reports you have completed indicate he continues to struggle at home, which is understandable. It takes more time before we can expect the skills he's learning to be used at home. I know that feels scary and that his behaviors are frustrating.

In both of these examples, the play therapist works to see the world through the parent's eyes, to think about what the parent is really asking, and how the parent is feeling. Line and Ray (2022) recommend thinking through possible options for what questions parents are genuinely asking and feeling in order to create responses that will facilitate the relationship. Play therapists who are prepared to view parent questions and concerns in this way are more likely to respond with empathy rather than react defensively.

Working With Other Professionals

The content of this particular chapter has made it very clear that working with children lends itself to more complicated and nuanced work than seeing individual adults. All children have adults in some capacity that require attention and help from the play therapist. Foster parents, Child Protective Services caseworkers, Court Appointed Special Advocates (CASA), attorney ad litems, and parents' attorneys are some of the legally involved professionals play therapists may find themselves working with. Other professionals are teachers, medical doctors, occupational therapists, and other mental health professionals, such as coordinating with the parents' marriage counselor or a family counselor. One of the most important things for play therapists to remember in working with these other professionals is that they are not your enemy. They are not trying to make your life difficult or purposely being obstructive. These professionals have a job to do, and they are focused on their piece of this puzzle that involves the child client. It is the job of the play therapist to appropriately inform other professionals regarding the child client; however, the play therapist is not a case manager. This may require that the therapist set boundaries with the other professional and maintain the focus to keep the child's best interest in mind as related to the therapy process. Be aware that these other professionals do not know the ethical guidelines or legal requirements by which play therapists must abide. The play therapist is knowledgeable of their own rules and ethics and can articulate them to others.

Entering into these relationships with a posture of humility and focusing on how you can be helpful in this process to advocate for your client will facilitate these dynamics. Utilizing consultation with other play therapists who have experience with the type of professional you are working with could be helpful if you are navigating uncharted territory. Have compassion for yourself; it is complicated, challenging, and stressful to work with many other people who have different goals. Keep yourself regulated so that you can speak to the issues important to your client, and the case, calmly, and professionally.

The golden thread cannot be forgotten. Documentation is critical when there is a phone conversation, voicemail, meeting, text or email from another professional regarding the child. Keeping a contact log of the date and time, type of communication, and a summary or exact copy of the communication is required for the child's record. When there is a great deal of communication, this added step of documentation may feel tedious. And, if you have separate files for parents, keep contact logs respective to each. Remember, this documentation protects you, the play therapist.

Divorced Parents

The stress cortisol levels of play therapists increase each time a parent reports they are divorced or in the process. The family dynamics of a divorce, or pending divorce, adds a level of complexity that the play therapist must manage. The ethical and legal requirements of working with families of divorce can be intense, and it is the play therapist's responsibility to navigate these in addition to the case dynamics. Parents who are in the painful process of a divorce, or even divorced for several years, are likely experiencing unresolved emotions. Co-parenting may be one of the most conflictual aspects of a parent's life. A significant amount of control is relinquished when they begin co-parenting with a former partner. There are many experiences their child has now that they know nothing about and may have no influence over. Many of these parents worry their child is not safe with the other parent and feel powerless in their ability to do much about that concern. Even in the best co-parenting situation, it is difficult; parents must try to put their child above any feelings they may have about the other parent.

As already discussed, the play therapist must consult the custody paperwork to determine each parent's legal rights. Knowing what the court requires will give the play therapist a starting point for how to proceed. Play therapists have differing opinions on how they choose to work with divorced parents. It is generally agreed that involving both willing parents is best practice for the child; however, how that is done is based on the clinical judgment of the therapist and the legal requirements of the divorce. It is also possible that as parents grow in their roles as single parents, they may come to a place where they can focus on co-parenting more. Therefore, the therapist might adjust the parent consultation structure. If the parents need extensive help and support in their co-parenting, consider referring them to a therapist who specializes in this area so that your work can focus on the child. Ask yourself if you have structured your parent consultations based on what is easiest for you or what the family needs. Process this with a colleague, make the best clinical judgment you can, and remember that if it isn't working, you can always change the structure.

There are general recommendations regarding working with divorced couples, especially if they are at the beginning of their co-parenting relationship. These parents are often in a state of panic, and defensiveness, and their amygdala has taken over their rational brain. They are reacting and not responding. Parents need to be reminded that managing their relationship is a blueprint for how their children may view relationships as they become adults. Helping parents create a coherent divorce narrative to share with the children is a piece of the process with which play therapists can help. Parents may not intentionally put their child between them; it happens. The pressure, stress, and consequences for their child will likely impact them for the rest of their life. Challenging parents to resist the urge to punish the other parent by "making them figure it out" or to think, "my ex is just trying to control what I do with the kids." Encouraging parents to see that cooperative communication regarding their children sets them up for success. For example, if the children are young, keep them on a consistent schedule, make sure they have their "lovie," have familiar toys and books in both homes. Provide as much consistency in routines and rituals as possible to help children regulate their brain. The less energy children use, wondering what will happen next, the more safe, secure, and regulated children feel. Feeling regulated will enable children to manage their own behavior more consistently.

Joint Parent Consultations

Play therapists who prefer to have both parents in parent consultations do so for various reasons. One of the primary reasons is to avoid triangulation. No therapist likes to be caught between parents. Therefore, having both parents in the room reduces that possibility. These therapists also require that both parents are copied on every communication, facilitating transparency between therapist and parents. This transparency can assist in facilitating trust in the therapist-parent relationship. This approach also makes documentation cleaner; there is one set of parent consultation notes, all of which are kept in the child's file. With joint notes, it is most likely that notes would be focused on both parents, for example, *Therapist recommends parents use reflection of feelings at home.* A play therapist who works with both parents may have a statement in their informed consent that states that if one party requests records, then both parties receive records simultaneously. In this situation, the play therapist maintains strong boundaries and is prepared to manage conflict during the parent consultation. Sending parents an agenda, so they know what to expect may be helpful to keep the session focused and possibly reduce parent anxiety and defensiveness. For play therapists who do not have a lot of experience setting boundaries between clients, these sessions may feel less therapeutic. The therapist may find themselves taking a posture of teaching or telling and have difficulty displaying the core conditions. This approach may make parent-specific work more challenging, as parents may be less likely to be transparent with their struggles with the child. It might be challenging for the play therapist to help these parents think introspectively. However, this approach can also be very helpful in parents learning to truly co-parent. These are all important factors to keep in mind in making a clinical treatment decision for the clients.

Separate Parent Consultations

Conducting separate parent consultations allows the play therapist to work individually with each parent and focus on that parent's relationship with their child. Play therapists choose to do individual meetings for many different reasons, some of which may be if there is a history of domestic violence between parents, if the divorce is fresh, or if the conflict is too high and parents are unable to co-parent. Many play therapists who prefer to meet with parents individually find separate consultations more productive in that they do not have to navigate the tension between parents. These sessions focus on the relational and behavioral issues within that parent-child dyad without attention to the other parent-child dyad. In these cases, firm boundaries are still needed to make sure the parent consultation is focused on therapeutic work and does not turn into one parent complaining about the other parent. The play therapist must remain neutral.

Documentation is handled differently in this situation. Play therapists may have parents sign their own informed consent, in addition to the consent for the child, and then keep separate parent consultation notes for each parent rather than notes in the child's file. This is cleaner and easier when one parent requests records. The records released are two files: the requesting parent's consultation notes file and the child's file. If both parents' consultation notes are kept together in the child's file, the play therapist would need to redact all notes related to the other parent. When therapists choose to work with parents separately, billing arrangements must be clearly stated in the informed consent so that parents understand these sessions will be billed separately. The custody paperwork may already establish requirements regarding which parent is financially responsible for therapy services.

Parents Who Live Out-of-Town

Parents who live separately from their child often feel left out as they do not have day-to-day knowledge of their child. The out-of-town parents are minimally, if at all, involved with educationalandextracurriculardecisionsfortheirchild.Somemaybeunawareoftheirparental rights. These parents may come from a defensive and angry position. Involving these parents in the therapeutic process may result in them feeling respected. When there is a parent who lives out of town, it is critical to consult the custody agreement, as the therapist may be required to reach out to this parent. The animosity between the local parent and the out-of-town parent may be high. The local parent may feel alone, isolated, and overburdened; the out-of-town parent may feel disenfranchised. Therefore, empathy and understanding from the play therapist are critical to involving these parents in the therapeutic process. If your goal is to see these parents together, inviting the out-of-town parent to do so by video conference allows them to be a part of the conversation. Be aware of your licensure requirements if the out-of-town parent is out of state. If the custody orders require both parents' consent to treat their child, knowing your state's licensure rules is necessary. This might be when a consultation with an attorney is warranted to determine best practice, given that the parent is legally the client. If you decide it is in the parents' and child's best interest to see the parents separately, you can see one in person and video conference with the other. Seeing the parents either together or separately, the best practice of keeping notes still applies.

Familiar Parent Profiles

There are some profiles of parents who have similar worldviews. These become familiar as we encounter them in our practice. While we caution against overgeneralizing, these profiles can help develop an approach to understanding and interacting with parents who present with similar dynamics. This is by no means an exhaustive list but will hopefully give you some general direction on responding to parents.

"Pull Yourself Up by the Boot-Strap" Parent

These parents may not see the need for therapy. They are likely only in your office because the other parent sees the need for therapy, or a court requires it. This parent often says things like:

> **Boot-Strap Parent**
>
> "They will get over it."
> "I don't want to coddle them."
> "They just want attention."
> "They just have to work harder."

♦ *They will get over this.*
♦ *I don't want to coddle them.*
♦ *They just want attention.*
♦ *They just have to work harder.*

These parents are likely emotionally unavailable and want to avoid any suggestion of vulnerability. It feels safe to be angry and blame the child rather than look at the deeper issues. This boot-strap response may be how the adults in this parent's world responded when they were hurting as a child. Consequently, they lack the modeling to respond differently to their own child. It is also possible that this boot-strap response is one that served this parent well as they worked through their own life challenges.

What reactions do these responses bring up in you? Many play therapists are triggered or activated by a boot-strap parent. They feel protective of their child client if they experience the parent as critical of the child. It is not uncommon for play therapists to have a protective "mamma bear" type reaction to a boot-strap parent. Some play therapists may feel inadequate with a boot-strap parent and fear they will not be able to meet the parent's expectations. First, give yourself compassion, working with parents is hard, very hard. Then, ask yourself: How can I regulate myself so that I can connect with this parent? Is there someone in my life that this parent reminds me of? What conditions of worth, cognitive distortions, or mistaken beliefs does this parent have? From what primal emotion is this parent functioning? How can I develop empathy for this parent? It is often our tendency to try to convince the parent with research, expertise, and confidence that play therapy is effective, yet a defensive response is not therapeutic. Modeling an emotional and empathetic response first may be more effective. We must regulate ourselves and come from a place of empathy for the parent's fears and struggles. Consider what the parent is genuinely asking or saying. Address those first and then share with them how play therapy is helping their child. Do not forget to have compassion for yourself in this process also.

Pseudo-Agreeable Parent

During the initial contact, this parent seems like a parent with whom you dream of working. They are eager to come to the session and to learn new skills, they may ask,

> **Pseudo-Agreeable Parent**
>
> "Yes, I will try that."
> "Yes, I will do that."
> "What else can I read?"
> "What do I do when . . .?"

- ♦ *What should I do when my child does . . . ?*
- ♦ *What books should I read?*
- ♦ *What do I need to do differently?*
- ♦ *Yes, I will do that.*
- ♦ *Yes, I can do that.*
- ♦ *Yes, we will try that next week.*

However, it becomes evident that this parent does not follow through over time. They have not made the calls to teachers or other referrals you have recommended; they are not utilizing new skills at home. It feels like they are only telling you what you want to hear, and you observe the child continue to struggle. This parent may feel overwhelmed. They have the best of intentions but struggle with implementation. This parent is fearful of disappointing you, fearful of what you think about them as a parent. This parent may feel like a failure and is frozen in their ability to make changes. This parent's Window of Tolerance may be very small, and their pleasing response is an attempt to self-protect, as a confrontation with the therapist is too stressful.

What response do you have to this parent? Do you feel betrayed because, at the beginning, you were so encouraged? Are you frustrated by the lack of honesty and confused about why this parent has not said, "*I just can't do that right now.*" Are you frustrated that they ask, "*what would you do when ___ happens?*" repeatedly, and yet they are surprised this behavior continues to happen. First, give yourself compassion, as working with parents is hard, very hard. Then ask yourself, who does this parent remind you of in your life? What does this parent need most from you? What do you need to do to regulate yourself so you can provide the core conditions for this parent? When you conceptualize this client from your theory, how does this inform your work with them?

This parent needs compassion from you, and maybe even permission from you not to be the best, most perfect parent. Reflecting their fear, helping them regulate so they feel confident to try your recommendations. This may be a situation where the therapist misread how capable the parent was and inadvertently overprescribed the number of techniques to do at home. This parent may need the play therapist to take responsibility, apologize for overburdening them, and repair the relationship. Modeling this acknowledgment of imperfection may be therapeutic for this parent. Working with parents is hard, and parenting is hard; both you and the parent need empathy and support. Providing the parent with one very simple and achievable thing to focus on facilitates success. For example, a simple touch on the shoulder may be the most doable and straightforward connection with the child they can provide. Once parents feel successful with simple tasks like touch and eye contact, more challenging skills such as limit-setting and reflection of feeling can be introduced.

Defensive Parent

Parents have a lot of various reasons to be defensive with a play therapist. Often this parent perceives the play therapist as holding all the power in the relationship. Defensive reactions usually stem from a place of fear. It might also be a deflection, based on the inability to be responsible, or imperfect. This parent may say things like,

> **Defensive Parent**
>
> "I didn't say that."
> "I would never say that."
> "Don't you think there is something wrong with him?"
> "It's never enough."

- *I did not do that. I would never say that to my child.*
- *I set the limit and he still did it again.*
- *Don't you think there is something wrong with my child?*
- *Don't you think he has ____ disorder?*
- *It's never enough for him, I give him toys, but he is still a problem.*

A defensive parent is quick to blame their child or look for a diagnosis to explain their behavior. These parents may feel angry that their child's behavior dictates life for the rest of the family. Being a parent is not what they expected. They may feel confused by their child's behavior. They may be afraid you are going to tell them this is all their fault. They may feel pressure from the school, day care, or family. They likely have tried many things suggested by others, and nothing worked, leaving them feeling incompetent. And they probably do not understand the repercussions of trauma, challenges in development, or general behavioral difficulties children encounter.

How do you react to this parent? What thoughts are running through your head? Are you feeling protective of your child client? Are you angry that this parent is so self-centered? Do you find yourself absorbing their dysregulation? Who in your life does this parent remind you of? Are you frustrated that this parent wants you or the child to do all the work? Are you worried you will not be able to meet their expectations? Are you irritated that this parent has no empathy for such a young child? First, give yourself compassion, working with parents is hard, very hard. Then ask yourself, How can I gain empathy for this parent? How do I conceptualize this parent from my theory? How do I understand why this parent is having this response to their child? How can I address their fear and concern? What feeling can I reflect on first? A play therapist might say,

Parenting is not what you expected it to be. I know you wonder when things will get better, and you are worried they may not.

Just as we co-regulate with an angry and defensive child, an angry and defensive parent also needs co-regulation. Engaging the right side of their brain before you move to the left will enable you to connect with them and help them feel heard and seen. This parent needs to perceive you are on their side, that you know parenting is challenging, and that you are here to support them just as much as you support their child. Working to help these parents feel safe enough so vulnerability is not quite so scary is a significant focus. Reflecting feeling and encouraging the good things they are doing can help them feel supported to be more open to therapeutic parenting skills. For parents who struggle with vulnerability, a parenting skill such as choice-giving may help them feel more in control of themselves and the situation. This parent may struggle with reflecting feelings as they likely are not in touch with their own feelings, so seeing their child's feelings may be challenging for them.

Inadequate Parent

These parents present as helpless. They don't know what to do, how, or when to do it. They feel ineffective. Perhaps they grew up in a dysfunctional home with no modeling of good-enough parenting. These are parents who say things like:

♦ *I do know what else to try.*
♦ *I just want it to go away.*
♦ *Parenting is harder for me than for other people.*
♦ *No matter what I do it doesn't work.*
♦ *I'm just so tired.*
♦ *I can't make my kid do anything.*
♦ *My kids are harder than others.*
♦ *I've given up asking—doing chores, getting dressed for school, or anything.*

One overwhelming feeling from these parents is exhaustion. There is low energy. These parents feel like failures and are trapped and frozen in their ability to think of other options. How do you react to this parent? Are you exhausted by their complaining and sense of inadequacy? Is there someone in your life this parent reminds you of? Are you frustrated and feel like

> **Inadequate Parent**
>
> "I don't know what else to try."
> "No matter what I do, it doesn't work."
> "I'm just so tired."
> "I can't make my kid do anything."
> "I've given up asking, doing chores, getting dressed for school, anything."

they are not even trying? Are you shocked that someone could give up on their child? Do you fear you cannot meet their expectations or hopes for therapy? First, give yourself compassion, working with parents is hard, very hard. Then, conceptualize this client from your theory, and work to gain empathy for them so that you can be more regulated in session. Consider what the parent is genuinely asking or saying. A challenge with the inadequate parent is to assist them in finding places of success. This might be in their roles and experiences outside of parenting. However, finding even the most minor areas of success can begin the process of expanding and scaffolding their role as a parent. Encouragement is the beginning experience. These parents often then respond well to psychoeducation and skill-building. Begin with teaching them to reflect feelings and then utilizing self-esteem-building statements. Next might be limit setting. The play therapist will be most effective with coaching basic skills one at a time, building confidence and success.

The Cognitive-Behavioral Play Therapist might begin with simple reward charts to use at home. Don't assume that the parent can create and execute this activity. Perhaps the reward chart can be created together in a parent consultation. Discuss appropriate levels of activity to reward and what those rewards will be. In every case, regardless of the clinical theory, the play therapist models good-enough parenting.

Referring Parents for Their Own Counseling

As we work with a child and their parents, it frequently becomes apparent that the parent needs their own intervention. Their level of need is beyond what we can provide during parent consultations. This may be for several reasons. Perhaps the parent has personal struggles for which counseling is needed, present before their child's current presenting issues, such as their life experiences, possibly in their own childhood. Perhaps they are dealing with substance abuse issues. The parent may have experienced the same trauma as their child, like a natural disaster, or it activates the memory of previous trauma. It becomes clear that the child's prognosis is negatively impacted by the parent's current level of functioning. For the child to make progress in therapy, the parent may also need to begin therapy. Consider recommending counseling for parents when their distress is overwhelming, and your support and encouragement are not enough to help them regulate. When you find yourself thinking about this parent frequently, a referral may be necessary. These parents may contact you frequently between appointments. Their anxiety does not decrease after a parent consultation. They do not seem hopeful about treatment progress. They seem engaged during the parent consultation and problem solve with you but cannot follow through between sessions. Their emotion overwhelms their ability to see their child objectively. Their own trauma reaction interferes with their own daily functioning. Parents in these situations need more support than can be expected or is possible in parent consultations.

These parents need more support than they are able to access in their existing environment. Society is full of judgment for parents: their own family, friends, other professionals, social media, and even strangers in the grocery store. Many of these individuals may mean well but are not helpful with their advice or criticism. Parents need to hear messages like this:

♦ *Parenting is hard and anyone would need support in your situation.*
♦ *Your child has experienced something horrific and you need a place to talk about that and support for you as you heal.*
♦ *You want so much to be healthy enough to be the kind of parent you want to be.*
♦ *The trauma you experienced is overwhelming you, and you are unable to be there for your child without additional support for yourself.*

Even after hearing these empathic statements, parents may be resistant to engaging with their own counseling. Again, think deeper. Think about *why* they might be resistant. Is it time? Cost of therapy? A perception that all the focus should be on the child? There is a multitude of reasons parents may be hesitant, but play therapists need to make recommendations in the best interest of the child and parent. It may be the parent needs intervention before the child.

It is essential to have a list of therapists who work with various presenting issues for referrals. This may include community agencies that can provide reduced fee services. Often there are specialized agencies with counseling services such as child advocacy centers, family violence centers, sexual assault agencies, and bereavement centers. The play therapist might require regular attendance at Alcoholics Anonymous, Narcotic Anonymous, or other support groups as a condition for continued work with the child. Notate recommendations or requirements in the child's record (part of the treatment plan) or parent consultation file to continue the golden thread.

When Parents Activate You

Play therapists need to look inward when a parent is particularly challenging—asking yourself what you do for yourself to stay more regulated during the session. Managing your schedule is an essential skill as a therapist and occasionally a simple fix. Making sure you have time between sessions to complete notes, eat lunch, and drink enough water. You are not serving your clients by "getting through the day." In order to have the capacity to be with clients, you must take proper care of yourself. Being self-aware enough to know that you do best with a break after three sessions or you are a better therapist if you start early in the morning rather than working late in the evening. Managing parent consults throughout your schedule is critical in being fully present for both your child and adult clients. For example, it might not be wise to schedule a challenging parent consultation immediately after a play therapy client who tends to have significant trauma play. Knowing yourself and what you need allows you to establish healthy working boundaries. Then sticking to the boundaries you set for yourself is critical. It is easy to feel resentful toward a parent when you believe a situation results in you having to violate your boundaries. Our own boundaries are part of what protects us from burnout and vicarious trauma. We became therapists because we want to help. However, it is not helpful to our other clients when we bend our boundaries for one, and then we cannot be our best.

Self-reflect on your own thoughts and feelings about a challenging parent. Are you activated when thoughts of a particular challenging parent intrude throughout your day? Identifying and working through this trigger may require work outside of the session, in consultation with another play therapist, and, at times, your own work in therapy may be warranted. Self-awareness is essential; ask yourself:

- *What am I feeling?*
- *What about this behavior is a problem for me?*
- *Who does this parent remind me of?*
- *What about this parent triggers me?*

- *Why do I struggle to have compassion for this parent?*
- *What about my own life reminds me of this parent?*
- *What am I afraid of?*

As you answer these questions, have compassion for yourself, working with parents is hard, very hard. Is there a pattern that you are noticing in your answers? Process these with a colleague. Once you reflect on your own feeling and have regulated yourself, then ask:

- *Where is the parent's behavior coming from?*
- *Where is their hurt?*
- *What are they afraid of?*
- *What is my theoretical conceptualization of this parent?*

There is so much about the parent we may not know or understand. There is little time to gather information directly about them. As you answer these questions and conceptualize the parent from your theory, gain empathy for that parent. Utilizing sand tray or expressive arts may help you determine how to connect with the parent. Create a plan for your subsequent parent consultations so you can be regulated and empathetic. *The Parent Consultation Preparation Form* in Appendix E will provide you with some structure to your plan to be more regulated with parents in session. A focused plan will help you to speak to their fears and hurts and help them see hope as they continue in the therapeutic process.

While in a parent consultation session, it is critical therapists respond rather than react when triggered by a parent. As we have discussed, there are many useful, creative methods to help you gain empathy and understanding for a parent outside of the session so that next time you are prepared and can respond more effectively. But what do you do at the moment when a parent surprises you? Robyn Gobbel (Personal communication, July 14, 2021) recommends several steps to staying regulated and connected with a dysregulated parent in the moment.

First, notice yourself and have compassion for yourself. As we have discussed, working with parents is hard. Take a breath and notice how you are feeling. Next, reflect and match the parents' feeling, energy, and intensity, focusing on helping the parent feel heard. Then, ask the parent to tell you more, reflect more, and ask if they feel understood? If parents say *no*, ask, *how will you know when I understand?* Gobbel warns against arguing or convincing, even when you want to.

As discussed earlier in this chapter, Line and Ray (2022) encourage play therapists to think about what the parent is really asking, what the parent is feeling, and respond to those first. The parent's behavior is communication, just as their child's behavior is communication, so look deep into their hearts to touch the hurt or fear that this parent is feeling.

Gobbel encourages therapists to consider the following: Do the parents need more information? Do they feel you believe them about how difficult it is at home? Do they think they have already done everything you suggest? Do they believe they cannot do any more right now and what you ask is too hard? (R. Gobbel, personal communication, July 14, 2021). As play therapists, this is what we do best, looking deep into the heart of the client and seeing them and touching them in a way that no one else ever has. Remind them that you are here with them to help and support them.

In Closing

As you read and personally reflect on the parents or situations discussed, which most challenged you? Did you find yourself thinking, *Oh, I don't think I could work with this one!*

What patterns are you noticing in your reactions? What is it about that particular type of parent that brings up such strong emotions in you? Who can you talk to that can help you sort out your feelings? Having another play therapist with which to consult is essential. Both Linda and I have colleagues with whom we consult as needed. Even after years of practicing play therapy, there are cases that befuddle us. Often it is simply talking it through with an experienced, trusted colleague. Sometimes that colleague may help us realize we need some sessions with our own counselor (just like we see that parents may need some counseling). This is healthy. This is ethical practice. The more we can look inward with compassion for ourselves, we can offer the same compassion to the parent. When this works well, we can impact the entire family system. The parent changes, develops new skills, greater self-awareness, a more robust and healthier relationship with their child. Having this broad, inclusive view of the importance of being a therapeutic agent within the child client's family environment changes everything.

Resources

- *Linking Parents to Play Therapy*, Debbie Killough McGuire & Donald E. McGuire, Routledge, 2000.
- *When Parents Are at War*, Lynn Louise Wonders, 2019.

References

Kottman, T., & Meany-Walen, K. (2016). *Partners in play* (2nd ed.). American Counseling Association.

Line, A. V., & Ray, D. C. (2022, February 4). *Getting ready to work with parents: Activities to build competencies for play therapists*. Texas Association for Play Therapy Annual Conference, Austin, TX.

Ray, D. C. (2012). *Advanced play therapy*. Routledge.

Rogers, C. (1957). The necessary and sufficient conditions of therapeutic personality change. *Journal of Consulting Psychology, 21*(2), 95–103. https://doi.org/10.1037/h0045357

Sanders, M. R., & Burke, K. (2014). The "hidden" technology of effective parent consultation: A guided participation model for promoting change in families. *Journal of Child and Family Studies, 23*, 1289–1297. https://doi.org/10.1007/s10826-013-9827-x

Chapter 9

Difficult Parenting Issues

Parenting is full of challenges; parents are rarely prepared for the bumps and bruises of the journey. Play therapists are equipped to help parents navigate difficult conversations. Providing empathy and warmth couched with developmentally appropriate information can help parents. Often parents are fearful of talking with their children about sensitive topics because no one talked with them as children. Therefore, these parents need support and encouragement navigating troubled waters is essential in the parent-child relationship. If parents do not provide the answers, children will find the information somewhere else. We live in the information age, and information is always available; however, it might not be factual or developmentally appropriate for their child.

The Importance of Co-Regulation

The idea of co-regulation is a relatively new concept for parents. For many parents, co-regulating is counterintuitive. A toddler screaming because their favorite purple bowl is dirty is not exactly someone a parent wants to press into, offer comfort, and rock at this moment. Co-regulating with young children ultimately trains their bodies to internally regulate and learn to understand their feelings and get their needs met in appropriate ways. When our brains are not connected with others, and we do not feel seen, heard, and understood, our brain is in protect mode and therefore is not as flexible and cannot internally regulate. Rocking, running, and physical touch are great avenues to co-regulation. Allowing children to create a calm corner with books and favorite stuffed animals can give them a place to go when they are beginning to feel dysregulated. Teaching parents to watch for the signs that their child is starting to dysregulate is essential. Helping parents identify the types of play that are soothing and regulating for their children can be helpful. There was a season in my (Mary's) family when my husband traveled on short business trips. My children were young, under 6 at the time, and while he was gone, they were generally regulated. However, when he would return, one of my children struggled with re-entry; he had a short temper and had a lot of big feelings over seemingly insignificant things. His play would move from puzzles to building blocks where he could gain control over his environment

DOI: 10.4324/9781003258766-11

and his emotions. As he gained more control over his emotions, he was able to move to more imaginative, free-flowing play. Helping parents see those patterns so that they can join in and help co-regulate rather than place limits on this play will help them tune into their child's world.

Equipping parents with general knowledge of Interpersonal Neurobiology, co-regulating, and how our brains respond to each other's mirror neurons is valuable. Parents can feel confident that a simple reflection of feeling can help a child manage the unmanageable. The role of the parent is not to prevent life's challenges but to struggle with their child and sit with emotion so that, ultimately, the child gains self-regulation skills. Disappointment, hurt, and loss are all part of life, and if children can learn to process these experiences, they will develop even more self-regulation skills as they mature.

Helping Parents Talk With Their Children About Difficult Topics

Adults often fear talking to children about hard or sad things; they worry the news will take away the child's innocence. Remind parents that ignorance is not the same as innocence, that a child with information does not mean that the wonder and joy of childhood are lost. In situations where there is difficult news, often children are aware something is different. They are not as oblivious as the adults in their life often think. When parents have not shared the truth, children may fill in the blanks and create a narrative that often blames themselves and may be worse than the truth. Play therapists can help parents reframe the bad news so that the child can understand. For example, parents who are worried about telling their child about a medical diagnosis or learning disability need help explaining it so that the child can understand. For example,

Honey, you haven't been feeling well lately, and we need to go to the doctor to figure out why your brain and your stomach are not working very well together. The doctor is going to do some tests and look at how your body is working and why it isn't doing what we would expect.

Giving children information about what is happening and focusing on how the body is working (rather than what is wrong) provides understanding and security.

Talking to Children About Death

Death is sad; while it is a part of life, there is always distress for those who are left behind. Helping parents talk to children about death is often difficult because the parent is also grieving over the loss of a person or pet. Reassure parents that it is fine for children to see that adults are sad and know that adults may even cry from time to time about this loss. Parents may need help telling their children about death. Here are things to keep in mind. It is important that the information is shared as soon as possible to prevent children from overhearing it from someone else. The Dougy Center, a nationally renowned grief counseling center in Portland, Oregon, has an excellent website with resources for parents, children, and therapists on various topics related to grief (dougy.org). Regardless of the type of death, The Dougy Center recommends giving specific factual answers and avoiding euphemisms such as "passed away" or "went to sleep." Children need sufficient information, including age-appropriate language, whether the death was sudden, violent, suicide, sickness, or expected. It is not helpful to tell a child one story and then change it when they are older. Instead, how much detail is given is based on the child's age. For example,

I have very sad news. Uncle Brian died, his heart stopped working and the doctors could not make him better, so he died.

If the child is older,

Uncle Brian had a heart attack when he was at home, and an ambulance took him to the hospital, where doctors could not restart his heart, and he died.

Encourage parents to allow children to ask questions and allow those to lead the conversation. Specific details give children the information they need to make sense of the situation. When parents talk in more generalities such as, "he got sick," it can cause children to feel more anxious the next time they get sick and wonder if they will die. Play therapists can help parents feel comfortable answering questions as children process this death and have a deeper understanding of death in general. Play therapists can help parents by answering questions to avoid the fear of their child's questions. In particular, prepare parents that younger children may ask more detailed questions at seemingly odd times. Children process events at different times and rates and often need only one bit of information to make sense of things until the next question comes up. Look for a grief center for children and families in your area; these centers are wonderful resources for families facing these challenges.

Talking to Children About Adoption

Play therapists work with a variety of families and family structures. However, we can never assume that parents have shared how their family came to be with their children. In the *Child Background Form*, we ask parents about adoption. However, we cannot assume the child knows this information about themselves. In the initial parent consultation, play therapists ask parents about their adoption process and what the child knows about their adoption. Children need a cohesive narrative about their adoption. Some children want a longer narrative that includes as many details as their parents have, while others are only interested in a short version. Encourage parents to allow their child to take the lead with as much or as little detail as the child is interested in. All children need a narrative that they can share with friends or teachers when asked. For example, a child adopted from the foster care system may have a narrative that sounds like,

My biological mother couldn't take care of me, and there are people who help take care of kids. They saw she couldn't do it, and they stepped in so I would be safe. They found my mom and dad, who love me and take good care of me.

It is always surprising and hurtful when other children say something mean regarding adoption, and while it's distressing, it happens, and parents need help equipping their child with a response. Parents need to understand it is likely that their child thinks about their adoption more frequently than the parent thinks about it.

Adoptive parents are rarely prepared for the impact their child's adoption will continue to have throughout their life. There is a misconception that a child adopted as an infant will not have the attachment and relationship struggles an older child may have. Play therapists may need to have candid conversations with parents regarding adoption's impact on their child. Play therapists who are well versed in attachment styles can help educate parents on their own attachment style and that of their child's. There are many children's books therapists can recommend to parents regarding adoption. These books can help parents with words or phrases and keep the conversation at home open and flowing. See the Resources section at the end of this chapter for a list of children's books.

A family who has both biological and adopted children, may not have thought about how having an adopted sibling impacts the biological children. These children need the opportunity to process their family structure and their role in that structure, just as the adopted child does. A coherent family narrative of how the family came to be and how families are formed in many different ways. Children may need an opportunity to make sense of the fact that one child looks like one parent but the others do not share those physical traits. Children need help responding when another child says, *he can't be your brother, he doesn't look like you*. Helping parents point out personality traits that are similar within the family and the shared family values they all have is important. For young children the idea of a forever family is important, that none of the children in this family can be a part of another family, they are all family together. It might be shocking, for example, for a parent to learn that their biological child fears being given up, just as her adopted brother was given up. The play therapist can help bring awareness to the many possible thoughts children may have in making sense of and gaining mastery over understanding their family structure.

Talking to Children About World Events

News regarding world events is readily available on any and every screen around us, at the gas station, grocery store, restaurant, and in our pockets. Encouraging and helping parents share the news with children regarding world events is essential. While we all want to live in a world where horrible things do not happen, sadly, it is not the case. Children will hear about events at school from friends or overhear adults talking. We cannot assume we can shelter children from this information.

When talking about world events, natural disasters, and school shootings, there are several things to keep in mind. First, help parents work to regulate themselves and be ready to hold their child's feelings. Coach parents to give direct, concrete answers and validate the feelings their child may express. Play therapists will likely need to caution parents about dismissing their child. In general, parents want their child to feel better, but they may dismiss their child's feelings in the process. For example,

a parent says, *There was a hurricane in Houston; there was a lot of rain and water everywhere, on the streets and even in people's homes.*
The child responds, *I'm scared.*
The parent says, *There's nothing to be afraid of.*

To validate the child's fears, a parent might say,

Hurricanes are scary. We have watched the weather, and the hurricane is over; now we are safe.

It is important to tell parents not to watch videos and news reports of the disaster with their children. Children cannot differentiate that each video may be of the same event, just viewed from different angles. Therefore, they think the disaster is happening over and over again. Some parents are anxious to understand what is happening and watch the news for long periods of time, resulting in children seeing the event repeat over and over.

Play therapists can help parents know how to use art or play at home to provide their child a space to process this information. This is an opportunity to remind parents of the importance of co-regulation and the skills you have previously taught them to hold their child's emotions. And the importance of providing a place to play or talk. Encourage parents that if they see play that is a direct reenactment of the disaster, to let you know so that you can be prepared to process it in session with the child.

Creating a Divorce Narrative

Divorce is a common occurrence. No matter the circumstances, there are a lot of feelings. As with all sensitive topics, children need to know the truth in a developmentally appropriate way. The amount of detail that is appropriate for parents to share depends on the child's age. Gathering details and helping parents discern what to share with children is a very delicate balance for the play therapist. In situations where the play therapist can gather information from both parents, presenting a coherent narrative both parents agree with can be challenging. The focus is for the child to maintain a relationship with both parents. Therefore, offering a balanced divorce narrative is the goal. However, there are times when a parent can no longer, and should no longer, be involved in their child's life, which requires a different narrative.

Divorce Narrative When Both Parents Are Involved

Working with divorcing parents is a challenge. Our heart rates and stress cortisol levels rise anytime divorce is mentioned in our offices, even for the most seasoned therapist. Emotions are elevated, parents are raw, and the stakes are high. Everyone has a lot to lose. As discussed in Chapter 8: Parents Who Challenge Us, play therapists have different preferences in working with divorcing parents. Whatever your preference, the goal at first is to gather information from both parties so that a coherent divorce narrative can be created for the children to hear the same message from both parents. Parents can use phrases with a similar theme:

> **Parents Never Stop Loving Kids**
>
> You did nothing wrong to cause this. We are one family with two homes. These are not the kind of problems we can work out.

We are one family with two homes, both of us love you, parents can never stop loving kids, there is nothing that you did to cause this, and we have problems that we cannot work out.

Reflecting the child's feeling is also important,

- ♦ *You are sad.*
- ♦ *You are angry.*
- ♦ *You don't want it to be like this.*
- ♦ *You are confused, and you miss mom/dad.*

For young children, the message is very short, simple, and concrete. As these children develop, more information may be provided, but, for now, keeping things short and simple is better.

For children under 5 years of age, parents often think the divorce will not impact them. These children may not even remember their parents being married; however, the impact of divorce means disrupted attachments. The change is very real, as these children will now live a life transitioning between families. There is a loss for these children that parents often do not understand. The divorce narrative for these children needs to be brief and concrete. For example,

We are getting a divorce, this means we will live in two different homes. We each still love you, and we will be living in two homes. At my home, I will give you hugs, play with you and tuck you in at night And at my home (the other parent), I will give you hugs, play with you, and tuck you in at night.

Children in this age range will likely ask very concrete questions about why,

Why can't we still live together?

Parents need to first reflect on the child's feeling, *you are sad,* and pause to see if the child will talk more. Then answer the question,

We are now divorced, which means we live in different homes.

Parents reflect more feeling, *I know this is really hard.*

Children this age will likely express their feelings through behaviors. Parents may experience their child as more demanding, resistant to doing things independently, and more challenging. These children may also be clingier and cry more often over seemingly insignificant things. These behaviors are even more challenging when the parent has a smaller Window of Tolerance. Preparing parents that these behaviors are typical and that what children need most is empathy and support in their struggle in their new circumstances.

Children ages 6 to 10 will require more details regarding why their parents are divorcing. Using the word *divorce* and phrases such as,

We are one family with two homes; there are some problems adults cannot work out; there is nothing you did to cause our divorce. I will still come to your games, and you will come to visit every other weekend, and you can call me anytime you want.

Children this age may know the word *divorce,* as they likely have a friend whose parents are divorced, so using it is important. For example,

Mom and I are getting a divorce, we have been fighting a lot, and it is not good for you. Things have been stressful at work, so I began drinking, and mom was angry, so she would yell. There are things adults can work out, like what color to paint the house or where to go to dinner. But mom and I have arguments that we cannot work out. That is why we think it is better for us and better for you for us to get divorced. We are still one family, and we have two homes. I will still come to your games, and you will come to visit every other weekend, and you can call me anytime you want.

Parents accepting their role and responsibility in the divorce is important. Children learn problem-solving and relationship skills based on how their parents handle this challenge. Giving children examples of what will stay the same and what will change is also helpful. Preparing them for what to expect, such as visitation schedule, who will attend games, take them to practices, and any other details specific to their lives. Play therapists can help parents think through different concrete questions their children may have about how this divorce impacts their life. Creating predictability will help facilitate security for children this age. Calendars of the month that note visitation, which parent is picking them up, and their activity schedule can be helpful.

Children 10 and older may require even more details and explanations regarding their parents' relationship. Preadolescents and adolescents will likely be most concerned about how the divorce will impact their life: Will they go to the same school, have the same friends, live in the same home, and so forth. The same phrases recommended for younger children can also be helpful in this age range. The play therapist can help parents accept their role in the divorce as they work together to create a coherent divorce narrative.

We are getting a divorce, things have been really hard around here for all of us, and we have decided that being married is not the best thing for our family. We are still one family with two homes. I will live here, and you will stay with me during the week, and I (the other parent) will live in a new apartment, and you will visit me every other weekend. I know you have seen us fight a lot.

Children at this age may need more general information about what was good at the beginning of the relationship and what was happening as things got more complicated. Helping children see this was not an overnight decision is helpful to them as they make sense of their world. Parents may say,

When we were dating, we fell in love. I loved dad because he was fun, and he loved me because I supported him. As we got older, things got more stressful; work was hard, so I started drinking, and dad avoided me. We started fighting more and more, and we realized that we had hurt each other deeply and could not stop fighting, so it would be better if we got divorced. Some things will stay the same, and some things will change.

Play therapists may need to caution parents to be sure to monitor themselves and ask, *"Is this important for my child to know, or is it that I want someone to know?"* If the answer is the parent wants someone to know, encourage them to work through those things with their own therapist. Play therapists caution parents to be aware of when they want the child to know how much their ex hurt them. This kind of information is not helpful to the child.

Play therapists can help parents be prepared for the different responses their children may have. Children may be angry, sad, or may appear disinterested. Play therapists teach parents to reflect their child's feeling and be empathetic to the child's struggle in the divorce. This can be hard for parents who are deeply hurt by their ex-spouse.

Divorce Narrative When One Parent Is Involved

When one parent is no longer in a parenting role or available to the child, it is usually sad and confusing for the child. Even in the most volatile marriages, children do not always understand or think the divorce is a good idea. It is common for children to believe their behavior caused the parent to leave. Therefore, addressing this concern directly is very important. In these situations, the developmental information provided in the preceding section still applies, but the narrative details are a bit different. Parents might say,

Your dad (or mom) left. They will not live with us anymore. There are times when parents cannot work out their fights, and this is what happened to us. This has nothing to do with you; there is nothing you did or said that caused them to leave. I am not going to leave; you and I will always be together; for now, we will live here, and you will still go to school, and I will still go to work.

Or, in the case of abuse or other legal situations, still being aware of appropriate developmental language,

Your dad (or mom) will be in jail because they hurt someone. We will miss them and still love them. We will visit them when we can. Or,

Your dad (or mom) is going to prison because they abused you. Remember, it is not your fault; grown-ups know they are not supposed to do that to children.

Help parents respond and reflect their child's feelings of being confused, scared, relieved, and so on. Children may have a wide range of feelings, and they may have conflicting feelings at different times, which can be surprising and challenging for parents.

General Support for Divorced Parents

Divorced parents may need help learning to communicate with each other. While most play therapists choose not to do couples counseling for many reasons, we find ourselves with parents in the most stressful places. It is not uncommon for play therapists to avoid working with these parents. However, our child clients need us to help these parents learn to co-parent. Play therapists need to help parents with wording in how to respond when their child is sharing something that has happened at the other parent's home. Equipping parents with responses such as,

Thank you for telling me. I know it is hard for you. I am so sorry that happened.

Parents need to focus on responding from a place of understanding rather than anger at the other parent. Certainly, situations may require a parent to report to Child Protective Services. It may be helpful for the play therapist to initially process these situations with the parent to avoid unnecessary reporting. In situations when parents know their child is safe. Yet, they still complain about trivial matters at the other parent's home. Play therapists encourage parents not to engage with the child about these issues but instead respond with,

hmm, let me talk with mom about that.

When parents can engage in basic communication, play therapists may encourage parents to bring issues into their parent consultations to work them out together. A boundary some parents need to maintain is that they only speak to each other on logistical issues regarding the children. While more significant family issues can be brought into parent consultations. Often these cases require more frequent parent consultations than parents who are not in conflict.

Parents who are in significant conflict may need firm boundaries around communication with each other. It is not uncommon for parents to be required to rely entirely on an online site or app to manage their communication. Some play therapists may refer parents out for additional therapy around co-parenting, allowing the play therapist to stay focused on the child.

The play therapist may also help the parents see the world through their child's eyes. Sometimes parents are surprised that children are angry at one parent for "making the other parent leave" or "for leaving." The child knows nothing about the lengthy decision-making process or understands why their parents would want to change their family. These beliefs often hold true, even when there has been an abusive parent. Children love their parents, and while it may not make sense to love someone who has hurt them, it is the only parent this child has likely known.

Rituals are helpful and provide consistency, which promotes safety and security. Parents can easily create rituals around food or activities. For example, taco Tuesdays or Friday game night can help children tolerate the transition between families more smoothly. To make the exchange less stressful, I (Mary) encourage families to share a joke with the other parent. This allows everyone to laugh; it gives the children something to focus on as they wait for their parent to arrive. A joke can reduce tension and anxiety and with a laugh, the brain is flexible and more responsive rather than reactive. A calendar at each home can provide a visual for children to know their visitation schedule. Weekly calendars may be more appropriate for younger children. Older children may prefer a monthly calendar that gives them a bigger picture of their visitation schedule.

Every family has a different story, and the impact of the divorce on their child is unique. There is no way to prepare for every situation; even the most seasoned therapist will be surprised by a story, custody requirements, or a parent's behavior. Keep yourself regulated and remember that these parents are hurt, dysregulated, and need a lot of help. Play therapists provide empathy, unconditional positive regard, and genuineness to facilitate the therapeutic process. While support for the parent is necessary, the child is always the clinical focus. A referral may be needed so the parent has a professional to focus on caring for them. See Chapter 8: Parents Who Challenge Us for a discussion on when to refer parents for their own counseling.

Introducing a New Partner

Parents are often eager to introduce new partners. Praise parents who even ask for help in introducing a new partner; this is a parent putting their child first. Encouraging parents to take things slowly and be mindful of their child's response. Making their first meeting very casual, for example, running into them at a park several times, so it feels spontaneous and gradual to the child. After several short park run-ins, ask the children to see if the new friend would like to have dinner together. Creating an opportunity for the children to get to know and slowly experience the new friend allows their relationship to develop more organically. Play therapists can remind parents that adjusting to a new person is difficult for children. Bringing in a new person creates yet another change in the whole family system to which the child must adapt.

Talking With Parents About Trauma

Parents of traumatized children are living a life they never imagined and do not know how to navigate. Particularly if the parents and entire family experienced the same trauma. It is not unusual for parents to avoid talking about the trauma. They believe that if they don't talk about it, the child will not remember. "I feel like I am playing a part in a movie I don't want to be in," said the parent of a traumatized child. It is critical that play therapists remember the parent is also traumatized; the feelings these parents experience are incredibly diverse: anger, guilt, fear, and many others. These parents are often dysregulated and need their own therapist to process their trauma.

Educating parents about trauma can be challenging, especially if the parent is dysregulated and has difficulty tracking the information you are providing. Parents who are struggling in this way most definitely need their own therapist. In some cases, intergenerational trauma may be a significant factor in the parents' response to their child's trauma. Due to their own traumatic childhood, it is possible that the parent may not perceive their child has experienced trauma but think these experiences are normal and part of growing up. The play therapist will need to be very empathetic with this parent before educating the parent about trauma. The primary goal in this situation is to increase the parent's trust in the therapist.

Once the therapeutic relationship is strong, teaching parents how to respond to their child at home is essential. Beginning with the concept of felt safety and the skill of reflection of feeling is a good starting place. Felt safety is different from being safe; one can be safe yet not feel safe. Explaining to the parent that the child's perception of safety is most important. Attempting to convince the child they are safe is likely not very effective. It is more effective to reflect the child's feeling, engage the right/feeling brain, and then move to the left/logical brain to talk about how they are actually safe. Parents will need help with this skill repeatedly as it is not intuitive for most parents.

Teaching parents about the Interpersonal Neurobiology of how the brain works and responds to felt safety is helpful. The brain is wired to protect when it senses danger, and this is why children respond in a fight, flight, freeze, or feign response. Helping parents understand their child's behavioral responses enables the parent to feel more in control. Play therapy is where children develop more productive skills to protect themselves and make sense of their experiences.

Talking With Parents About Sensitive Topics

Not all parents realize all that a therapist can offer. Just as a pediatrician can help parents with more than ear infections and strep throat, a play therapist can help parents with general parenting struggles beyond the specific reason the child came to therapy. As pediatric professionals, it is part of our role to ask parents about screen use, protecting their children from sexual abuse, eating, sleeping, and pooping. These topics should be approached gently; parents may be triggered or feel defensive or inadequate. The primary goal with parents continues to be to maintain the therapeutic relationship, the primary agent of change.

Technology

The family's use of technology may impact the child's progress in therapy. Remember, in the *Child Background Form*, there are questions about the families' technology use that may apply to the child's treatment. Inquiring about a family's technology use can be a touchy subject for some families. As part of a child's healthy development, managing screen time is an important part of modern parenting. However, not all parents know about the dangers and benefits of technology. Providing parents with information on appropriate uses of technology and boundaries to keep children safe is a critical conversation. The American Academy of Pediatrics has general recommendations on media use for children.

- ♦ Age 18 to 24 months, if parents want to introduce media, AAP recommends only high-quality media (such as Sesame Street) that parents watch with children.
- ♦ Age 2–5 years, only one hour of high-quality material that parents watch with children to link what they see to the world around them is recommended.
- ♦ For children age 6 and up, the AAP recommends parents create limits on media and be careful not to let media take the place of physical activity or relationships with others. (AAP, 2016, www.aap.org/en/news-room/news-releases/aap/2016/aap-announces-new-recommendations-for-media-use/)

Technology is a part of our culture. Being intentional about its use in the family is a part of modern parenting. There are a plethora of resources for parents on creating a family media plan. Play therapists need to have a perspective of helping parents create safety. This includes the rising number of children addicted to pornography and online predators. Resources and products are designed to help families create a media plan and keep children safe. See the Resources at the end of this chapter for websites to assist in developing family media plans.

Protecting Children From Sexual Abuse

Parents are uncomfortable talking with their children about protecting themselves from sexual abuse. Many parents were sexually abused and are triggered or activated when even thinking about having this conversation. Other parents may be unaware of the statistics on the frequency of child abuse. Some parents fear talking about abuse would destroy their child's innocence. No matter the reason, this topic needs to be addressed with compassion, so parents feel supported in broaching this topic with their children. If the child's safety or the family's living situation, is in question, the play therapist should be prepared to discuss sexual abuse prevention with the parent. Offering to help parents is often well received. Teaching children the correct words for their body parts is a significant first step. While some parents may be embarrassed to use anatomically correct language, their children are not usually embarrassed. Guiding parents to teach their children, there are no secrets in their family and that if anyone asks them to keep a secret, they should respond,

We don't have any secrets in our family.

Coaching parents to explain what a secret is can sound like this:

Secrets, like what we are getting grandma for her birthday, should make you feel excited inside; secrets that make you feel scared, lonely, or unsure should never be kept. If a secret makes you feel like that, you should tell me immediately.

Bibliotherapy is helpful here. There are many books written for various age levels that both teach the importance of setting boundaries and telling someone if abuse occurs. See the Resources section in this chapter for some of our favorites.

Sleeping, Eating, and Pooping

Proper sleeping, eating, and pooping are important for all children. Healthy amounts of each can significantly impact a child's day. It is not uncommon for a child with mild behavioral challenges to need to adjust their sleep patterns, and then magically, behavior improves! Sleeping, eating, and pooping can be stressful topics for parents. Therefore the play therapist should approach these topics gingerly. A posture of curiosity is critical to help the parent feel supported rather than judged is the goal.

Play therapists do not need to be sleep experts. However, knowing the recommended amount of sleep children at different ages need is helpful. The American Academy of Pediatrics (AAP) has this foundational information on its website www.healthychildren.org. The AAP recommends that children ages 3 to 5 years get 10 to 13 hours of sleep each day, including naps; children 6 to 12 years old need 9 to 12 hours a day. Play therapists can help parents make proper sleep a family priority. This includes going to bed early enough and stopping screens one hour before bed. While it may seem counterintuitive, many children who wake very early in the mornings may be doing so because they did not go to bed early enough the night before. Yes, early enough. Children who have trouble going to sleep may be overtired and have difficulty winding down. Play therapists can help parents talk through bedtime routines and be a sounding board to make minor adjustments in their lives. Suppose minor adjustments are not addressing the sleep challenges. In that case, the play therapist may combine this piece of the puzzle with others to determine if a referral to a sleep specialist or occupational therapist is in order.

Children who eat red food on Tuesday or sometimes eat chicken but just not today can cause significant stress for their parent. Empathy for the parent is in order here, as when this is a problem, it is a problem multiple times a day, and it is exhausting for the parent. Parents of children who are picky eaters often share this struggle in the initial parent consultation. The source of picky eating may be due to development, sensory issues, power and control needs, among other things. Ask parents about patterns in the picky eating, textures, types of food, and so on. As you listen to parents talk about the child's general behavioral struggles, look for patterns. If the picky eating seems to be a piece of a bigger sensory processing puzzle, refer the family to an occupational therapist. Once again, the play therapist does not need to be an expert in these issues, nor does the play therapist need to treat sensory processing issues. A referral is what is warranted. I (Mary) often find myself saying, *I wonder what an occupational therapist would say about this*. Picky eating issues may also center more around the child's need for control which can then be addressed in play therapy.

Play therapists problem-solve with parents, think of ways children can have more control, or ways to make dinner more fun. For example, children can be involved in meal planning, influencing one item of their meal while the parent is still in charge of the child's nutrition. This may result in unusual combinations such as goldfish crackers with chicken and broccoli. Creatively thinking parents cut food into fun shapes, or use a dip such as hummus or ketchup. At my (Mary's) house, a favorite was playing the crunch game to see who could make the loudest crunch at the table. Or the mystery food game to see if the parent can guess what the child is eating. An eating story, where everyone takes a bite when the narrator says the magic word. Problem-solving with parents to think outside of the box, have more fun at dinner, and connect with their child during meals can ease the tension in the family. More relaxed brains can connect and be more flexible in challenging situations, including dinner.

Toileting struggles can be the result of several underlying issues. In very young children, general potty training could be the source of the conversation. Products on the market make it easier for parents but often more challenging for children to feel wet and therefore can delay potty training. For children over four years old who have difficulty potty training, it is essential to encourage parents to talk to their pediatrician to rule out any medical issues. Often toilet training is a symptom of a mental health struggle; anxiety, trauma, and perfectionism are all possible sources of toileting challenges. Play therapy will likely be helpful in these cases. Play therapists should be aware that regressive toileting issues due to trauma or stress may resolve as treatment progresses. In addition to play therapy, children with encopresis may benefit from a structured-sit several times a day. Encourage parents to be playful and relaxed. Stress and consequences or punishments are not helpful here. Most children do not wet themselves on purpose, despite their parents' feelings. Children also need to be set up for success. Is there a footstool, can they fit on the toilet seat without falling in and get their own clothes off easily? These are issues parents may not consider.

Coach parents to chat with their children about being a good detective about their bodies, and learning to listen to the clues their bodies give them. Parents might say,

What clue is your body giving when your tummy growls or your mouth is thirsty, or you need to potty?

For children with encopresis, scheduled sits may be helpful to train the body to relax and for the child to take time to make a bowel movement. Kristen Bemis (Personal Communication, May 13, 2015) encourages children to have a sit every three to four hours for five minutes. This is at least three trips a day. Parents may use a timer and provide books for children to read, songs to sing, or paper to draw; electronics are prohibited during the sits. Once the child sits, the parent responds,

This is how we take care of our bodies, everybody goes poop on the potty, or *everyone goes to the bathroom* (if you think the child hates the "poop" word)
    if bowel movement, *You did it*
    Or, if not, *You worked really hard*
    Parents always say, *You did your job and took care of yourself! Way to go!*

Parents can use sticker charts for sitting; each sit earns one sticker, and for every five stickers, there is a reward. Rewards should be relational, for example, special time with mom, extra time outside, a family game, and so on. Remind parents this is a process and it will take time and compassion for themselves and their child to be successful (K. Bemis, Personal Communication, May 13, 2015). Practicing Limit Setting around the bathroom will also be helpful for parents. Helping parents notice their tone of voice during limit-setting and choice giving is critical as very few parents in this situation are not frustrated with their child. That frustration is evident in their voice tone. An example of a limit would be,

You are scared to go to the potty. I know you do not want to go to the potty. Going to the potty is not a choice. You can choose to race me to the bathroom or hop like a bunny to the bathroom.

Some children will resist going to the bathroom and help parents mentally prepare for this possibility. After all, why would a child willingly and with a good attitude want to do something so hard? I (Mary) certainly do not have a good attitude about hard things in my life. If the child resists, the parent can restate the choice in a calm and peaceful voice,

Going to the bathroom is not a choice; you can choose to slither like a snake or dance with me to the bathroom; which do you choose?

Parents may have to restate the choice many times, which is exhausting. Play therapists need to be sure to encourage and support parents as they work in this process also.

In Closing

Play therapists are great resources for parents. Sometimes parents ask for help first, and other times the play therapist may ask some questions that cause a parent to realize they lack information or skill in an area. An attitude of curiosity is paramount in every parent consultation as the play therapist works to help families identify challenges and think through different options to address the challenges. Respecting parents' knowledge, culture, and capacity is critical, as maintaining the therapeutic relationship continues to be of primary importance to parents. Parents need support and encouragement to tackle challenging topics. Often they are fearful of saying the wrong thing, play therapists can give parents the space to practice what to say and the courage to take the risk. Parents who are willing to engage in tough conversations with their children provide added safety and security in the parent-child relationship, laying the groundwork for difficult conversations as the child develops.

Resources

There are a lot of great children's books on a variety of topics. This is not an exhaustive list, but a few of our favorites.

- ♦ Children's books on divorce
  - *Mama and Daddy Bear's Divorce*, Cornelia Maude Spelman, Albert Whitman & Company, 1998.
  - *Dinosaurs Divorce*, Laurene Krasny Brown & Marc Brown, Little, Brown and Company, 1986.
  - *Fred Stays With Me*, Nancy Coffelt, Little, Brown and Company, 2007.
  - *Do You Sing Twinkle*, Sandra Levins, Magination Press, 2010.
- ♦ Children's books on families
  - *Families Families Families*, Suzanne Lang & Max Lang, Penguin, 2015.
  - *And Tango Makes Three*, Justin Richardson & Peter Parnell, Little Simon, 2015.
  - *My Family Is Forever*, Nancy Carlson, Puffin Books, 2006.
  - *Rosie's Family*, Lori Rosove, Asia Pr, 2001.
  - *We Adopted You Benjamin Koo*, Linda Walvoord Girard, Albert Whitman & Company, 1989.
  - *The Family Book*, Todd Parr, Little Brown and Company, 2003.
- ♦ Books for parents and children on sexual abuse
  - *Body Safety Education*, Jayneen Sanders, Educate2Empower Publishing, 2015.
  - *I Said No!*, Zack & Kimberly King, Boulden, 2010.
  - *The Secret That Should Never Be Kept*, Jayneen Sanders, Educate2Empower Publishing, 2011.
  - *No Means No!*, Jayneen Sanders, Educate2Empower Publishing, 2015.
- ♦ Children's books on death
  - *When Dinosaurs Die*, Laurie Krasny Brown & Marc Brown, Little Brown and Company, 1996.
  - *The Invisible String*, Patrice Karst, DeVorss, 2000.
  - *Kids Book About Death*, Taryn Schuelke, A Kids Company About Inc., 2020.
  - *A Terrible Thing Happened*, Margaret Holmes & Sasha J. Mudlaff, Magination Press, 2000.
  - *Trauma Is Really Strange*, Steve Haines & Sophie Standing, Singing Dragon, 2015.
  - Dougy.org (The Dougy Center Website)
- ♦ Resources for Parents on Understanding Trauma
  - *Helping Traumatized Children: A Brief Overview for Caregivers by Bruce Perry*
  - *www.childtrauma.org/_files/ugd/aa51c7_237459a7e16b4b7e9d2c4837c908eefe.pdf*

- *RobynGobbel.com*
  - *Parenting After Trauma Podcast*
- *Adopting a Child With a Trauma and Attachment Disruption History: A Practical Guide*, Theresa Fraser & William Krill, Loving Healing Press, 2011.
- *The Whole Brain Child*, Dan Siegel & Tina Payne Bryson, Bantam Books, 2012.
- *The Power of Showing Up*, Dan Siegel & Tina Payne Bryson, Bantam Books, 2020.
- Screens, online, social media for children
  - *Good Pictures Bad Pictures Jr*, Kristen A. Jenson, Glen Cove Press, 2017.
  - *Good Pictures Bad Pictures*, Kristen A. Jenson, Glen Cove Press, 2018.
  - Fight the New Drug, fightthenewdrug.org (Docuseries for parents and children)
- Media contacts and other resources for parents
  - *Waituntil8th.org*
  - *Mediatechparenting.net*
  - *Commonsensemedia.org*
  - *Healthychildren.org*
  - *Screenfreeparenting.org*

Chapter 10

A Deeper Look at Play

We have a PLAY circuit in our brain! Jaak Panksepp, a neuroscientist and psychobiologist, located and identified seven emotional circuits in brains (Panksepp, 2006). He discovered that the urge to play is an instinctual action in all mammalian brains. Also labeled as *social joy*, it is an experience-expectant system that promotes social activities and joy (Panksepp, 2006). Emergent emotions from the PLAY circuit are joy, glee, and happy playfulness. (Note: Panksepp capitalized the name of each circuit to clearly identify these as biologically inherited primary affective systems.) We are wired to play, joyfully, and in connection with others. Our neurobiological state motivates play.

Knowledge of child development is the initial key to our understanding of children. Play therapists' grounding in child development provides the constructs to assess the children in our playrooms. Play is used by child developmentalists to identify children as being on-target in meeting developmental markers. As a refresher, refer to Dee Ray's, *A Therapist's Guide to Child Development: Extraordinary Normal Years*. It provides a review of several developmental theories, then chapters for specific age ranges. It also has handouts for parents. It goes into greater detail than is possible here. Neurodivergent children also are identifiable by their play. Providing mental health and play therapy interventions with various neurotypes requires specialized training. We refer play therapists to the work of Robert Jason Grant, and his book, *The AutPlay Therapy Handbook: Integrative Family Play Therapy for Neurodivergent Children*.

In Chapter 5, Treatment Phase: Session Notes, we discussed identifying the type of play in which the child engages for documentation on the *Play Therapy Session Note*. The list of types of play is also found in Appendix D. These are tied to cognitive development during child development. A couple of these will be further explained here: regressive and solitary play.

Regressive play is a construct that indicates a child is playing at an earlier stage of development. This is differentiated from a neurodivergent play. Regressive play is frequently initially noted in young children in childcare centers. When this stress-related regressive play intensifies and begins to interfere with functioning, children come to play therapy. Play therapists identify regressive play in the playroom by also noting a child playing at a younger developmental level. I (Linda) had a 4-year-old child-client who, when in an intense play sequence, would leave the play, get a baby bottle, fill it with water, and suck on it, then re-engage in his distressing play. This was a self-selected coping skill that he developed to meet his own regulation need. It is play reflective of an earlier developmental stage (being fed a bottle), easily seen as regressive play. We know sucking and drinking soothe the child's nervous system, so the neurobiological basis of the self-soothing is understood.

DOI: 10.4324/9781003258766-12

Solitary play is typical for children up to two years of age. It may be identified as regressive play for older, neurotypical children. Our clinical understanding of the purpose this play serves for this particular child is what is clinically meaningful. What is the child communicating through their chosen play? Is it because there is no felt safety? Is the child afraid that they will not be accepted if that play is observed by the play therapist? The play therapist makes a clinical hypothesis of its meaning as with other play behaviors. And documents it.

When coping skills become overwhelmed, children often engage in a play behavior of an earlier time, re-creating a feeling of well-being, safety, and comfort. For example, a child may be playing a domestic-violence scene in the dollhouse and abruptly change the play where the young child doll they have been playing with is replaced by a baby doll. The story of the play changes to the mother who becomes a nurturing, caring mother, feeding the baby and putting her to bed. The aggressor in the domestic violence is no longer in the play sequence. This change in play may occur subtly and simply seem to have less dissonance. The attentive play therapist, however, notices the shift and makes meaning of it in context. This is a subtle variation of the previous example with the baby bottle. The child acts out a play sequence of a safer time. It also neurobiologically soothes and regulates.

Other children may have a *play disruption*. While appearing to manage a distressing play sequence, a child might abruptly leave her domestic violence play in the dollhouse and moves to the sandbox. The child then pours sand back and forth into containers in the sandbox and onto their hands. It is neurobiologically soothing and regulating. When the child senses regulation has sufficiently returned, they frequently return to the distressing dollhouse play. The child learns to manage their Window of Tolerance through their play. In this case, the child may not have previously played in the sand, so it's not regressive play. It's not playing out an earlier, safer life-stage experience. But the tactile, sensory play directly soothes the lower brain.

Therapeutic Powers of Play

Play itself is therapeutic. Athena Drewes and Charles Schaefer state:

> Play is not just a medium for applying other change agents, nor does it just moderate the strength or direction of the therapeutic change. It is not an ancillary add-on to the treatment approach, but is rather a key component essential within the treatment approach. (Drewes & Schaefer, 2016, p. 36)

Mary Anne Peabody and Charles Schaefer define the therapeutic powers of play as "the mechanisms in play that actually produce the desired change in a client's dysfunctional thoughts, feelings, and/or behaviors" (2019, p. 5). The identified 20 therapeutic powers of play assist the play therapist in understanding how the play process is therapeutic. This connection between play and how it serves the play therapy process is vital to know in-depth. This knowledge provides the framework upon which we explain how play therapy works to other mental health professionals, other professionals (e.g., doctors, school personnel, attorneys), and parents. How play is therapeutic is explained in detail by Charles Schaefer and Athena Drewes (2014) and the other chapter authors in their edited book, *The Therapeutic Powers of Play: 20 Core Agents of Change*.

Their now-classic work interweaves the understanding of the play therapy process and continues to be written about by many others. The Association for Play Therapy (APT) requires knowledge of the therapeutic powers of play as part of their credentialing process. It is also required to be interwoven by the APT-approved trainers in their training.

Figure 10.1 is the graphic developed by Judi Parson of Deakin University in Australia. It visually organizes the 20 powers of play into the four categories identified by Drewes and Schaefer (2016). These powers of play and corresponding categories provide words to use in session notes and treatment planning. But perhaps more importantly, to help us make meaning of the therapeutic work the children are doing in the playroom.

Here is a brief review and definitions of the 20 therapeutic powers of play. While these powers of play are transtheoretical, some are identified more frequently as change agents for specific play therapy theories. While reading through the following list and explanations, we challenge the reader to identify the ones that resonate most with them and their approach to doing play therapy. Even highlight or underline them. (This experience will also be used as one of the steps in identifying your clinical theory. More about that in Chapter 11: Finding a Theory.) These therapeutic powers of play can also be used in identifying a deeper understanding of play when documenting the session.

Figure 10.1 Therapeutic powers of play

Source: Copyright, 2017, Parson & Renshaw. Used with permission.

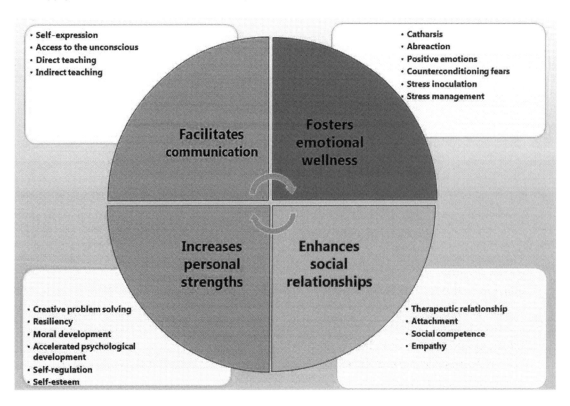

Facilitates communication

1. Self-expression: "Children speak play!" (Parson, 2021, p. 7) and this is where "toys are the words and play is the language" fits. Mary Morrison Bennett and Stephanie Eberts additionally identify components of self-expression in play as the opportunity to talk in third person (e.g., through dolls and puppets); acting "as if" during role play; expression of the unspeakable; and the safety to facilitate expression (2014, pp. 12–13).

2. Access to the unconscious: The child is able to use defense mechanisms as a way to communicate meaning. These defense mechanisms include projection, displacement, symbolism, sublimation, and fantasy compensation (Drewes & Schaefer, 2016). Children use play within each of these defense mechanisms to communicate to their play therapist.

3. Direct teaching: "The play therapist imparts knowledge or skills through strategies as instruction, modeling, guided practice, and positive reinforcement" (Fraser, 2016, p. 41). Drewes and Schaefer (2016) state that making learning fun and enjoyable increases the child's motivation and effort to learn. They also indicate other components of direct learning are capturing attention, using sensory input, providing a safe environment, active involvement, consolidating of skills, and learning by example.

4. Indirect teaching: The play therapist uses stories and metaphors to provide guidance (Drewes & Schaefer, 2016). This may be the use of bibliotherapy or creating stories the during the play session, such as therapeutic storytelling and mutual storytelling. The play therapist may also provide indirect teaching through their facilitative responses and reflections to the child on the meaning of the play.

Fosters emotional wellness

5. Catharsis: Children use play to release pent-up negative affect in a safe space. This play might be punching a "Bobo" or pounding clay. Cathartic play in a safe environment also provides psychological distancing. Children can play out more intense experiences through toys than they could verbally tell a therapist about. Catharsis offers the opportunity for increasing conscious awareness and control of those emotions. The fun of play helps balance the discharge of strong emotions (Drewes & Schaefer, 2016).

6. Abreaction: In play, a "forgotten" memory of a traumatic event becomes sufficiently consciously aware for the child to re-experience it through play. Drewes and Schaefer (2016) indicate that the miniaturization of the experience in the playroom provides the child a sense of power. Children actively control replaying the trauma event leading to the cognitive restructuring of the incident, or a corrective emotional experience, during abreactive play. Finally, the child can deconstruct the event into workable, doable segments, gaining mastery one segment at a time. Or, as trauma is stored in the mind in fragments, each fragment is played out individually.

7. Positive emotions: Play provides the child with the feeling of relief needed from the heaviness of stress. Positive feelings can be the healing force that precipitates change in psychotherapy (Drewes & Schaefer, 2016). As indicated in the beginning of this chapter, the PLAY circuit in the brain engenders social joy.

8. Counterconditioning of fears: Play gradually exposes a child to identified fears using specific techniques to desensitize children by introducing more desirable responses (Drewes & Schaefer, 2016; Parson, 2021). For example, playing in the felt safety of a dark playroom can inhibit or weaken the fear of the dark

of the child who is afraid of the dark at home (Van Hollander, 2014). Playing a superhero helps a child embody the feeling of power while reenacting a bullying scenario at school, counterconditioning the bully's fear. Other procedures noted by Tammi Van Hollander (2014) include the use of emotive imagery (counterconditioning), game play (extinguishing), laughter therapy (desensitization), and replay (desensitization).

9. Stress inoculation: Play proactively prepares a child to meet an identifiable upcoming novel situation. This might be using toys to play out an upcoming court appearance or medical procedure. The play rehearsal exchanges the strange or novel situation with familiar ones, provides time to develop coping mechanisms, and makes the rehearsal fun and enjoyable, reducing activation of negative emotions (Drewes & Schaefer, 2016). It also makes use of the therapeutic power of play of positive emotions.

10. Stress management: Play provides the opportunity for momentary relief (fantasy escape) from stressful situations and develops stronger self-concept and resilience. This might be as simple as using humor in the playroom, where the play therapist acts in silly and laughter-inducing ways (Drewes & Schaefer, 2016). Children often initiate play that demonstrates what they wish their situation would be, called fantasy compensation. Others use self soothing play after a play disruption, using something tactile such as water or sand play (Drewes & Schaefer, 2016). Additional forms of play for stress management are social play and exploratory play (Bemis, 2014).

Enhances social relationships

11. Therapeutic relationship: The child's play provides a means for connection with the therapist. Children use toys such as the medical kit instruments or puppets to come close to the play therapist and initiate a play interaction to sense if the therapist feels safe. Others invite the play therapist into their play to see if they can be trusted to interact in a playful yet respectful manner. A child may use play to test the therapeutic relationship, to sense if the therapist hold and contain their story, or do they shut the child down as other adults do. Most therapists, including play therapists, agree that a therapeutic relationship is required for change to occur (Drewes & Schaefer, 2016; Stewart & Echterling, 2014). The resulting therapeutic relationship "garners its healing power in the way that it embodies the characteristics of a healthy parent-child relationship . . . there exists a shared goal or purpose to the relationship, an attuned and known way to engage with one another, and a positive affective connection" (Stewart & Echterling, 2014, p. 158).

12. Attachment: Play enhances and develops attachment. "In secure and playful interactions the therapist delights in the child and demonstrates non-threatening behaviours such as smiling and laughing. These actions replicate early life secure attachment behaviours and aim to enhance and strengthen the therapeutic attachment" (Parson, 2021, p. 8). Play therapists may tell the child what they recall about what they did together in a previous session (Drewes & Schaefer, 2016). This brings to the child's attention that the therapist remembers the child between sessions and further develops attachment. This can be as short and simple as, *"I remember you did that last time you were here."* Other joint play like blowing bubbles together is a fun way to develop connection.

13. Social competence: Play is the primary way children learn social skills, leading to social competence. Socio-dramatic play, where children take on various roles, might

occur through using puppet play, sand tray play, or role-playing. Game play, where the child and play therapist practice keeping rules or working to reach a common goal and facilitates social competence is effective with older children. Positive emotions naturally emerge in these types of play, further enhancing the positive interactions and reinforcing social skill development (Nash, 2014).

14. Empathy: Play provides the means through which the child can discover and develop the skill of taking the perspective of others. This occurs especially during role-play and storytelling (Drewes & Schaefer, 2016). As in social competence play, the same types of play are effective for developing empathy. The play therapist's facilitative responses assist in enhancing and reinforcing the child's experiencing and expressing empathy.

Increases personal strengths

15. Creative problem solving: "In play, a wide range of unique ideas and stories can be brought to life; these in turn stimulate and extend the imagination to consider alternative possibilities in a safe and carefree way" (Parson, 2021, p. 9). Problem-solving can be trying a different way to build the tower, it might also be helping a horse family find a way to avoid the tigers and dinosaurs. The play therapist uses facilitative responses of encouragement and returning responsibility, trusting the child can develop divergent thinking, flexibility, and insight. Another example is the Adlerian Play Therapy form of limit setting in which the play therapist and child work together to agree on alternate options also develops problem-solving skills.

16. Resiliency: Using play to recover from unexpected or difficult situations and to expand the capacity for resilience (Parson, 2021). John Seymour (2014) lists eight resilience processes provided by play: reducing anxiety and increasing problem solving, reducing self-blame, reducing blaming by others, reducing isolation and enhancing attachment, increasing self-esteem and self-efficacy, creative play fosters creative problem solving, improving nurturing relationships beyond the playroom, and learning to make meaning of life's experiences.

17. Moral development: Stages of moral development are tied to cognitive development. Children at all developmental levels play at their current level of social consciousness. Judi Parson (2021) writes that "working out right from wrong, or things being fair or unfair, may be played out in role-play where power and control themes or games with rules predominate" (p. 9). Puppets are especially useful for this. Examples might be the child who has a helper-figure be the perpetrator, such as the doctor puppet making children vampires rather than healing them, or firemen not rescuing another toy in danger. Or in the sandbox when adult animals ignore child animals in danger. Or the mother who treats one of her children differently from the others.

18. Accelerated psychological development: Through play, children "are able to extend their play and consider and explore more complex play possibilities without fear. Play can also help foster the mastery of physical, cognitive and emotional regulation" (Parson, 2021, p. 9). Vygotsky (1978) calls this the zone of proximal development, where the child uses play to scaffold their development. "The assistance (scaffolding) provided by the more advanced play partner helps the child advance to the next higher developmental level" (S. Prendiville, 2014, p. 259). The playroom's wide range of toys and

materials allow the child to continue to scaffold more advanced play. More directive play therapists may gradually introduce more complex, advanced play (Stagnitti, 2021).

19. Self-regulation: The ability "to control impulses and to motivate one-self when bored and calm one-self when hyperaroused" (Parson, 2021, p. 9) is enhanced during play. It's important to note here that the play therapist co-regulates with the child before the child develops the ability to self-regulate. The play therapist profoundly connects with the child, using the "Being-With" stance. As the child acquires the ability to self-regulate, they also use play to both up-regulate and down-regulate.

20. Self-esteem: Using play, children learn to understand, integrate, and value their entire selves. Children are delighted as they develop new and higher levels of mastery within their play. Deconstructing, understanding, and integrating resolved trauma through play is satisfying and increases competence. The play therapist can enhance this through esteem-building facilitative responses, such as *"you figured that out," "you know just what you need,"* and *"you know how to make it work."*

As the play therapist identifies the therapeutic powers of play the child is using, this awareness can link the play therapy session to the treatment plan. It informs the play therapist in crafting more therapeutic facilitative responses. It provides understanding of the play, which can be shared in parent consultations. The therapeutic powers of play are the fibers of the web that weave together to produce and hold the therapy process.

The reader is encouraged to read more detailed and in-depth explanations of the therapeutic powers of play. In addition to several works by Charles Schaefer is the book *Clinical Applications of the Therapeutic Powers of Play: Case Studies in Child and Adolescent Psychotherapy* by written and edited by Eileen Prendiville and Judi Parson (2021). The case studies highlighted in each chapter provide insight into how the therapeutic powers of play are identified in the playroom.

View of Play Continuum

The play therapist's rationale of why they use play in their work must be clear and understood. One view is that play is the child's communication or language and, therefore, the play therapist must be bilingual in the languages of play and talking.

> *Toys are the words.*
> *Play is the language.*

Every play therapist knows the phrase, "child's play is his talk and the toys his words" as originally stated by Haim Ginott (1960, p. 243) and popularized by Garry Landreth (2012). A play therapist in the middle of this continuum uses play to connect with children, sometimes relying on play as communication and other times relying on it to facilitate verbalization. At the other end of the continuum, play is the medium or activity through which therapeutic concepts are taught, and play is used with the goal to facilitate increased verbalization. Play is used to teach and help children verbalize, develop new coping skills, change cognitive distortions through role-playing, psychoeducation, and more. Some play therapists will primarily work on one end of the continuum; others will move fluidly along it.

Directive Versus Nondirective Continuum

Another component is the play therapist's position on the directive-nondirective continuum. This continuum is about the *role* of the play therapist in the play therapy session. Of course, given the clinical theory, one might quickly identify with a specific spot or range on this continuum. Other theories will expect constant movement along the continuum. For example, Adlerian Play Therapists can be in various places depending on Adlerian Play Therapy (AdPT) phase and even within any given session. On the other hand, a Child-Centered Play Therapist (CCPT) will consistently take the nondirective stance and views play as communication. This directive-nondirective lens aids documenting the interaction between the child and therapist, and the child and the play. It also helps the play therapist to be aware of the stance they are taking as the therapist and why it is appropriate for this particular child at this specific time in the therapeutic process.

Neurobiology in the Playroom

Lorraine Freedle, a sandplay therapist, and pediatric neuropsychologist, conceptualized the process of healing in Kalffian-Jungian Sandplay Therapy. Freedle developed the *Sandplay's Neuro-Sensory Feedback Loop*® (Figure 10.2) during a sandplay therapy research project. While documenting

Figure 10.2 Sandplay's neuro-sensory feedback loop
Source: Copyright, Lorraine Razzi Freedle. Used with permission.

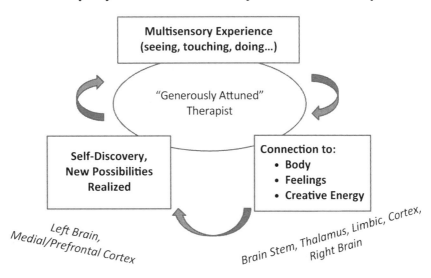

Sandplay's Neuro-Sensory Feedback Loop

when the change occurred, she identified an emerging repetitive, continuous pattern. I (Linda) believe this same model applies to the child in the playroom. Lorraine has generously given us permission to introduce readers of this book to her model. The application of the feedback loop to play therapy is mine.

Note the feedback loop has as its hub the *generously attuned* therapist. Throughout this book, the importance of the focused, attuned, regulated play therapist is emphasized. Without this attunement, and subsequent understanding, the ability for insightful documentation is very limited. The feedback loop is entered through the child's multisensory experience. The child's senses are activated as they connect with the toys and materials in the playroom. This occurs when touching, feeling, and doing play. In the playroom, they also use fine and gross motor skills, physical movement throughout the room, and expansive play with the toys and materials. This results in the child experiencing a connection with their body and feelings, creating energy. Polyvagal theory informs us here (Porges & Dana, 2018). The child might also become neurologically hyperactivated or hypoactivated, encompassing the expression of strong emotions. When connected with self and the generously attuned play therapist, the child's brain is activated through the brain stem, limbic system, and cortex, resulting in vertical right-brain integration. As the play therapy experience continues, so does the feedback loop. The child and the therapeutic responses provided by the generously attuned play therapist serve to energize continued movement along the loop. The child begins self-discovery and new possibilities are realized. This is a left-brain process, integrating the medial and prefrontal cortex. As the generously attuned play therapist enters the child's world and their play, translating the language of play to the spoken word, the child's left brain hears and makes sense of their play. This translating of play language does not need to be interpretive; it can be the reflection of understanding. The child's right brain neural networks open as they are immersed in their play; the facilitative responses provide meaning-making into that played-out and remembered experience. And so, the neuro-sensory feedback loop continues.

In-the-Moment: The Play Therapist's Response to Play

As part of the therapeutic relationship in the playroom, the play therapist is involved in the play in many ways and at many levels. It might be observing the child's play while profoundly resonating with the child and in the child's world. We sense what the child is feeling, see it through the child's eyes, and even imagine the feelings and thoughts regarding the play sequence and metaphor. The child may invite us into the play to role-play them and thus experience their nightmares in the dark of night; playing out the terror they feel when put to bed at night and without having enough protection. We are *in* the play, experiencing and reacting. It's a full-body experience. These levels of engagement provide healing for the child as they have a shared experience of meaning-making and feel deeply understood. They feel felt at the moment as our MIRROR neurons are in complete resonance. Their neural nets are open to having a corrective emotional experience. So powerful.

Or, perhaps the play therapist feels bored, confused, or detached. This can also happen. This is when self-awareness on the part of the play therapist is paramount. What is happening in the child's play might activate or trigger in the play therapist? Is the sense of detachment a self-protective reaction? It can be a neurobiological, polyvagal reaction to protect ourselves from some previous personal trauma or stressor. Our neurological system is reacting. In these moments, we have broken the connection with the child. That interrupts the therapeutic process. In these cases, connecting with our supervisor or seeking consultation to explore these reactions is an appropriate course of action. Our experience in doing years of supervision and consultations is that we begin the exploration of underlying dynamics with the play therapist. Sometimes we suggest they engage in their own therapy. For example, I (Linda) supervised a new play therapist in her practicum experience. With every client she saw sexualized content in their play, regardless of presenting issues. Observing these same sessions live, I did not attribute the child's play to sexual abuse. During supervision, she shared she had experienced sexual abuse as a child. She stated, "I thought I had already worked through all of that in my own therapy!" Children's play can result in a visceral reaction of physical and emotional reactions totally out of our awareness. This is why *self-awareness* is critically important. Self-awareness in the moment.

In Closing

Counseling theory, therapeutic powers of play, types of play, the therapist's view of play, and the child therapist experience in play therapy are all important factors to document. It is the deep understanding and knowledge of these play characteristics that therapists need to see the moment and understand the child's world. It is not uncommon for therapists to doubt their effectiveness in play therapy, but when therapists use these tools as their guide, they can see the movement and progression in the play, and change and growth in the children. These nuances in a child's play are essential and often impossible to capture without a detailed study of video recordings of a child's sessions. (With appropriate consent and explicit details of the purpose, storage, and destruction of the videos.) Therefore, when possible, we strongly encourage therapists to occasionally video record sessions. One of the biggest challenges is the pressure therapists get from parents, and it is easy to cave into that pressure. Therefore, in-depth knowledge and understanding of how play is the agent of change is critical to our ability to communicate to parents and see the child's perspective and the growth and change in our clients that their parents may not be able to see.

Resources

- *Clinical Applications of the Therapeutic Powers of Play: Case Studies in Child and Adolescent Psychotherapy*, Eileen Prendiville & Judi Parson (Eds.), Routledge, 2021.
- *The Therapist's Guide to Child Development*, Dee Ray (Ed.), Routledge, 2016.

- *The Therapeutic Powers of Play: 20 Core Agents of Change* (2nd ed.), Charles Schaefer & Athena Drewes (Eds.), Wiley, 2014.
- *The Autplay Therapy Handbook: Integrative Family Play Therapy for Neurodivergent Children*, Robert Jason Grant, Routledge, 2022.

References

Bemis, K. S. (2014). Stress management. In C. Schaefer & A. Drewes (Eds.), *The therapeutic powers of play: 20 core agents of change* (2nd ed., pp. 143–153). Wiley.

Bennett, M., & Eberts, S. (2014). Self-expression. In C. Schaefer & A. Drewes (Eds.), *The therapeutic powers of play: 20 core agents of change* (2nd ed., pp. 11–23). Wiley.

Drewes, A., & Schaefer, C. E. (2016). The therapeutic powers of play. In K. O'Connor, C. Schaefer, & L. Braverman (Eds.), *Handbook of play therapy* (3rd ed., pp. 35–60). Wiley.

Fraser, T. (2016) Direct teaching. In C. Schaefer & A. Drewes (Eds.), *The therapeutic powers of play: 20 core agents of change* (2nd ed., pp. 39–50). Wiley.

Ginott, H. G. (1960). A rationale for selecting toys in play therapy. *Journal of Consulting Psychology, 24*(3), 243. https://doi.org/10.1037/h0043980

Landreth, G. (2012). *The art of the relationship* (3rd ed.). Routledge.

Nash, J. (2014). Social competence. In C. Schaefer & A. Drewes (Eds.), *The therapeutic powers of play: 20 core agents of change* (2nd ed., pp. 185–195). Wiley.

Panksepp, J. (2006). Emotional endophenotypes in evolutionary psychiatry. *Progress in Neuro-Psychopharmacology and Biological Psychiatry, 30*(5), 774–784.

Parson, J. (2021). Children speak play: Landscaping the therapeutic powers of play. In E. Prendiville & J. A. Parson (Eds.), *Clinical applications of the therapeutic powers of play: Case studies in child and adolescent psychotherapy* (pp. 3–11). Routledge.

Parson, J., & Renshaw, K. (playandfilialtherapy). (2017, September 27). *Therapeutic powers of play* [Video]. YouTube. https://youtube.com/watch?v=wuu59E97igU&feature=share

Peabody, M. A., & Schaefer, C. E. (2019). *The therapeutic powers of play*. PlayTherapy.

Porges, S., & Dana, D. (2018). *Clinical applications of the polyvagal theory*. Norton.

Prendiville, E. (2014). Abreaction. In C. Schaefer & A. Drewes (Eds.), *The therapeutic powers of play: 20 core agents of change* (2nd ed., pp. 11–23). Wiley.

Prendiville, E., & Parson, J. A. (2021). *Clinical applications of the therapeutic powers of play: Case studies in child and adolescent psychotherapy*. Routledge.

Prendiville, S. (2014). Accelerated psychological development. In C. Schaefer & A. Drewes (Eds.), *The therapeutic powers of play: 20 core agents of change* (2nd ed., pp. 255–268). Wiley.

Schaefer, C. E., & Drewes, A. A. (2014). *The therapeutic powers of play: 20 core agents of change* (2nd ed.). John Wiley.

Seymour, J. (2014). Resiliency. In C. Schaefer & A. Drewes (Eds.), *The therapeutic powers of play: 20 core agents of change* (2nd ed., pp. 225–242). Wiley.

Stagnitti, K. (2021). Learning to play. In E. Prendiville & J. A. Parson (Eds.), *Clinical applications of the therapeutic powers of play: Case studies in child and adolescent psychotherapy* (pp. 87–98). Routledge.

Stewart, A., & Echterling, L. G. (2014). Therapeutic relationship. In C. Schaefer & A. Drewes (Eds.), *The therapeutic powers of play: 20 core agents of change* (2nd ed., pp. 157–168). Wiley.

Van Hollander, T. (2014). Counterconditioning fears. In C. Schaefer & A. Drewes (Eds.), *The therapeutic powers of play: 20 core agents of change* (2nd ed., pp. 121–131). Wiley.

Vygotsky, L. S. (1978). *Mind in society: The development of higher psychological processes*. Harvard University Press.

Chapter 11

Finding a Theory

The importance of having an underlying clinical theory has been a consistent message throughout this book. Many of you reading this book already have a clinical theory with which you align. Others may not. Or, you have heard it is important, but you are not sure how to begin the process and figure it out. This chapter is written to you. We walk you through a process that we have found helpful to graduate students and other professionals we meet at conferences and trainings. Our hope is that this will be helpful to you as well. While working through this process, we also know that you may find it beneficial to discuss this with other more experienced play therapists. Referring back to textbooks on theories of counseling and psychotherapy from your graduate program may also be helpful. Also, read case studies written from various play therapy theories. There are *Resources* at the end of the chapter to help begin this process. Worksheets are included to help facilitate that process. Let's begin.

Therapeutic Powers of Play

"Starting with the therapeutic powers of play lays a solid foundation and provides a learning progression onto which therapists then may overlay seminal or historically significant theories or add techniques" (Drewes & Schaefer, 2016, p. 6). Chapter 10: A Deeper Look at Play, discusses the 20 therapeutic powers of play. Perhaps as you read those explanations, you resonated with some more than others. This awareness can be one way to identify your values and beliefs, which help form the basis for selecting a clinical theory.

Which of the therapeutic powers of play stood out to you? Refer back to the therapeutic powers of play chart (Figure 10.1). Take a moment to review those powers. On the worksheet, Table 11.1, list the therapeutic powers that are the most important to you. Or the ones you believe are the most powerful for clinical change. Organize these by the four corresponding categories. Once you have finished this process, take a moment to reflect on which category has the most powers. What do you believe are the similarities? What might this imply on how you view play as therapeutically important? What do you believe about play therapy? Complete the question on the worksheet: *What do I notice about the powers of play I selected.* Keep this in mind as you continue to work your way through this chapter.

DOI: 10.4324/9781003258766-13

Table 11.1 Worksheet of my important therapeutic powers of play

FACILITATES COMMUNICATION	FOSTERS EMOTIONAL WELLNESS
INCREASES PERSONAL STRENGTHS	ENHANCES SOCIAL RELATIONSHIP
WHAT DO I NOTICE ABOUT THE POWERS OF PLAY I SELECTED:	

Exploring Counseling Theories

During the beginning of mental health graduate programs, most students study a wide range of various theories of counseling and psychotherapy. Mental health graduate programs and disciplines vary in the emphasis on encouraging or requiring students to select a theory-of-choice that most closely harmonizes with one's own personal belief system. In the Professional Counselor Program where we taught, this is an essential beginning step of the graduate student's professional development. The understanding and application of clinical theories continue to be scaffolded as the student moves throughout the program. Additionally, it is not unusual in our experience to challenge a student to reevaluate their selection during their clinical practicum experience. Watching students with their first clients as they *do* therapy may reveal dissonance. A deeper exploration of matching their belief system with who they are in the therapy room is appropriate. This is all part of their expected and continued professional development.

We understand that this is not the educational experience of many mental health professionals who become play therapists. However, this understanding of an initial, basic clinical theory is essential. Identifying a clinical theory with which to align is an intensively personal and professional process. The first step is self-awareness of one's own belief system and worldview. Kevin Fall et al. state,

> In essence, a counseling theory is *the story of a person*. It is the theorist's story of each human being's life, including your life—and each of your client's lives. Like any good piece of literature, a good counseling theory provides good character development. In the case of counseling theory, this means an explanation of how each person was innately endowed and developed through one's lifetime so far: how one became who one is today. (2017, p. 2)

Play therapists, like other therapists, identify the dysfunction that brings the client to us and focus on the intervention to return the child and family to healthy functioning. The story plot has taken a difficult turn, to continue Fall's imagery, and the play therapist is the action figure to bring about the happy ending. Or in more clinical terms, "theories provide a broad conceptual framework for understanding how psychopathology develops in humans and how to remedy it" (Peabody & Schaefer, 2016, p. 198). Kevin O'Connor, a co-founder of the Association for Play Therapy (APT) and developer of Ecosystemic Play Therapy, writes, play therapists "can be effective only when they consistently work from an organized theoretical framework" (2011, p. 254; cited in Kottman & Meany-Walen, 2018, p. 39). Terry Kottman, the founder of Adlerian Play Therapy, states, "play therapists . . . should have a consistent method for systematically conceptualizing clients and coming up with a 'Big A agenda' (your long-term goals and objectives for your clients) and a 'small a agenda' (a plan for specific sessions)" (Kottman & Meany-Walen, 2018, p. 39).

The following questions are helpful in this exploration. These were posed to us throughout our doctoral program. Once we became professors, we continued to ask them of students in our graduate courses and continue to do so during professional development training. Similar questions are found in various professional publications (Fall et al., 2017; Jones-Smith, 2021; Kottman & Meany-Walen, 2018; O'Connor & Braverman, 1997; Peabody & Schaefer, 2019). They are philosophical in nature, so there are no right or wrong answers; only what matches what *you* have come to believe about people and the world. Each primary question has several sub-questions to assist in your exploration. How do characters in your story develop? How did you develop?

1. *View of human nature: What are people like when they enter the world?*
   What is the role of epigenetics? Intergenerational trauma? Nature vs. nurture? Are we born to innately self-actualize or be irrational? Do you believe in the unconscious? Are people propelled by drives or goal-directed? Which is most important—thinking, feeling, or doing?

2. *View of environmental influence on personality: How do environmental factors influence how we function? How does dysfunction occur?*
   Think about the physical environment—how is a person impacted if they have access to resources or struggle with poverty? Live with neighborhood violence, drugs, and gangs? Live in a food desert? What about the home environment— attachment, bonding, positive and adverse childhood experiences? How do these impact childhood development? How do they impact adult functioning?

3. *View of change: What does the client need to experience during therapy to change?*
   How does change occur? Is insight needed into childhood experiences or thought patterns? Is learning coping skills sufficient? Will changing behavior change thinking? Or is it the other way around, change thinking to change behavior? How does a person decide or is influenced to want to change? What therapeutic conditions are required for change to be made? Is it essential to understand neurobiology and the window of tolerance? To understand the cycle of violence? How to be trauma-informed?

4. *View of the therapist: What is the role of the therapist?*
   Is the therapist an expert and must take charge of and direct the session? Or is the therapist an equal on the journey toward health and functioning? Or do you believe the client will self-actualize and self-heal within the provided

secure and a safe therapeutic relationship? Does the therapist help explore past experiences? Some of these? All of these? Which are the primary functions of the therapist? Which are essential?

5. *Unique to play therapists, View of play: How does the child use play? How does the play therapist use play?*

Is play the form of communication for the child? Is it the means through which new skills are learned? Does the play therapist play with the child? If so, how does that happen? Initiated by the child, the play therapist, or both?

Now that you have read through the questions make some quick notes on the worksheet (Table 11.2) of your initial thoughts and reactions. (Pause here. Do it!) Next, take some time to reflect, chat with other counselors and play therapists, refer back to the theory of counseling and psychotherapy textbooks, or read other play therapy literature. See the *Resources* section for some suggestions.

Table 11.2 Finding your clinical theory worksheet

View of human nature: What are people like when they enter the world?
View of environmental influence on personality: How do innate or environmental factors influence our functionality? How does dysfunction occur?
View of change: What does the client need to experience during therapy to change?
View of the therapist: What is the role of the therapist?
View of play: How does the child use play? How does the play therapist use play?

Indicators for Selecting Your Play Therapy Theory

As this is a play therapy book, we will focus next on clinical theories applied to play therapy. Chapter 1: Introduction noted that several counseling theories have been applied to play therapy. (Refer back to Figure 1.1 Play Therapy Theories.) As the figure shows, eight are identified by APT as seminal and historically significant theories. APT also recognizes two explicitly developed for play therapy: Ecosystemic Play Therapy and Theraplay. For the purpose of this chapter, five of the historically significant play therapy theories will be explored. These five represent three major movements in psychotherapy: Psychodynamic, Cognitive-Behavioral, and Humanistic. This same exploration can apply or lead the reader to any additional nascent applications of play therapy. The many emerging play therapy approaches reflect the field's viability and energy, and the work of academics and practitioners developing new perspectives and methods to serve specific populations. Sometimes, the burgeoning number of approaches and models and the number of online and face-to-face training can be overwhelming. Mary Anne Peabody and Charles Schaefer state:

> Eager practitioners currently have access to a range of education content across various delivery formats. While this explosive growth is certainly cause for excitement and celebration, it is also cause for reflection and caution. We argue without understanding specific foundational play therapy content prior to undertaking advanced training, play therapists could find themselves in the middle of an expansive buffet of "too many choices" and, perhaps more alarming, practicing in a haphazard fashion. (2019, p. 4)

Terry Kottman has a chapter titled "Pick a Theory, Any Theory" in her book, *Doing Play Therapy* (Kottman & Meany-Walen, 2018). She is not endorsing random selection, which is evident in reading the chapter, but that any (every) theory is viable. So, choose one!

Here is another process that may help you identify a play therapy theory. These are the five basic questions you have already explored. Under each are various statements. As you read through the list, mark the one with which you most strongly agree.

1. View of human nature: *What are people like when they enter the world?*
   a. People are forward-moving, goal-directed, positive self-concept, self-actualizing.
   b. People are process-oriented, possessing organismic self-regulation.
   c. People are socially embedded, goal-directed, creative, and unique.
   d. People have a psyche, made up of the conscious and unconscious; the person introjects views of self from others; people have the capacity for self-healing.
   e. People are primarily thinking beings, can be rational or irrational.
2. View of environmental influence on personality: *How do innate or environmental factors influence our functionality? How does dysfunction occur?*
   a. Modeling by others during childhood develops patterns of thinking that are then disputed or reinforced; for children, irrational patterns of thinking and feeling result in problematic behavior.
   b. Given a safe-enough environment, the person will self-actualize; incongruence between the ideal self and the real self results in dysfunction.
   c. Interpreting life experiences from a subjective perspective, mistaken beliefs are formed that impact personality priority and private logic; discouragement to meet life tasks leads to dysfunctional behavior.
   d. Uses the boundary of self to develop preferences and make choices; dysfunction is the disturbance of boundary contact between self and other.
   e. Uses defense mechanisms when the self is weak and is threatened with disintegration; unable to maintain the individuation process because of school, family, and society demands.

3. View of change: *What does the client need to experience during therapy to change?*
   a. The child develops awareness of their own choices that were made, takes responsibility, and develops homeostasis.
   b. The child's self-healing potential is reactivated; to come to terms with or overcome distressing life experiences.
   c. The child has an innate ability to move toward health given a safe therapeutic environment and the therapeutic relationship.
   d. The child reduces irrational thoughts and subsequent behaviors through developing new coping skills and strategies.
   e. The child develops insight into the goals of misbehavior, leading to understanding and choosing to change.
4. View of the therapist: *What is the role of the therapist?*
   a. The play therapist develops a therapeutically safe, sacred space to allow for transformation.
   b. The play therapist is the expert who identifies irrational and distorted thinking patterns and then introduces experiences to dispute and correct those patterns.
   c. The collaborative relationship with the play therapist is most important to experience a healthy boundary contact; provide engagements and experiences that raise awareness in the here and now.
   d. The play therapist is an equal who travels through the therapeutic process together with the child creating unique experiences and metacommunicating meaning of the play and behavior to the child.
   e. The play therapist focuses on who the child is capable of becoming, not who the child was or must be; trusts the inner wisdom of the child.
5. View of play: *How does the child use play? How does the play therapist use play?*
   a. Play is used to introduce therapist selected activities or engagements upon which to build awareness leading to change.
   b. Play is both the means through which to teach a child new behavior and new thinking; how a child communicates.
   c. Play is the child's natural language.
   d. Play is a means to communicate with the child and teach new skills and thought patterns.
   e. Play is how a child discharges tension, externalizes struggles and traumas, and is primarily self-directed.

The preceding statements are short and simplistic, out of necessity for this purpose. Each of the five theories selected is much more in-depth, complex, and sophisticated. These brief statements are used to highlight some aspect of the theory. These statements are drawn from our own understanding of the play therapy theories and informed by John Allan (1997), Felicia Carroll and Violet Oaklander (2009), Terry Kottman and Kristin Meany-Walen (2018), and Garry Landreth (2012).

The next step is to organize the identifiers you selected onto the worksheet, Table 11.3. Once this is done, see which theory has the most identifiers. This is a rudimentary process to assist you in identifying a possible play therapy theory of choice. Finding discordance between two or more theories may be valuable: take time to see where the dissonance is. Read more, talk more, be more self-reflective on what you believe.

Table 11.3 Worksheet to sort play therapy theory identifiers

Child-Centered Play Therapy	Gestalt Play Therapy
1.a	1.b
2.b	2.d
3.a	3.a
4.e	4.c
5.c	5.a
Adlerian Play Therapy	Jungian Play Therapy
1.c	1.d
2.c	2.e
3.e	3.b
4.d	4.a
5.c	5.e
Cognitive-Behavioral Play Therapy	
1.e	
2.a	
3.d	
4.b	
5.d	

In Closing

Many play therapists are utilizing Integrative Play Therapy and Prescriptive Play Therapy. Each of these approaches requires the play therapist to be competent (i.e., knowledgeable, skilled, and supervised) in more than one play therapy theory.

Integrative Play Therapy blends various elements from different play therapy theories.

Transtheoretical play therapy entails having a solid theoretical base with which you initially view the whole treatment case, symptoms, and so on. Once solidly grounded in this one theoretical frame, play therapists can begin to select and add to their repertoire the best change agents from among all the major theories of play therapy. (Drewes & Schaefer, 2016, p. 37)

Indeed, this precludes an in-depth knowledge of several play therapy theories, the change agents, and how to combine these to serve a specific child with specific presenting issues. This is *not* selecting and stringing together techniques. "Counselors should be careful of trying to integrate theories that might be incompatible theories of human nature and possible change mechanisms" (Jones-Smith, 2021, p. 10). One way to keep the perspectives of human nature and change mechanisms consistent is to use theories of the same category of psychotherapy movements: Psychodynamic, Cognitive-Behavioral, Humanistic, Postmodern, and Systemic (see Figure 1.1). That would be a helpful beginning point. This is also a purpose behind APT's requirement to become a Registered Play Therapist, to have education in all the historically significant play therapy theories.

Prescriptive Play Therapists believe "certain theories of play therapy work better than others for specific disorders of clients" (Peabody & Schaefer, 2016, p. 200). This necessitates the Prescriptive Play Therapist to be competent in more than one play therapy theory or approach. In addition, it requires a working knowledge of play therapy research. They need to know the evidence-based and efficacious play therapy research for various disorders. "In addition . . . the prescriptive play therapist seeks to individualize the treatment by tailoring it in accord with a comprehensive initial assessment of the characteristics of the individual client, including the client's strengths, weaknesses, motivations, and treatment preferences" (Peabody & Schaefer, 2016, p. 200). This is a complex task based on knowledge, experience, and competency.

These approaches, conceptualized by Charles Schaefer, are based on individualizing the selection of a play therapy theory or components and techniques for a specific child. Both require understanding and competency in two or more play therapy theories. Understanding the philosophical basis of a clinical theory is the first step. Then, how change occurs, and the role of the play therapist and play are added layers for the play therapist. The need for competency in one or more play therapy theories is clear.

We hope this chapter has helped you begin the process of selecting a theory of choice. We hope it has energized your curiosity. And encouraged you to a new level in your professional development.

Resources

♦ *Doing Play Therapy*, Terry Kottman & Kristin Meany-Walen, Guilford, 2018.
♦ *Foundations of Play Therapy*, Charles Schaefer, Wiley, 2003.
♦ *Play Therapy: A Comprehensive Guide to Theory and Practice*, David Crenshaw & Anne Stewart (Eds.), Guilford, 2015.
♦ *Play Therapy Theory and Practice: A Comparative Presentation*. Kevin O'Connor & Lisa Braverman, Wiley, 1997.

References

Allan, J. (1997). Jungian play psychotherapy. In K. J. O'Connor & L. M. Braverman (Eds.), *Play therapy: Theory and practice* (2nd ed., pp. 100–129). Wiley.

Carroll, F., & Oaklander, V. (2009). Gestalt play therapy. In K. O'Connor & L. M. Braverman (Eds.), *Play therapy: Theory and practice* (2nd ed., pp. 184–202). Wiley.

Drewes, A., & Schaefer, C. E. (2016). The therapeutic powers of play. In K. O'Connor, C. Schaefer, & L. Braverman (Eds.), *Handbook of play therapy* (2nd ed., pp. 35–60). Wiley.

Fall, K. A., Holden, J. M., & Marquis, A. (2017). *Theoretical models of counseling and psychotherapy*. Routledge.

Jones-Smith, E. (2021). *Theories of counseling and psychotherapy* (3rd ed.). Wiley.

Kottman, T., & Meany-Walen, K. (2018). *Doing play therapy*. Guilford.

Landreth, G. (2012). *The art of the relationship* (3rd ed.). Routledge.

O'Connor, K. J. (2011). Ecosystemic play therapy. In C. E. Schaefer (Ed.), *Foundations of play therapy* (2nd ed., pp. 253–272). Wiley.

O'Connor, K. J., & Braverman, L. M. (1997). *Play therapy theory and practice: A comparative presentation*. Wiley.

Peabody, M. A., & Schaefer, C. E. (2016). Towards semantic clarity in play therapy. *International Journal of Play Therapy*, 26(4), 197–202. http://doi.org/10.1037/pla0000025

Peabody, M. A., & Schaefer, C. E. (2019, September). The therapeutic powers of play. *PlayTherapy*, 14(3), 4–6.

Chapter 12

Professional Growth Considerations

Professional growth is a lifelong process. Professional growth is ever-changing, ever progressing, and moving forward. It includes many ways of expanding who we are as play therapy professionals. We find new ways to explore our love of play therapy and connect to other play therapists. It includes collegial relationships, looking deeper at known areas, and expanding in new areas. Sharing skills while developing advanced skills. Reading new play therapy publications, staying current with professional journals and research, and enjoying reading seminal play therapy works. Paul Bloom, a Yale professor of cognitive psychology (2010), researches and writes about *pleasure*. He found that extended study of an area increases pleasure. Many play therapists have well-developed pleasure in the area of play therapy. We are amongst them.

Seekers and Finders of Continuing Education

Some play therapists are *seekers*, lifelong learners who are always excited when they become aware of any related conference, training, or webinar. Seekers pre-order professional books as soon as they are aware of them. They are on several social media platforms and groups to stay up with all the new training possibilities. Seekers have more continuing education hours each year than they need to maintain licensure and certifications. Others are *finders* who know the importance of keeping up with the field but carefully select what they attend to build and expand on current knowledge and new developments. Finders also log continuing education hours each year, however, most are carefully identified to meet their licensure and certification requirements.

Continuing education is required for all mental health disciplines in the United States and many other countries. Each mental health discipline and jurisdiction establish its own requirements and rules about the number of hours required and from whom one can obtain those hours. Continuing education hours are required for maintaining licensure; it is also necessary for ethical practice. While playful and at times fun, the practice of play therapy is life-changing for clients. Without proper education, training, and supervision, the mental health professional could be guilty of maleficence. Therefore, play therapists must spend

DOI: 10.4324/9781003258766-14

significant time growing, learning, and utilizing supervision or consultation throughout their careers.

The Association for Play Therapy (APT) was founded in 1982 by Dr. Charles Schaefer and Dr. Kevin O'Connor to establish the practice of play therapy as a professional treatment modality by mental health professionals. From its inception, APT has promoted the ethical, competent development of play therapists and the field of play therapy. Well aware of the complexities of working with various mental health disciplines, APT developed programs applicable to all. Ten years later, APT responded to the need in the field to establish minimum training standards leading to a credential, the Registered Play Therapist™ (RPT) and Registered Play Therapist—Supervisor™ (RPT-S). At the end of 2021, APT reported 5,005 play therapists holding their credentials.

Play therapy associations around the world have also established credentials. Even those who have not established a credential have developed minimum criteria for the ethical practice of play therapy. In 2022, the International Consortium of Play Therapy Associations was formed. The initial Board of Directors is made up of representatives of six national play therapy associations from around the world. The IC-PTA also have aspirational standards for play therapists.

We are both RPT-Ss. We have developed a supportive, fun, thought-provoking group of play therapy colleagues throughout the years. We continue to participate in serving on a branch and national committees and boards. We have life-long friendships on this life-long professional journey. We strongly believe in gaining and maintaining competency in play therapy. Some mental health professionals may choose to do so without completing the RPT credentialing process. However, being totally transparent, we highly recommend being credentialed.

Becoming a Registered Play Therapist™

A Registered Play Therapist™ (RPT) is a credentialed, licensed mental health professional with specialized training, education, and supervision in play therapy. The Association for Play Therapy (APT) states,

> Moreover, play therapy is regarded as an evidence based practice (SAMSHA, 2014) and should only be provided by licensed clinical mental health professionals with a graduate mental health degree and extensive specialized play therapy education, training, and supervised experience. (APT, www.a4pt.org/AboutAPT)

APT created a three-phase approach that includes education and supervision built upon a graduate degree in mental health. Licensed mental health professionals, who meet the requirements of the three phases and master the three competencies along with graduate education in specific areas, can apply to become an RPT. This is a registration, not a separate license, as play therapy is not intended to be the primary focus of a professional but rather a specialty of a licensed mental health professional.

The play therapy credential of RPT was established in 1992 to develop national standards and required supervision for mental health professionals in play therapy. In 2019 the standards were updated to the three competencies and three phases of training and supervision to focus more on professional accountability and require ongoing professional growth. All supervision for RPT must be completed by a Registered Play Therapy-Supervisor™ (RPT-S). Professionals seeking to earn the RPT credential must demonstrate competency in three areas: (1) knowledge and understanding of play therapy, (2) clinical play therapy skills, and (3) professional engagement in play therapy. The graduate coursework required includes child development, theories of personality, principles of psychotherapy, child and adolescent psychotherapy, and legal, ethical, and professional issues. The three phases of the clinical experience include education, clinical experience, and supervision. Within each phase, the education topics include play therapy history, play therapy seminal or historically significant theories, play therapy skills and methods, play therapy special topics, and applicants' choice.

- ◆ Phase 1 requires 35–55 hours of play therapy education, 50–75 hours of supervised play therapy experience, and 5–10 hours of play therapy supervision, including observation or viewing of a minimum of one play therapy session by the RPT-S.
- ◆ Phase 2 requires 55–70 hours of play therapy instruction, 100–150 hours of supervised play therapy experience, and 10–15 hours of play therapy supervision with a minimum of two observations by the RPT-S.
- ◆ Phase 3 applicants complete 45–60 hours of play therapy instruction, 100–175 hours of supervised play therapy experience, and 10–20 hours of clinical supervision with a minimum of two sessions observed or viewed by the RPT-S.

This three-phased approach provides play therapists in training with a gradual exposure and integration of both training and clinical experience. Ongoing supervision is required to ensure play therapists are competent to work with the most vulnerable of our population, children. Each phase requires a specified amount of education and training from the five-play therapy education topics to ensure a balanced approach to education. Please read the Credentialing Standards by APT (www.a4pt.org). Criteria may change over time; please refer to the APT website to confirm current standards and requirements.

School Based-Registered Play Therapist™ (SB-RPT) was a credential added in 2020 by APT. These professionals are licensed or certified school counselors or school psychologists in their state and then have the added training, education, and supervision in play therapy. The SB-RPT is a post-graduate, post-licensure credential. The education and training required to be an SB-RPT include 150 hours of education in play therapy. While not required, APT strongly recommends the hours are distributed between these areas: play therapy history (four to five hours), play therapy theories (40–50 hours), play therapy techniques or methods (40–50 hours) and play therapy applications/special populations (40–50 hours). Supervision by an RPT-S is also required for the SB-RPT designation. Supervision must occur for at least one school year. A minimum of 600 direct client hours utilizing play therapy under supervision, with 50 hours of supervision by an RPT-S is required. The three phases are not a part of the SB-RPT requirements. Continuing education requirements are similar, 24 hours every 36 months with an additional requirement of three hours of training on the *Diagnostic and Statistical Manual of Mental Disorders*. As stated above, continue to check the APT website for current requirements.

Play Therapy Consultation and Supervision

Clinical supervisors have an ethical obligation to protect the integrity of the mental health field as gatekeepers of the profession. APT requires those who hold an RPT-S designation to be licensed mental health supervisors by their specific credentialing board. The requirements to become an RPT-S include three years in good standing as an RPT; 3,000 hours of client contact post licensure; 500 play therapy client contact post-RPT, and 30 hours of supervision instruction, of which six hours are required to be play therapy specific. It is critical to find a competent supervisor who shares your theory and compliments your learning style. We strongly encourage you to take the time to interview potential supervisors. Asking questions such as:

- ◆ Where did you get your mental health degree?
- ◆ Where did you get your play therapy training?
- ◆ What is your guiding theory in play therapy?
- ◆ What type of clients do you typically see?
- ◆ What experiences do you attribute to your growth as a play therapist?
- ◆ What are your areas of specialty?
- ◆ How do you structure supervision?
- ◆ What do you require of your supervisees?

Licensed supervisors have an ethical obligation to supervise within their bounds of competency. Just because someone is a supervisor does not mean they have expertise in the theoretical perspective or client population you work with. It is in the best interest of the supervisee to ask questions regarding the supervisor's education and clinical experience to determine who will best facilitate growth.

Professional growth occurs throughout one's professional career, "Every day's a school day," as my friend would say. APT differentiates consultation and supervision. APT defines consultation as an activity for credentialing when both the more experienced play therapist and the person seeking consultation each hold clinical mental health licenses that allow for independent practice. The consultant shares expert advice and wisdom specific to play therapy with the consultee during consultation. Consultation may not have the same legal liability as supervision. Some states and disciplines have specific rules regarding each. APT allows consultation to meet APT credentialing requirements (APT Credentialing Standards, www.a4pt.org).

Ongoing consultation is a best practices activity, well beyond the credentialing process. Throughout one's play therapy practice, there will be clients who surprise you when you feel stuck and question your effectiveness. Therefore consultation is critical in our work with clients. One of the significant nuances in working with children is the vast nonverbal movements, interactions, play behaviors, and play patterns in a play therapy session. Video recorded play sessions provide an opportunity to watch the intensity, pace, and emotions involved in the play that are easy to overlook while in the playroom. Even the most experienced and seasoned play therapist benefits from watching themselves on video and consulting with a colleague. We watch sessions through our own lens; other perspectives can help us see things we might not have noticed in the session.

Association for Play Therapy's Play Therapy Best Practices

All licensed mental health providers have ethical guidelines that govern their practice. Ethics must be followed to maintain nonmaleficence in working with clients. Best practices are guidelines that, if broken, may not be an ethical violation but rather, when followed, are in the client or therapist's best interest. The APT *Play Therapy Best Practices* (2020) were created to provide guidance for many unique aspects of working with children and families that may not be addressed in state licensure ethical guidelines.

One of the critical nuances in working with children is the dual relationship. For example, it is not uncommon for a play therapist's friend to request help for their child. As discussed in Chapter 3: Initial Parent Consultation, this is a dual relationship and must be avoided. A more nuanced situation is when a parent may want the play therapist for their son to also see their daughter. While this is not a direct ethical violation in most states, APT recommends providing parents with the advantages and disadvantages of the play therapist entering into a therapeutic relationship with both children. There are confidentiality issues between siblings, and occasionally children are possessive of "their" play therapist. It could be counterproductive for siblings to share a therapist. It may also be a situation where there are few other play therapists to refer to, so you must see the child (APT Play Therapy Best Practices, 2020, A.8). Sibling play therapy is also a very effective intervention, particularly when the presenting issue involves the sibling relationship. Family play therapy may also be the treatment intervention of choice. These are all options that need clear expectations and boundaries.

Confidentiality is handled slightly differently with minors in that, legally, confidentiality is not extended to minors. However, minors deserve respect and have a right to privacy. APT recommends play therapists balance the minor's right to privacy and the parent's legal right to information (see APT Play Therapy Best Practices, 2020, C.1.). The client's right to privacy is included in the client's artwork. Play therapists may not publicly display any artistic expression of the client's in a public place without the client's written permission (APT Play Therapy Best Practices, 2020, C.3). This includes not hanging client artwork in your office. We discourage play therapists from hanging anything that looks like it could have been created by a child so as not to cause clients, or their parents, to wonder if you will or could display their artwork. It is not unusual for young children to ask you to display artwork. At home, proud parents display their artwork on walls and the refrigerator. An easy limit to set is,

It would be so special to have your art on the wall. And one of the rules of the office is that I cannot hang artwork on the wall.

Before seeking permission, the play therapist should explore the purpose and motivation for this request. This self-awareness may provide alternative possibilities.

As discussed earlier in this chapter, supervision, and consultation are critical to the effectiveness and competency of the play therapist. APT places a high value on play therapists' continued growth and development by requiring play therapy specific continuing education, encouraging consultation, and for therapists to monitor competency and effectiveness (APT Play Therapy Best Practices, 2020, D.2). The same level of importance is placed on the quality of supervisors and the importance of supervisors getting continuing education to stay current and challenge themselves in their own growth as both a clinician and supervisor.

Utilizing technology in session with minors has unique best practice policies. APT recommends therapists ensure that the client is developmentally capable of using technology and would reap the therapeutic benefits of the technology. Play therapists keep in mind the child's developmental and chronological age and culture to make sure technology is an appropriate choice. Specific statements in the *Informed Consent* explaining risks and benefits and the rationale for technology supporting treatment goals should be obtained from parents. Play therapists ensure the child's identity and other aspects of confidentiality that could be breached in using technology are protected (APT Play Therapy Best Practices, 2020, J.4).

In Closing

Despite the use of the word *play* in our profession, the practice of play therapy is a professional activity. Professional development, adherence to an ethical code, obtaining continuing education, and participating in supervision and consultation are required. Beginning in 2023, Registered Play Therapists™ must earn 24 hours of continuing education every 36 months; two of those hours are required to be in social and cultural diversity specific to play therapy. In addition, RPT-S must have six hours of continued education in supervision each cycle. The joy we have in our profession is directly related to our effectiveness and our confidence in our abilities to help our clients. Again, the reader is referred to the Association for Play Therapy website (www.a4pt.org) for up-to-date requirements.

References

Association for Play Therapy. (2020, June). *Best practices*. www.a4pt.org/page/Publications

Association for Play Therapy. (2022, January). *Credentialing standards*. www.a4pt.org/page/CredentialsInfo

Bloom, P. (2010). *How pleasure works: The new science of why we like what we like*. Norton.

Appendices

Sample Intake Forms

Intake Form*

Informed Consent for Play Therapy*

Professional Disclosure Statement*

Professional Disclosure Statement—Sample

Child Background Form*

Consent for Release of Information (ROI)

*These forms are also available on the Routledge Website.

To locate these forms:

- Go to *Routledge.com*
- Search for this book title: THE GUIDE TO PLAY THERAPY DOCUMENTATION AND PARENT CONSULTATION
- When on the book page, look for the menu choice labeled: SUPPORT MATERIALS
- This will be the link to the COMPANION WEBSITE where the downloadable forms are located
- *www.routledge.com/9781032193427*

Intake Form

Date of Inquiry: _____ Date of Follow-up: _____

Inquiring Parent:

_____   _____

Name   Contact preferred: phone/text/email

_____ Permission to leave messages

Client Information:

___ Age of Client
___ Dual Relationship
___ Presenting Issue

_____
_____
_____
_____
_____
_____
_____
_____
_____
_____
_____
_____

___ Within Scope of Practice & Competence
___ Method of Payment: Insurance/Private Pay/Other _____

Initial Intake Parent Appointment: _____

People attending (and role): _____
___ Forms sent; Date: _____
    ___ Informed Consent for Treatment
    ___ Child Background Form
    ___ Professional Disclosure
    ___ Release of Information as needed for stepparent, etc.
    ___ Other: such as HIPAA, Privacy Policies, etc. _____
___ Confirmed who is authorized to consent for treatment (circle status below)
Married/Divorced/Never married/Widowed/Other: _____
___ Requested divorce decree, custody orders

Informed Consent for Play Therapy

(Name & Degree, Credentials)
(Spell out credentials in words)
(phone number/email)

Confidentiality: Everything we talk about in our parent consultation sessions and your child's play therapy sessions is confidential. The session notes and other paperwork regarding our work together on behalf of your child are also confidential and part of the clinical file. However, Texas law requires certain exceptions: If I learn of abuse/neglect of children and/or the elderly; if you (or your child) are a danger to self; if you request (in writing) that I release information/records; or if I receive a court order to release information and/or records. We will discuss what occurs in your child's play therapy session in parent consultations.

I cannot ensure the confidentiality of any form of communication through electronic media, including email and text messages. You are advised that such communication has the potential to be seen by others, including internet providers. I am ethically and legally obligated to maintain written documentation of each time we meet, talk on the phone, or correspond via electronic communication such as email or text messaging. These records include a brief summary of the telephone conversation and printed copies of texts and emails. Therefore, I request you *not communicate personal information by text or email*. A judge can subpoena your records for various reasons, and if this happens, I must comply. *If, however, you prefer to communicate via email or text messaging **only** regarding appointments, I will do so*. Please initial that you understand the risks involved: _____. Communication through the Client Portal of my electronic health records program are confidential. This is my preferred form of communication. These interactions automatically become part of your child's clinical file.

Sessions: Sessions are typically once a week for 45–50 minutes. Although our sessions may be very intimate psychologically, ours is a professional relationship rather than a social one. Our contact will be limited to when you bring your child in for play therapy sessions except in the case of emergency, when you may contact me by phone. You will be best served if our sessions concentrate exclusively on your concerns.

Potential Risk and Benefits of Play Therapy: In play therapy, children explore and discuss issues through their play and their words. Sometimes symptoms worsen before they improve as you and your child work through this process. Parents and children may at times feel uncomfortable levels of sadness, anxiety, guilt, frustration, helplessness, and other negative feelings as part of the healing process. Children often express this through increasing their problematic behavior. This is seen as part of the process of moving toward health. We will discuss these occurrences in parent consultations.

Potential benefits of play therapy include a decrease in problem and distressing symptoms, greater self-awareness and verbalization of feelings, increased understanding of life situations, increased skills in coping and self-regulation, and improvement in relationships.

Fees: My fees for sessions are $_____ per session.

Cancellation: If you cannot keep an appointment, please notify me at least 24 hours in advance. Unless you do so, you will be charged a cancellation fee that is the same as your session fee.

Counselor Change of Employment, Incapacity, or Death: If I become incapacitated, die, or cease to provide counseling your counseling files and records can be obtained from _____. In accordance with the laws of the State of Texas and HIPAA requirements, the clinical file is destroyed seven years after your child's play therapy is completed.

Complaints: If you have a complaint about my services, I hope that you will bring this up with me and make every attempt to work through the issue. However, if this does not work, you have the right to make a formal complaint to my licensing board:

_____.

Emergency Procedures: In case of emergency, please contact your family physician, 911, or _____.

Also, please provide me with an emergency contact. This person is would only be contacted in an emergency situation (medical or psychological) and by signing below you give permission for me to contact this person directly.

Emergency Contact

_____

Name   Phone Number

Agreement: By signing this document, you are indicating that you have read the contents, asked any questions you may have regarding the contents, and have received a copy for your own records. You also verify you have received a copy of our Privacy Practices.

_____

Child's Parent/Guardian   Date

_____

Play Therapist's Signature and Credentials   Date

Professional Disclosure Statement

(Name & Degree, Credentials)
(Spell out credentials in words)
(phone number/email)

Qualifications

Education, certifications

Experience

Licensure, length of time practicing

Nature of Counseling

Explain play therapy and theoretical approach

Professional Disclosure Statement—Sample

LINDA E. HOMEYER, PH.D., LPC-S, RPT-S
TEXAS LICENSED PROFESSIONAL COUNSELOR—SUPERVISOR
REGISTERED PLAY THERAPIST—SUPERVISOR
(phone number/email)

Qualifications

I have been the Director of the Door of Hope Counseling Center since it opened in 2014. I am also a retired Professor in the Professional Counseling Program in the Department of Counseling, Leadership, Adult Education and School Psychology at Texas State University. I received my Master of Science in Counseling and Guidance from East Texas State University (now Texas A&M Commerce) in 1985 and my doctorate in Counseling and Student Services from University of North Texas in 1994. My specialty area of study was children (play therapy) and art therapy. My formal education has prepared me to counsel individuals, groups, children, parents, couples, and families. I also have additional certification as a Registered Play Therapist and Supervisor issued by the Association for Play Therapy. This includes additional training and clinical supervision to obtain the certification and ongoing continuing education to maintain this certification.

Experience

I received my Texas Licensed Professional Counselor (LPC) license in April of 1994. I have extensive training and experience in working with children with a variety of problem behaviors. Working with sexually abused children in both assessment and therapeutic settings is a particular area of specialty. I have testified in court on numerous occasions on behalf of children. I also research and write professionally in play therapy, sand tray therapy, and supervision. I am a frequent presenter at state, regional, national, and international conferences in the area of counseling, play therapy, sand tray therapy, and/or child sexual abuse. I am also an LPC Supervisor.

Nature of Counseling

I believe that we all are created to be in healthy relationships. Many of us have less than optimal role modeling as we grew up and may need assistance from time to time to create and maintain healthy relationships in our own lives, and those of our children (if parents). As we experience our lives growing up we make sense of our experiences, developing beliefs about who we are in that world. Because we are children, and lack full reasoning skills, these sometimes develop as misbeliefs. The misbeliefs, in turn, result in how the child behaves in order to belong in their world. Some of these behaviors interfere with being able to make healthy connections, have the courage to move forward in life, and feel competent and capable.

We are also created with innate needs. When these needs are met or unmet beginning in our own childhood and throughout our lives, resulting in beliefs about who we are and how we relate to others. Unmet needs will affect our beliefs about ourselves and our behaviors. I view play therapy as a developmentally appropriate approach to work with children.

I believe play is their talk and toys are their words. Play, the child's natural and familiar world, provides the opportunity to *play out* their issues, much like an adult *talks out* issues. During parent consultations we will work together to make plans, improve and increase needed parenting skills.

I view serving you and your child in play therapy as a joint venture in which, together, we identify behavior and beliefs that are not working for you and your child and find ways to understand unmet needs and needed changes. You always have the right to discuss what I hope to accomplish with any given technique and to decline to do so on behalf of you or your child.

Child Background Form

GENERAL INFORMATION

Date form completed: _____

Completed by:_____ Relationship to child _____

Child's Name _____

Address: _____

Child's Ethnicity_____

Child's Gender_____

Child's Date of Birth_____

Child's Grade:_____ School Child Attends:_____

School District_____

Name of Parent/Legal Guardian(s) _____ _____

Phone number (May we leave a message?) _____

Email address _____

Child's parent's status: Married, Divorced, Never Married, Widowed

[NOTE: If child is NOT living with both natural parents, or adoptive parent(s), the State of Texas REQUIRES a copy of the file-marked court order from the District Clerk's Office of the divorce decree and any subsequent/most recent custody order. These must be received 24-hours before the first session.]

GUARDIAN INFORMATION

Parent/Caregiver with whom the child has primary residence

Parent Name_____

Relationship to Child_____

Parent's Gender_____

Parent's Ethnicity_____

Cell Phone (May we leave a message?)_____

Address_____

Email Address_____

Relationship Status_____

Parent Name_____

Relationship to Child_____

Parent's Gender_____

Parent's Ethnicity_____

Cell Phone (May we leave a message?)_____

Address_____

Email Address_____

Relationship Status_____

Child's Primary Household Members:

Please list, beginning with the eldest, all those who live in your household. Please list name, age, and relationship (step, adopted, foster, etc.) siblings, significant adults. How long has this been the living situation?

_____

Are there any significant adults who spend time in your home regularly? How often?

_____

If co-parenting, describe your relationship with the other parent.

_____

Caregivers/parent in secondary household (such as divorced parent with visitation rights; stepparent)

Parent Name_____

Relationship to Child_____

Parent's Ethnicity _____ Parent Gender_____

Cell Phone (May we leave a message?)_____

Address_____

Email Address_____

Relationship Status_____

Parent Name_____

Relationship to Child_____

Parent's Ethnicity _____

Cell Phone (May we leave a message?)_____

Address_____

Email Address_____

Relationship Status_____

Child's secondary household members:

Please list all members of the household, beginning with the eldest member name, age, relationship to child (step, adopted, foster etc.). How long has this been the living situation?

_____

CHILD'S HISTORY

Please identify any developmental milestones that were NOT met at the typical time. Has your child now met those milestones? _____

Has your child ever repeated a grade in school? If so, which grade. _____

Is, or has, your child received Special Education Services? _____

Has a diagnosis been given?_____

Is your child receiving counseling services anywhere else at this time? If so, with whom and phone number. _____

Has your child *previously* had counseling? If so, with whom and when.

_____

Has your child been hospitalized for a mental health concern? If so, where and when.

_____

Child's previous mental health diagnosis _____

Child's previous medications _____

Are you seeking services because your child is a victim of a crime? If so, what crime? Did it result in legal action? Explain. _____

Is your child currently on probation? Explain. _____

Any significant medical concerns or surgeries for your child? _____

_____

CURRENT CONCERNS

What is the primary reason you are seeking counseling for your child now? _____

_____

Have you had this concern before?

_____

Does your child have a current diagnosis?

_____

Is your child currently taking any medication? Who prescribed this medication?

_____

If yes, enter previous therapist(s) seen for this concern and describe treatment.

_____

What have you found has helped dealing with this?

_____

What have you found that has made this situation more difficult?

_____

Current Symptoms (check all that apply) and note how often (times per day or week)

Anxiety	Nightmares or Night Terrors
Appetite Issues	Suspiciousness
Avoidance	Toileting Issues
Crying Spells	Current or Past Neglect
Depression	Current or Past Physical Abuse
Excessive Energy	Current or Past Sexual Abuse
Eating Challenges	Suspected Sexual Abuse
Education Concerns	History of Abandonment or Separation
Fatigue	Current or Past Family Domestic Violence
Hallucinations	Suicidal Thoughts/Attempts
Impulsivity	Substance Abuse
Irritability	Technology/Gaming Addiction
Loss of Interest	Exposure/Addiction to Pornography
Panic Attacks	Feelings of Guilt and Shame
Racing Thoughts	Parent-Child Relationship Problems
Risky Activity	Separation/Divorce
Sleep Difficulties or Changes	Grief and Loss

FAMILY HISTORY

Was the child adopted? If yes, at what age? Domestic, kinship, international?

_____

Any family members with significant medical conditions? _____

_____

Family members with mental health conditions?

_____

HISTORY OF TRAUMA and/or STRESS

Please check any of these that your child has experienced. These are used to identify how many stressors are experienced.

- ☐ Did a parent or other adult in the household often . . . swear at your child, insult your child, put your child down, or humiliate your child? Or, act in a way that made your child afraid that they might be physically hurt?
- ☐ Did a parent or other adult in the household often . . . push, grab, slap, or throw something at your child? Or, ever hit your child so hard that your child had marks or were injured?

- ☐ Did an adult or person at least 5 years older than your child ever . . . touch or fondle your child or touched their body in a sexual way? Or, try to or actually have oral, anal, or vaginal sex?
- ☐ Did your child often feel that . . . no one in their family loved them or thought they were important or special? Or your child's family didn't look out for each other, feel close to each other, or support each other?
- ☐ Did your child often feel that . . . they didn't have enough to eat, had to wear dirty clothes, and had no one to protect them? Or, their parents were too drunk or high to take care of them or take them to the doctor if they needed it?
- ☐ Were your child's parents ever separated or divorced?
- ☐ Was your child's mother or stepmother often pushed, grabbed, slapped, or had something thrown at them? Or, sometimes or often kicked, bitten, hit with a fist, or hit with something hard? Or ever repeatedly hit over at least a few minutes or threatened with a gun or knife?
- ☐ Did your child live with anyone who was a problem drinker or alcoholic or who used street drugs?
- ☐ Was a household member depressed or mentally ill or did a household member attempt suicide?
- ☐ Did a household member go to prison?

Please check any of these that occurred during *your* own first 18 years of life.

- ☐ Did a parent or other adult in the household often . . . swear at you, insult you, put you down, or humiliate you? Or, act in a way that made you afraid that you might be physically hurt?
- ☐ Did a parent or other adult in the household often . . . push, grab, slap, or throw something at you? Or, ever hit you so hard that you had marks or were injured?
- ☐ Did an adult or person at least 5 years older than you ever . . . touch or fondle you or have you touch their body in a sexual way? Or, try to or actually have oral, anal, or vaginal sex with you?
- ☐ Did you often feel that . . . no one in your family loved you or thought you were important or special? Or your family didn't look out for each other, feel close to each other, or support each other?
- ☐ Did you often feel that . . . you didn't have enough to eat, had to wear dirty clothes, and had no one to protect you? Or, your parents were too drunk or high to take care of you or take you to the doctor if you needed it?
- ☐ Were your parents ever separated or divorced?
- ☐ Was your mother or stepmother often pushed, grabbed, slapped, or had something thrown at her? Or, sometimes or often kicked, bitten, hit with a fist, or hit with something hard? Or ever repeatedly hit over at least a few minutes or threatened with a gun or knife?
- ☐ Did you live with anyone who was a problem drinker or alcoholic or who used street drugs?
- ☐ Was a household member depressed or mentally ill or did a household member attempt suicide?
- ☐ Did a household member go to prison?

RELIGION/SPIRITUALITY

Is spirituality important to you and your family? _____

If so, what faith community do you attend or belong to? _____

Please describe the importance of your family's spiritual activities (attendance to religious services, prayer, reading spiritual texts, etc.)

_____

TECHNOLOGY USE

How much time does your child use technology at home each day?

_____

How much time does your child use technology at school each day?

_____

Does your child have a gaming addiction?

_____

Has your child been exposed to pornography that you know of?

_____

What is your family's media plan? What limits if any are on games/screen time?

_____

Are you happy with your child's current technology usage?

_____

FAMILY CULTURE

What are some of the things your family values most?

_____

How would you describe your parent-child relationship?

_____

What are some expectations you have of your child?

_____

ADDITIONAL INFORMATION

What was the pandemic like for your family?

_____

What do you enjoy most about your child?

_____

What do you find most challenging about your child?

_____

What is the one thing we need to know to help your child today?

_____

Anything else you want your counselor to know?

_____

Consent for Release of Information

(Name & Degree, Credentials)
(Spell out credentials in words)
(Phone number/email)

I hereby authorize

Name/Agency/Organization _____

Address_____

City, State, Zip _____

Contact information: email/phone: _____

to release records, reports, and file to

Play Therapist Name _____

Address_____ _____

City, State, Zip _____

This release pertains to: _____ DOB: _____

I DO—DO NOT (circle one) authorize the above-named person/agency to also discuss their information regarding this case with my above-named counselor.

I DO—DO NOT (circle one) authorize my counselor to discuss my child's case information with the above-named person.

This authorization for the release of information may be revoked, in writing, at any time. Otherwise, this release will automatically expire six months from the date signed.

_____
Client or Legal Guardian

_____
Date

Initial Parent Consultation Session Notes

Initial Parent Consultation Preparation Form*

Initial Parent Consultation Session Note*

Initial Parent Consultation Session Note—Sample

*These forms are also available on the Routledge Website. See Appendix A for detailed instructions.

Initial Parent Consultation Preparation Form

Parent Names_____   Intake Appointment Date _____

Child's Name/Age _____

Review Informed Consent/Professional Disclosure:

- Introduce self, education, licensure, certifications or additional trainings
- Explain supervision (if applicable)
- Limits of confidentiality
- Reporting of abuse
- If I run into you in public—I will wait for you to say hello
- How records are kept (length, parent records vs. child records if applicable)
- Required statement on complaints
- Both parents included in all email (all communication is part of the record)
- Explain play therapy
- Structure and Frequency of parent consultations
- Payment/Good Faith Estimate
- Best way to contact me between sessions
- Appointments/cancellations
- Impact of play therapy including risks and limits

Information to Gather:

- ROI for previous counseling or other services if necessary
- Request assessment reports from parents (if applicable)
- Parents' concerns
- Establish treatment plan goals
- Gather information to make a diagnosis
- Follow-up questions from *Child Background Form*
- Follow-up questions regarding trauma or significant events in the child's life
- Status of client's current relationships (parents, siblings, friends, teachers, other significant adults)
- How is the child functioning at school?
- What are some things your family values most?
- Walk me through your family's typical weekly schedule
- Habits, routines at home/school/after school/bedtime
- Screen time and safety
- Emotional regulation (what makes them afraid, angry, sad, joyful, hurt?)
- Frequency and intensity of behaviors
- Family time (what do you do together?)
- Responsibilities/chores for the child, do they differ from other children in the home
- What does discipline look like in your home?
- Pandemic's impact on the family, child's education, peer relationships
- Significant childhood events (loss, moves, pets, illness, trauma)
- Parental roles/style (who/how handles discipline, how do you show love, how do you handle arguments or challenges?)

- Medication
- Sleep patterns
- Strengths of child
- What do you want your child to get out of counseling? What will it look like when things are better? What are you hoping to get out of counseling?
- Broach the family's cultural identity and how it might impact your relationship with family given your cultural identity.

Information to Give:

- Explaining play therapy to the child
- What parents say to the child after sessions
- Child development
- Information on their specific situation (e.g., children's books on divorce, etc.)
- Therapist's expectations of parents at sessions (stay in waiting room/involved in sessions, length/frequency of sessions)
- Explain *Weekly Parent Feedback Form*

Treatment goal ideas:

Follow-up questions to determine diagnosis:

Questions parents may ask—what are they really asking, what are they feeling?

ASK: Is there anything you haven't shared yet? Do you feel like I understand your child and family?

Initial Parent Consultation Session Note

Child's Name_____ Date of Parent Consultation_____

Child's Date of Birth_____

Parent(s) Attending:

Name & Role _____

Name & Role _____

Ethical and Legal Documentation covered:

___ Informed Consent and Professional Disclosure Statement

___ Limits of Confidentiality

___ Custody Agreements/Orders (if necessary)

___ Explanation of Treatment Approach

___ Development Information

Parent Reported Concerns:

Treatment Focus:

Treatment Approach (individual, group, family play therapy, etc.) and frequency of sessions:

Referrals/Recommendations Made:

_____   _____

Play Therapist Signature with Credentials   Date

Initial Parent Consultation
Session Note—Sample

Child's Name: Noah   Date of Parent Consultation: May 15, 20XX

Child's Date of Birth: X/XX/XXX

Parent(s) Attending:

    Name & Role: Alicia (Biological Mother)

    Name & Role: Juan (Biological Father)

Ethical and Legal documentation covered:

    __x_ Informed Consent

    _x__ Limits of Confidentiality

    _NA_ Custody Agreements/Orders (if necessary)

    __x_ Explanation of Treatment Approach

    _x__ Development Information

Parent Reported Concerns:

Parents reported Juan has begun traveling again after being the primary parent for Noah after his sister was born. Since his traveling started, parents state Noah does not comply with limits set by the parents. Parents report he has frequent meltdowns and is emotionally dysregulated, they state he is jealous of the attention mom gives his sister. They also report that Noah is aggressive toward his sister and they fight daily at home. Noah is also having difficulty at day care with friends and parents reported being concerned about these behaviors as well.

Treatment Focus:

Emotional regulation
Compliance of limits
Relationship with sister and parents

Treatment Approach (individual, group, family play therapy, etc.) and Frequency of Sessions:

Weekly individual play therapy, sibling play therapy

Referrals/Recommendations Made:
Begin individual play therapy

Linda E. Homeyer   May 15, 20XX
Linda E. Homeyer, PhD, LPC-S, RPT-S   Date

Play Therapy Treatment Plans

Play Therapy Treatment Plan*

Adlerian Play Therapy (AdPT) Treatment Plan—Sample

Child-Centered Play Therapy (CCPT) Treatment Plan—Sample

Cognitive-Behavioral Play Therapy (CBPT) Treatment Plan—Sample

Gestalt Play Therapy (GPT) Treatment Plan—Sample

Solution-Focused Play Therapy (SFPT) Treatment Plan—Sample

Cues & Clues: Adlerian Play Therapy

Cues & Clues: Child-Centered Play Therapy

Cues & Clues: Cognitive Behavioral Play Therapy

Cues & Clues: Gestalt Play Therapy

*This form is available on the Routledge Website. See Appendix A for detailed instructions.

Play Therapy Treatment Plan

Client Name: Age: DOB:

Parent(s) Name:

Prepared by: (play therapist name)   Date:

Diagnosis: (DSM number & title)

Concern #1:
Long-term Goal #1:
_____

Intervention #1:
_____

Date completion expected: _____ Date achieved: _____

Concern #2:
Long-term Goal #2:
_____

Intervention #2:
_____

Date completion expected: _____ Date achieved: _____

Concern #3:
Long-term Goal #3:
_____

Intervention #3:
_____

Date completion expected: _____ Date achieved: _____

Other Professionals Involved: Name, contact information

_____   _____

Parent Signature   Date

_____

Play Therapist name & credentials Date

Adlerian Play Therapy (AdPT)
Treatment Plan—Sample

Client Name: Noah Rodriguez   Age: 3 yrs. 5 months   DOB: March 14, 20XX

Parent(s) Name: Alicia & Jessie Rodriguez

Prepared by: Linda E. Homeyer, PhD, LPC-S, RPT-S   Date: October 28, 20XX

Diagnosis: F43.24, Adjustment Disorder with Disturbance of Emotions and Conduct, Persistent

Concern #1:

Aggressive behavior between siblings as demonstrated by arguing, pouting, and dysregulation (six times daily); attempts to hurt his sister by throwing toys and other items at her (three times daily).

Long-term Goal #1:

Noah and his sister will develop a typical sibling relationship with appropriate levels of regulation, evidenced by one or two arguments a day and no attempts by Noah to hurt his sister.

Intervention #1:

Sibling play therapy: Strengthen the sibling relationship through increased self/sibling awareness; increase courage to connect; increase feeling vocabulary; increase relationship skills.

Parents: Improve family atmosphere; increase all family activities while decreasing parent-child dyads; increase skills to reflect children's feelings and intent; increase Noah's perception that he counts. Teach regulation skills through the Window of Tolerance.

Date completion expected: January 15, 20XX Date achieved: _____

Concern #2:

Noncompliance with parental requests and family rules, tantrums when responding to parental requests and family rules. This includes arguing, pouting, and dysregulation (four to six times a day).

Long-term Goal #2:

Noah complies with family rules and parental requests with only one tantrum a week. He can self-regulate 60% of the time and responds to parents' co-regulating.

Intervention #2:

Individual play therapy: Increase Noah's courage to develop relationships outside of the family: expand the ability to participate in co-regulation beginning with the play therapist and expand to self-regulation; expand creativity and increase problem-solving skills.

Date completion expected: February 15, 20XX Date achieved: _____

Concern #3:

    Aggression toward peers at day care; the possibility of being expelled; attacks (kicks) other children at nap time (daily), resulting in no friends and possibly harming them.

Long-term Goal #3:

    Noah will interact age appropriately with peers at day care, with typical disagreements but no attacks; Noah will develop peer relationships, evidenced by two or three friends.

Intervention #3:

    Individual play therapy: Expand types and complexity of play to increase frustration tolerance; expand social interest through experiencing joy within the therapeutic relationship. Increase ability to label and use a feeling vocabulary.

    Parents: Teach parents to use limit setting; learn and purposefully implement co-regulation skills; begin family meetings.

    Day-care staff: Provide consultation to encourage the use of limit-setting and reflecting feelings. This expands similar encouragement across Noah's environment.

Date completion expected: March 30, 20XX   Date achieved: _____

Other Professionals Involved:

Ms. Heather Jimenez, Day Care Director, EZ Kidz Daycare, 555–555–0011

_____   _____

Parent Signature   Date

Linda E. Homeyer   Nov. 3, 20XX_____
Linda E. Homeyer, Ph.D., LPC-S, RPT-S   Date

Child-Centered Play Therapy (CCPT) Treatment Plan—Sample

Client Name: Noah Rodriguez   Age: 3 yrs. 5 months   DOB: March 14, 20XX

Parent(s) Name: Alicia and Jesse Rodriguez

Prepared by: Mary Morrison Bennett, PhD, LPC-S, RPT-S   Date: October 28, 20XX

Diagnosis: F43.24, Adjustment Disorder with Disturbance of Emotions and Conduct, Persistent

Concern #1:

 Aggressive behavior between siblings as demonstrated by arguing, pouting, and dys-regulation (six times daily); attempts to hurt his sister by throwing toys and other items at her (three times daily).

Long-term Goal #1:

 Noah and his sister will develop a typical sibling relationship with appropriate levels of regulation, evidenced by one or two arguments a day and no attempts to hurt his sister.

Intervention #1:

 Sibling play therapy: Reflect feeling to identify and validate sibling's experience. Relationship reflections to facilitate sibling relationship and connection.

 Parents: Refer or teach Child-Parent Relationship Therapy (CPRT)

Date completion expected: January 15, 20XX Date achieved: _____

Concern #2:

 Noncompliance with parental requests and family rules, tantrums when responding to parental requests and family rules. This includes arguing, pouting, and dysregulation (four to six times a day).

Long-term Goal #2:

 Noah complies with family rules and parental requests with only one tantrum a week. He can self-regulate 60% of the time and responds to parents' co-regulating.

Intervention #2:

 Individual Play Therapy: Reflect feelings to identify and validate his feelings and increase his feeling vocabulary. Reflect themes of power and control to facilitate feelings of control. Set limits and use choices to help Noah learn to manage behavior. Co-regulate Noah in session so he can learn to self-regulate.

Parents: Highlight the parents using limit setting and choice giving from CPRT to assist in helping Noah manage his need for control. CPRT also teaches the six core conditions and how to implement them in interactions with Noah during special playtimes.

Date completion expected: February 15, 20XX Date achieved: _____

Concern #3:

Aggression toward peers at day care; the possibility of being expelled; attacks (kicks) other children at nap time (daily), resulting in no friends and possibly harming them.

Long-term Goal #3:

Noah will interact age appropriately with peers at day care, with typical disagreements but no attacks; Noah will develop peer relationships, evidenced by two or three friends.

Intervention #3:

Individual play therapy: Provide the six basic core conditions for Noah to facilitate his expression of emotion and perception of his world. Provide acceptance to Noah to establish a sense of worth without needing to use aggression. Facilitate decision-making and return responsibility for Noah to experience himself as capable. Utilize relational responses to facilitate Noah's understanding of his role in relationships.

Date completion expected: March 30, 20XX   Date achieved: _____

Other Professionals Involved: None

_____   _____

Parent Signature   Date

Mary Morrison Bennett   Nov. 3, 20XX_____
Mary Morrison Bennett, Ph.D., LPC-S, RPT-S   Date

Cognitive-Behavioral Play Therapy (CBPT) Treatment Plan—Sample

Client Name: Noah Rodriguez   Age: 3 yrs. 5 months   DOB: March 14, 20XX

Parent(s) Name: Alicia and Jesse Rodriguez

Prepared by: Elizabeth Kjellstrand Hartwig   Date: October 28, 20XX

Diagnosis: F43.24, Adjustment Disorder with Disturbance of Emotions and Conduct, Persistent

Concern #1:
    Day-care behaviors of aggression, noncompliance, and inability to manage self-control, with risk for expulsion.

Long-term Goal #1:
    Decrease aggressive behaviors, increase compliance to rules and expectations, utilize coping and self-regulatory skills to cope with feelings.

Intervention #1:
    Individual play therapy:
    - Directive:
        - Teach and build self-control through practice using music
        - Identify coping strategies to increase self-regulation and problem-solving through music and bibliotherapy
    - Nondirective:
        - Facilitative responses focused on feeling reflection, choices, effects of behaviors, problem-solving, self-control, and self-efficacy within client play themes
    Parents:
    - Gain understanding and utilize communication between parent and school
    - Teach, develop, and implement a parenting plan for reinforcing positive choices and behaviors at school as well as appropriate consequences

Concern #2:
    Noncompliance with family roles consisting of noncompliance to family rules and expectations demonstrated by client behaviors of pouting and aggression.

Long-term Goal #2:
    Increase compliance to family expectations and rules, increase the ability to appropriately communicate and express feelings, develop and utilize coping strategies

Intervention #2:
    Individual play therapy:
    - Directive:
        - Use of timer to indicate the transition of activities as well as the end of a session
        - Transition between counselor directed and client-led activities

- Nondirective:
  - Facilitative responses focused on reflecting observed rules and expectations, positive reinforcement of compliance, use of coping skills within client play themes

Parents:
  - Identify and explore family rules, expectations, and routine
  - Establish a routine with a transitional item for parent travel
  - Teach and utilize parent strategies of consistency, providing choices when applicable, and follow-through implementing consequences and privileges

Concern #3:
  Peer and sibling relationships with client demonstrating lack of social interest and connection with peers, aggression toward sibling

Long-term Goal #3:
  Increase positive interaction with peers and sibling based on developmental age, increase problem-solving skills and develop and utilize self-control when coping with feelings

Intervention #3:
  Individual play therapy:
  - Directive:
    - Play prompts with a focus on relationships to identify, practice, and model skills
    - Activities to identify feelings, express feelings, and collaboration
  - Nondirective:
    - Facilitative responses focused on reflecting problem-solving, communication, and social skills within client play themes

Parents:
  - Psychoeducation of developmental stages relating to communication, social relationships
  - Teach and develop skills to model problem-solving and communication
  - Develop strategies for coping with sibling rivalry including consequences for negative choices, observing and reinforcing positive choices

Interventions to include:
- Shift behavioral responses increasing ability to cope with situations to regulate emotions decreasing aggression
- Utilize self-regulatory skills such as: Stop, Think, and Make a Good Choice; Bibliotherapy
- Teach cognitive coping techniques to increase emotional awareness
- Teach problem-solving skills through bibliotherapy and prompted role-play with puppets or miniature figures

---

Parent Signature   Date

Lisa Remey   Nov. 3, 20XX
Lisa Remey, LPC-S, RPT-S   Date

Gestalt Play Therapy (GPT)
Treatment Plan—Sample

Client Name: Noah Rodriguez   Age: 3 yrs. 5 months   DOB: March 14, 20XX

Parent(s) Name: Alicia and Jesse Rodriguez

Prepared by: Linda E. Homeyer, PhD, LPC-S, RPT-S   Date: October 28, 20XX

Diagnosis: F43.24, Adjustment Disorder with Disturbance of Emotions and Conduct, Persistent

Concern #1:

Aggressive behavior between siblings as demonstrated by arguing, pouting, and dys-regulation (six times daily); attempts to hurt his sister by throwing toys and other items at her (three times daily).

Long-term Goal #1:

Noah and his sister will develop a typical sibling relationship with appropriate levels of reg-ulation, evidenced by one or two arguments a day and no attempts by Noah to hurt his sister.

Intervention #1:

Individual play therapy: Use nondirective play to provide new beliefs-of-self through the therapeutic relationship. Use directive play to express emotions and increase connec-tion with self and others. Example: Use Feeling Words handout and use instruments for full-body expression of feelings.

Parents: Teach to reflect feelings and use of games, including body movement to inte-grate body-emotion awareness.

Date completion expected: January 15, 20XX   Date achieved: _____

Concern #2:

Noncompliance with parental requests and family rules, tantrums when responding to parental requests and family rules. This includes arguing, pouting, and dysregulation (four to six times a day).

Long-term Goal #2:

Noah complies with family rules and parental requests with only one tantrum a week. He can self-regulate 60% of the time and responds to parents' co-regulating.

Intervention #2:

Individual play therapy: Provide directive activities to strengthen Noah's knowledge of himself and his own uniqueness. Artwork, clay, sand tray.

Parents: Raise parent awareness of child's perspective through therapeutic limit setting.

Date completion expected: February 15, 20XX   Date achieved: _____

Concern #3:

Aggression toward peers at day care; the possibility of being expelled; attacks (kicks) other children at nap time (daily), resulting in no friends and possibly harming them.

Long-term Goal #3:

Noah will interact age appropriately with peers at day care, with typical disagreements but no attacks; Noah will develop peer relationships, evidenced by two or three friends.

Intervention #3:

Sibling play therapy: Begin once Goal #1 has been met. Nondirective play and directive activities to assist in learning his own and others' boundaries and connections. Example: joint creating in the sand tray and collaborative drawings.

Date completion expected: March 30, 20XX   Date achieved: _____

Other Professionals Involved: None

_____   _____
Parent Signature   Date

Linda E. Homeyer   Nov. 3, 20XX
Linda E. Homeyer, Ph.D., LPC-S, RPT-S   Date

Solution-Focused Play Therapy (SFPT) Treatment Plan—Sample

Note the format change, which includes Client Resources. This is consistent with the SFPT (Hartwig, 2021). It is an example of how the play therapist's theory impacts not just the treatment but documentation as well.

Play Therapy Treatment Plan

Client Name: Noah Rodriguez   Age: 3 yrs. 5 months   DOB: March 14, 20XX

Parent(s) Name: Alicia and Jesse Rodriguez

Prepared by: Elizabeth Kjellstrand Hartwig   Date: October 28, 20XX

Diagnosis: F43.24, Adjustment Disorder with Disturbance of Emotions and Conduct, Persistent

What does client/caregiver want to change?

At home parents would like Noah to express his anger adaptively (e.g., taking breaks, sharing his feelings) and regulate his body when he gets dysregulated. Parents would like Noah to use words to express feelings and play collaboratively with his sister. His parents are open to supporting these changes in any way they can, even if that involves participating in family play therapy sessions or changing interactions at home.

At school parents would like Noah to use regulation skills and manage his anger when interacting with peers. They would like Noah to develop relationships with peers by playing and communicating with them. His parents would also like day-care staff to support Noah in changing his behavior.

Client Resources

What are client's internal strengths/abilities:

Noah is curious and creative. His well-developed language skills provide him an above average ability for verbal expression.

What are client's external resources/support system?

Noah's parents are engaged with the therapy process and available to be involved in family play therapy sessions and parent consultations. They are a stable nuclear family, both parents employed, and reside in their own single-family home. Extended family live nearby; they are involved in a faith community, and have social contacts.

Goals

Long-term Goal #1:

Noah and his sister will develop a typical sibling relationship with appropriate levels of regulation, evidenced by one or two arguments a day and no attempts by Noah to hurt his sister.

Objective/Short-term Goal #1a:
Noah and his sister will express three feelings in play therapy.

Objective/Short-term Goal #1b:
Noah's parents will be actively involved in supporting Noah's progress toward his goal by noticing and complimenting him at times when he is managing his anger and playing collaboratively with his sister.

Intervention #1:
Sibling play therapy: Use a nondirective approach to provide opportunities for Noah and his sister to express emotions and behaviors. Use SFPT skills of complimenting and amplifying solution talk to acknowledge strengths of each child and times when they are playing collaboratively and communicating. Use skills of reflecting behavior, content, and feeling to affirm childrens' perceptions and listen for who and what are important to each child.

Parents: Schedule a parent consultation to discuss the goal and what progress toward the goal would look like at home. Ask parents to describe times when Noah and his sister play together in adaptive ways at home. Give parents a mission to notice times when the siblings are communicating and playing collaboratively. Ask parents to compliment children when they notice these times. Schedule another parent consultation in a few weeks to check in on progress toward the goals.

Progress check in date: January 15, 20XX   Date achieved: _____

Long-term Goal #2:
Noah complies with family rules and parental requests with only one tantrum a week. He can self-regulate 60% of the time and responds to parents' co-regulating.

Objective/Short-term Goal #2a:
Noah will learn to express anger in adaptive ways and learn skills for regulating his body.

Objective/Short-term Goal #2b:
All family members will learn and practice regulation skills in play therapy and then apply this learning at home.

Intervention #2:
Individual play therapy: Use a nondirective approach to provide opportunities for Noah to express anger. Reflect content, feelings, and behavior when Noah expresses anger or frustration. Use directive activities to share regulation skills with Noah. These activities can include music, dance, belly breathing, sand tray, expressive art, and puppets. Use SFPT skills of complimenting and amplifying solution talk to identify Noah's strengths and capabilities of being able to regulate his body.

Family play therapy: Bring family together to practice regulation skills. Allow Noah to demonstrate belly breathing and have family members practice this with music. Ask family members to choose puppet characters and then role play with the puppets. The puppets will practice taking turns getting frustrated and then reminding each other to use the belly breathing skill. Give all family members a mission of practicing this regulation skill at home, reminding each other to use regulation during times when they feel frustrated, and complimenting each other when they choose to use this skill.

Progress check-in date: February 15, 20XX   Date achieved: _____

Long-term Goal #3:
    Noah will interact age appropriately with peers at day care, with typical disagreements but no attacks; Noah will develop peer relationships, evidenced by two or three friends.

Objective/Short-term Goal #3a:
    Noah will utilize his skills for expressing anger in adaptive ways and using regulation skills in the day-care setting.

Objective/Short-term #3b:
    Day-care teachers will be actively involved in supporting Noah's progress toward his goal by noticing and complimenting him at times when he is managing his anger and playing collaboratively with peers.

Intervention #3:
    Individual play therapy: Use empathy and practitioner's nonverbal behavior to acknowledge that Noah is capable of managing his anger and impulsivity in play therapy. Reflect content, feelings, and behavior when Noah expresses anger or frustration. Use limit setting as needed to give Noah opportunities to make choices to manage his behavior. Use complimenting and amplifying solution talk to highlight Noah's strengths and capabilities of being able to manage his anger and impulsivity.
    Day care: Consult with Noah's day-care teachers (with parent permission). Identify Noah's goal of reducing anger outbursts and developing peer relationships. Ask teachers to describe times when Noah does not have anger outbursts and also times when he chooses to play with peers. Ask teachers to compliment Noah at times when he is playing collaboratively with peers and chooses to not express anger in maladaptive ways. Schedule a time to check in with teachers on Noah's progress within one to two weeks.

Progress check in date: March 30, 20XX   Date achieved: _____

_____   _____
Parent Signature   Date

Elizabeth Kjellstrand Hartwig   Nov. 3, 20XX
Elizabeth Kjellstrand Hartwig, PhD, LMFT-S, LPC-S, RPT-S   Date

Cues & Clues: Adlerian Play Therapy

Need to Belong

Social Interest

Life Tasks

 School (Work), Friendship, Love

Encouragement—Discouragement

Mistaken Beliefs

Style of Life (Lifestyle)

Private Logic

 I am . . . . Others are . . . . The world is . . . . therefore, I . . . .

Personality Priorities

 Comfort, Control (of self/of others) Superiority, Pleasing

Goals of Misbehavior

 Attention, Power/Control, Revenge, Assumed Inadequacy

Crucial Cs

 Connect, Count, Capable, Courage

Family Constellation

Parenting Styles

 Permissive, Authoritative, Neglectful, Authoritarian

Cues & Clues: Child-Centered Play Therapy

Core Conditions

   Psychological Contact, Client Is Incongruent, Congruence; Unconditional Positive Regard, Empathy, Therapist Provides Conditions and Client Accepts Conditions

Real Self—Ideal Self

Congruent—Incongruent

Conditions of Worth

Organismic Valuing Process

Skills

   Tracking, Reflecting, Returning Responsibility, Encouragement, Self-esteem Building, Therapeutic Limit Setting

Cues & Clues: Cognitive-Behavioral Play Therapy

Cognitive Schemas

Core Belief

Rational and Irrational Thoughts

Logical and Illogical Thoughts

Cognitive Distortions—in children labeled as maladaptive thoughts

Bibliotherapy

Teaching—Developing Coping Skills

Modeling

Operant Conditioning

Positive Reinforcement

Systemic Desensitization

Praise

Tangible Rewards

Cognitive Triangle (thoughts, feelings, behavior)

Contingency Contracts

Behavioral Shaping

Cues & Clues: Gestalt Play Therapy

I-Thou Relationship

Awareness (internal and external)

Parts—Whole (fragmentation)

Contact Boundary

Unfinished Business (unmet needs)

Introjections

Self-Gestalts

Polarities

Homeostasis

Session Notes, Themes, and more Cues & Clues

Play Therapy Session Note—Nondirective*

Play Therapy Session Note—Directive*

Play Therapy Session Note Adlerian Play Therapy

Guidelines for a Cognitive-Behavioral Play Therapy Session Note

Cognitive-Behavioral Play Therapy Session Note*

Solution-Focused Play Therapy Session Note

Play Therapy Cues & Clues: Objective Information

Play Therapy Cues & Clues: Major Themes and Play Behaviors

Play Therapy Themes by Factor Analysis

Play Therapy Themes That Merit Special Attention

Play Therapy Session Cues & Clues: Other Useful Scales

*These forms are also available on the Routledge Website. See Appendix A for detailed instructions.

This appendix contains the forms and additional information from Chapter 5: Treatment Phase: Session Notes and Chapter 10: A Deeper Look at Play. This is all about documenting the play therapy session. Initially is a template for a nondirective play therapy session. It is a modified version of one used by Dr. Linda E. Homeyer and Dr. Mary Morrison Bennett at Texas State University.

Special acknowledgments to our friends and colleagues Dr. Elizabeth Kjellstrand Hartwig, Dr. Terry Kottman, and Lisa Remey. Elizabeth Kjellstrand Hartwig's *Solution Focused Play Therapy Session Note* from her book *Solution Focused Play Therapy* is used with permission. Terry Kottman graciously and playfully provided a sample *Adlerian Play Therapy Session Form*, also used with permission. Lisa Remey assisted in the development of the *Cognitive-Behavioral Play Therapy Session Form*. We are indebted to her for her input.

The *Cues & Clues: Analysis, Objective Data, Major Themes and Play Behaviors* are based on research by Dr. Linda E. Homeyer and Dr. Helen Benedict, Baylor University (retired). Dr. Benedict's information was from presentations at Association for Play Therapy International Conferences in 1997 and 2000 (used with permission). The information was adapted and put into a worksheet by Cindi Bockwitz, LPC, CPCS, RPT-S. We thank Dr. Benedict for her extensive research in play therapy behaviors and themes and Ms. Bockwitz for her work in making the information in a form to be accessible to play therapists. The format has further been adapted for this book by Dr. Homeyer.

Source: Play therapy session note

Play Therapy Session Note—Nondirective

Child's Name _____ Session #_____ Date: _____

Other's Present: _____ Length of Session ____minutes DSM _____

SUBJECTIVE

HAPPY: pleased, satisfied, delighted, excited, silly, elated, surprised, relieved

CONFIDENT: proud, strong, determined, comfortable, relaxed

SAD: disappointed, hopeless, pessimistic, discouraged, lonely, worthless, guilty

CONFUSED: ambivalent, hesitant, uncertain, timid, nervous, embarrassed

ANGRY: impatient, irritated, annoyed, frustrated, mad, mean, jealous, bored

CURIOUS: interested, focused

AFRAID: vulnerable, helpless, distrustful, fearful, fearful, terrified

ANXIOUS: nervous, worried, tentative, tense

QUALITY/INTENSITY: flat, broad, restricted, contained, ambiguous

OBJECTIVE INFORMATION

__sandbox/water

__puppets

__kitchen/cooking/food

__easel/painting

__bop bag

__dress up/jewelry/hats/masks/wand

__crafts table/clay/markers/etc.

__doll house/doll family

__baby dolls/bottle/pacifier

__cash register/money/telephone/camera/flashlight

__medical kit/bandages

__musical instruments

__games/bowling/ring toss/balls/ball & target

__building blocks/materials, boxes

__vehicles/planes

__animals: domestic/zoo/alligator/dinosaurs/shark/snake

__soldiers/guns/knife/sword/handcuffs/rope

__blocks

TOYS/PLAY BEHAVIOR

PLAY TYPE: solitary, parallel, onlooker, associative, cooperative, collaborative, competitive, combative

RELATING STYLE: egocentric, identifies w/other, helpless, seeks, rejects, confrontative, rescues

ASSESSMENT

_____
_____
_____

PLAY THEMES

Exploratory/Mastery

Relationship Building & Interpersonal

Power/Aggression/Helpless/Inadequate

Control/Safety Death-Loss-Grieving

Other:

Safety/Security/Protection

Family/Nurturance

Sexualized

Abandonment

CASE CONCEPTUALIZATION

_____
_____
_____

PLANS/RECOMMENDATIONS/HOMEWORK

_____
_____
_____

Next Appointment ____/_____/20__

_____   _____

Signature & Credentials   Date

Play Therapy Session Note—Directive

Child's Name _____ Session #_____ Date: _____

Other's Present: _____ Length of Session ____minutes DSM _____

SUBJECTIVE

HAPPY: pleased, satisfied, delighted, excited, silly, elated, surprised, relieved

CONFIDENT: proud, strong, determined, comfortable, relaxed

SAD: disappointed, hopeless, pessimistic, discouraged, lonely, worthless, guilty

CONFUSED: ambivalent, hesitant, uncertain, timid, nervous, embarrassed

ANGRY: impatient, irritated, annoyed, frustrated, mad, mean, jealous, bored

CURIOUS: interested, focused

AFRAID: vulnerable, helpless, distrustful, fearful, fearful, terrified

ANXIOUS: nervous, worried, tentative, tense

QUALITY/INTENSITY: flat, broad, restricted, contained, ambiguous

OBJECTIVE INFORMATION

__sandbox/water

__puppets

__kitchen/cooking/food

__easel/painting

__bop bag

__dress up/jewelry/hats/masks/wand

__crafts table/clay/markers/etc.

__doll house/doll family

__baby dolls/bottle/pacifier

__cash register/money/telephone/camera/flashlight

__medical kit/bandages

__musical instruments

__games/bowling/ring toss/balls/ball & target

__building blocks/materials, boxes

__vehicles/planes

__animals: domestic/zoo/alligator/dinosaurs/shark/snake

__soldiers/guns/knife/sword/handcuffs/rope

__blocks

TOYS/PLAY BEHAVIOR

Directive Intervention Name: _____

Materials Used: _____

PLAY TYPE: solitary, parallel, onlooker, associative, cooperative, collaborative, competitive, combative

RELATING STYLE: egocentric, identifies w/other, helpless, seeks, rejects, confrontative, rescues

ASSESSMENT

_____

_____

_____

PLAY THEMES

Exploratory/Mastery

Relationship Building & Interpersonal

Power/Aggression/Helpless/Inadequate

Control/Safety Death-Loss-Grieving

Other:

Safety/Security/Protection

Family/Nurturance

Sexualized

Abandonment

CASE CONCEPTUALIZATION

_____

_____

_____

PLANS/RECOMMENDATIONS/HOMEWORK

_____

_____

_____

Next Appointment ____/_____/20__

Goals for next week: Intervention for next week:

_____   _____

Signature & Credentials   Date

Adlerian Play Therapy Session Note

Date/Session # _____/_____   Child/Age_____

Counselor _____   Diagnosis_____

Underlying purpose of presenting problem: _____

Specific interventions used (circle): tracking, restating content, reflecting feelings, returning responsibility, asking questions, limiting, metacommunicating, metaphors/storytelling, bibliotherapy, spitting in soup, role-playing, art activity (_____), sand tray, didactic teaching, modeling, practicing new skills, _____

I. **SUBJECTIVE (Feelings Expressed) (underline all that apply and indicate predominant feeling(s) by circling them):**
HAPPY: relieved, satisfied, pleased, delighted, excited, surprised, silly
CONFIDENT: proud, strong, powerful, determined, free
SAD: disappointed, hopeless, pessimistic, discouraged, lonely
HESITANT: timid, confused, nervous, embarrassed, ashamed
ANGRY: impatient, annoyed, frustrated, mad, mean, jealous, enraged
CURIOUS: interested, focused, intense
AFRAID: vulnerable, helpless, distrustful, anxious, fearful, scared, terrified
FLAT: restricted, contained, ambiguous

II. **OBJECTIVE**

A. *Toys/Play Behavior* (put CH if child-initiated; put TH if therapist initiated)

_____ sandbox/water/sink
_____ kitchen/cooking/food
_____ bop bag/bean bag
_____ crafts/clay/markers/paint/ scissors/glue
_____ doll house/doll family bottle/pacifier/baby
_____ musical instruments
_____ games/bowling/balls/ring toss
_____ vehicles/planes/boats
_____ soldiers/weapons/handcuffs
_____ puppets/theater

_____ easel/paint/chalkboard/white board
_____ dress up/jewelry/hats/masks/wand
_____ sheets/blankets/fabric
_____ cash register/money telephone/camera
_____ medical kit/bandages
_____ construction toys (tinker toys, Legos, blocks)
_____ animals (domestic, zoo, alligator, snake, dino)
_____ sand tray/miniatures

B. *Significant verbalizations:*

_____

_____

C. *Set Limit(s) on:*

_____

_____

D. *Returned responsibility to child when:*

_____

_____

E. *Worked to help child gain insight/shift or adjust/move toward more constructive application of:*
- Functioning at life tasks (school, friendship, family, self, spiritual):
- Interpretation of family constellation/family atmosphere:
- Personality priorities:
- Crucial Cs:
- Goals of misbehavior:
- Impact of culture
- "Owning" assets:
- Mistaken beliefs:
- Self-defeating behaviors:
- Private logic:

III. ASSESSMENT

A. *Dynamics of the Session*
(circle the number on any scale that applies to child's behavior in session):

Low activity level	1	2	3	4	5	6	7	8	9	10	High activity level
Low social interest	1	2	3	4	5	6	7	8	9	10	High social interest
Low degree of self-regulation	1	2	3	4	5	6	7	8	9	10	High degree of self-regulation
Low level of intensity	1	2	3	4	5	6	7	8	9	10	High level of intensity
Little therapist inclusion	1	2	3	4	5	6	7	8	9	10	Much therapist inclusion
Destructive play	1	2	3	4	5	6	7	8	9	10	Constructive play
Chaotic/disorganized	1	2	3	4	5	6	7	8	9	10	Orderly/organized
Aggressive	1	2	3	4	5	6	7	8	9	10	Peaceful
Dependent	1	2	3	4	5	6	7	8	9	10	Independent
Too tight	1	2	3	4	5	6	7	8	9	10	Too loose
Immature/hyper-mature	1	2	3	4	5	6	7	8	9	10	Age appropriate
Scattered, impulsive, hyper	1	2	3	4	5	6	7	8	9	10	Focused, purposeful, calm

B. *Play Themes* (underline all that apply, describe play behaviors that fit into theme; circle predominate theme):

EXPLORATORY: RELATIONSHIP:
POWER/CONTROL: FEELINGS OF
AGGRESSION/REVENGE: INADEQUACY/HELPLESSNESS:
MASTERY: SAFETY/SECURITY/TRUST:
DEATH/LOSS/GRIEF: NURTURING:
REGRESSION: TRAUMA:
OTHER: SEXUALIZED:

Plans/Recommendations (including consultation with parents/teachers):

_____   _____
Play Therapist Signature & Credentials   Date

Guidelines for a Cognitive-Behavioral Play Therapy Session Note

These guidelines and explanations on using the form are provided by Lisa Remey, LPC-S, RPT-S. The Cognitive-Behavioral Play Therapy (CBPT) format reflects the directive-stance and is used to identify the dynamics of the session and therapeutic progress.

The CBPT session begins with a *check-in*. How this is done will vary based on the age of the child. The CBPT therapist is flexible and collaborative. While there are segments to cover during the check-in, the play therapist is flexible to use an activity or shift to nondirective play in the moment if it meets the broader therapeutic intention.

- *Check-in* consists of three areas:
  1. Update since the last session: notate what client reports they accomplished since last session. The opening question will vary depending on the age of the child, and might be a question like:
     a. *Tell me something good/happy about your week.*
     b. *Tell me something bad/hard about your week.*
     c. *Do you have something you want to talk about today?*
  2. Action plan review: established during and documented on the previous session note, typically checking on how a new skill was implemented
     a. *How did it go for you last week when you used your "calm-body-song"?*
     b. *Did you and your mom work on the sticker chart this week? How did it go?*
  3. Session goals: tied to treatment plan goals and identified to facilitate change in the child.
     a. *You can choose what to play with today.*
     b. *Today I'd like us to . . . (introduce activity or intervention).*
- *Affect:* The affective presentation of the child in the session may be documented in the same manner as the nondirective format.
- *Engagement:* This documents the style and level of engagement with the play therapist; how does the child respond to the play therapist's reflections, tracking; do they disengage, turn their back on the therapist, stay connected and interactive. What is the engagement with the play, activity, or intervention, maintaining the flow, expanding and extending, stopping, changing the direction?
- *Session Content*
  - Directive, *Counselor Led:* note the prompt, activity, or intervention the play therapist has selected. Lisa Remey, a CBPT play therapist, notes she uses the three following categories of directives (Personal communication, February 22, 2022):
    - Prompt—usually used in child-led play, with a focused prompt, such as:
      - *Play in the dollhouse to show me what is happening at home.*
    - Activity—is an informal, tentative suggestion of an activity to see level of engagement of the child, for example, offering a drawing activity to see the level of interaction with art, to note that for future selection of interventions.
      - *Feeling Faces: big and little, ability of holding more than one feeling at a time, etc.*

- ■ Intervention—more formal, more concretely structured; the play therapist selects this experience as one that will facilitate therapeutic growth. The play therapist displays *flexibility* to drop the intervention if the child doesn't engage. The play therapist and child can be *collaborative*, in adapting the intervention to suit both.
  - • Nondirective, *Client Led:* nondirective play, as this is an option based on the therapist's decision on what is needed therapeutically, either prior to the session or once in the session.
- ♦ Conceptualization: Just as on the nondirective session note, this is a brief statement on how the child is responding to the therapy. It might include automatic thoughts, distorted thinking/maladaptive thoughts/behavior, adaptive self-statements, rational/ irrational ideas/thoughts, and so on. It might sound like:
  - • *Client displayed problem-solving skills and ability to adapt chaotic play to calm, organized play.*
- ♦ *Action Plan & Next Session:* An action plan is developed with the client and shared with a parent, or with the child and parent together. (The nondirective play therapist might call this *homework*.) Examples might be:
  - • *Child will use keep your-body-calm song when he begins to become dysregulated*
  - • *Child and parent will develop a sticker chart for positive reinforcement of completing his chores*
  - • *Child will use the calm-down fidget made in session during the week*
  - • *Child will journal thoughts and emotions, using words, symbols, or art* (for an older child)

As part of the *action plan*, the directive play therapist may identify plans to bridge it to the *Next Session*. This is based both on the movement that occurred in this session, and the next therapeutic experience needed.

Cognitive-Behavioral Play Therapy Session Note

Child's Name _____ Session #_____ Date: _____

Other's Present: _____ Length of Session ____minutes DSM _____

Check-In

Update Since Last Session:

Action Plan Review:

Session Goals:

Affect

HAPPY: pleased, satisfied, delighted, excited, silly, elated, surprised, relieved
CONFIDENT: proud, strong, determined, comfortable, relaxed
SAD: disappointed, hopeless, pessimistic, discouraged, lonely, worthless, guilty
CONFUSED: ambivalent, hesitant, uncertain, timid, nervous, embarrassed
ANGRY: impatient, irritated, annoyed, frustrated, mad, mean, jealous, bored
CURIOUS: interested, focused
AFRAID: vulnerable, helpless, distrustful, fearful, fearful, terrified
ANXIOUS: nervous, worried, tentative, tense
QUALITY/INTENSITY: flat, broad, restricted, contained, ambiguous

Engagement

with therapist
with play, activity, intervention

Session Content

DIRECTIVE: *COUNSELOR LED*
Prompt, Activity, Intervention:
NONDIRECTIVE: *CHILD LED*
Toys/Play Behavior:

Conceptualization

_____

_____

ACTION PLAN & NEXT SESSION

Next Appointment ____/____/20__

_____   _____
Play Therapist Signature & Credentials   Date

Solution-Focused Play Therapy Session Note

Date: _____   Practitioner: _____

Child's Name _____ Client's age_____

Scaling

_____

| 0 | 1 | 2 | 3 | 4 | 5 | 6 | 7 | 8 | 9 | 10 |

_____

What client is doing to get to that point on the scale: _____

A—Amplify What's Better

SFPT Interventions

Toys Used

Physical Play
• bop bag, • swords, • tent, • tunnel, • dart board
• basketball hoop, • balls, • sensory toys

Language Play
• puppet/theatre, • action/animal figures,
• journal

Exploratory Play
• art supplies, • paints/easel, • musical instruments

Constructive Play
• blocks, • stacking toys, • play dough, • tools

Fantasy Play
• sand tray/miniatures, • dress up,
• dolls/dollhouse

Social Play
• kitchen/kitchen toys, • cash register, • medical toys,
• guns/handcuffs, • purse/phone/keys, • vehicles

Other Toys: _____
_____
_____
_____

Play Behaviors

R—Reinforce the Change
Client Strengths and Skills

_____

_____

S—Start Again

Solution Mission

_____

_____

Client Mission

_____

_____

Caregiver Mission

_____

_____

Recommendations

- ☐ Continue individual play therapy
- ☐ Family play therapy—with sibling(s), caregiver(s), or entire family
- ☐ Caregiver consultation
- ☐ Consultation with teacher, school counselor, or other academic professional—get release of information
- ☐ Consultation with pediatrician, psychiatrist, or other medical professional—get release of information
- ☐ Caregiver recommendation/referral for couples counseling or couples' resources
- ☐ Other treatment recommendations: _____

_____   _____

Practitioner signature and credentials   Date

Play Therapy Session Cues & Clues: Objective Information

Physical/Behavioral Aspects:
- **Eye contact** good/fair/poor/sporadic purpose: checking on therapist's attention/cautionary/relational
- **Engaged** with play: good/fair/poor/sporadic with therapist: good/fair/poor/sporadic
- **Works** systemically or trial and error/persistently or gives up easily/authentic effort or looks for direction
- **Cooperation** resistant or cooperative/secretive or open/deceptive or inclusive/exclusive or competitive

Affect:
- **Quality**: appropriate/inappropriate, flat/expressive, positive/negative, interested/indifferent, constricted/labile
- **Emotion**:
  - **Happy**: pleased, satisfied, delighted, excited, silly, elated, grandiose, elevated
  - **Sad:** disappointed, hopeless, pessimistic, discouraged, lonely, worthless, guilty
  - **Angry**: impatient, irritated, annoyed, frustrated, mad, mean, jealous, bored
  - **Afraid:** vulnerable, helpless, distrustful, fearful, terrified
  - **Confident:** proud, strong, determined, comfortable, relaxed
  - **Confused:** ambivalent, hesitant, uncertain, timid, embarrassed, ashamed, ambiguous, evasive
  - **Anxious**: nervous, worried, tentative, tense
  - **Other:**

Styles of Relating:
- **Egocentric** relates primarily to self, unable to see other perspectives
- **Identifies with others** supportive, validating
- **Helpless** solicits others to help without first trying
- **Seeks/rejects support** from others to help self
- **Empathetic** extends self to support others
- **Able to confront** direct but not attacking
- **Rescues others** to avoid emotions or to caretake

Play Types:
- **Solitary:** plays by self, away from others, birth to 2 years
- **Onlooker**: watches, may ask questions, no effort to join in, 2 years
- **Parallel:** plays along others but in a different activity, over 2 years
- **Associative:** plays the same activity as others, but no give-and-take, 3–4 years
- **Cooperative:** plays jointly with play therapist, sharing, compromising, helping, develops interdependence; 4 years and older

♦ **Collaborative:** plays in an organized, structured way with rules, procedures, role plays, but works independently but toward a common goal, 4 years and older

The following are of importance for social development and ages 4 and older

♦ **Constructive:** building, putting things together, problem solving·
♦ **Competitive:** plays to win, works to
  • beat others, winning is the goal, dominating, controlling
♦ **Combative:** uses intimidation or aggression to control others, fights, snatches, hits, throws

Play Therapist Skills and Interventions Used:
  ♦ **Limit setting:** (reason for limit)
    • protect child
    • protect therapist
    • protect property
    • structuring (end of session, staying in session, etc.)
    • socially unacceptable behavior
  ♦ **Nondirective**
    • tracking behavior
    • reflecting content
    • reflecting feeling
    • facilitating decision making, returning responsibility
    • facilitating creativity, responsibility
    • esteem building, encouraging
    • limit setting
  ♦ **Directive interventions**
    • complete feelings check
    • provide alternatives
    • problem solving
    • verbal redirection
    • encourage participation
    • provide simple directives
    • solicit feedback
    • credit the effort
    • physical restraint
    • reinforcement
    • validation
    • encourage listening
    • exploration of thoughts/feelings
    • cognitive reframe
    • initiated time out
    • recognition
    • therapeutic cradling/holding
    • confrontation

Play Therapy Session Cues & Clues: Major Themes and Play Behaviors

Exploration

____**exploration** curiosity, asking questions about what is available or how things work

Mastery

___ **reconstructs,** builds/constructs, masters a skill or ability, competence, resolution, integration

___ **failure to master**

Relationship Building and Interpersonal Relationships

___ **collaboration or cooperation**	___ **sharing**	___ **competition**
___ **refusal to cooperate**	___ **helping**	___ **protecting**
___ **affection**	___ **positive connection**	
___ **sadness**	___ **anger**	___ **rejection**

___ **independence** child refuses or rejects help in a setting of *realistic dependency* such as a child who cannot reach saying they don't need help putting a picture on the wall; also a child does something dangerous to avoid the help of the therapist; includes insisting on doing things alone

___ **boundary setting** child establishes boundary between two characters in a relationship including putting a physical barrier between them, demands that the therapist not talk, and so on.

___ **boundary violations** a character violates or oversteps a boundary (or set limit) set by another such as breaking down a door, pushing over a wall, talking when told not to

___ **roughhousing** child seeks to engage therapist or other in physical play such as tickling, wrestling, picking up, etc., that is POSITIVE in tone

___ **teasing** tricking or teasing of one character by another

___ **control** child or characters are bossy, controlling, dictating others' actions in play, announcement that child is "the boss," authoritarian actions

___ **imitation control** the therapist is directed to act like or do what the child is doing

Power and Aggressive, Helpless, and Inadequate

___ **good guy vs. bad guy** aggressive play in which there is a clear good vs. bad character, component, right vs. wrong, good vs. bad, cops and robbers, wars, superheroes against evil

___ **aggressor-victim** play in which there is a clear aggressor and a clear victim without the element of good vs. bad; one figure aggresses upon another—includes child shooting or killing therapist, throwing toys, biting, killing, knifing, shooting, verbal aggression, hitting

___ **general aggression** general unfocused throwing, hitting, kicking, etc., without being part of an explicit theme, a "room wreck/trash," scaring others

___ **powerful figure overcoming weaker figure** power assertion of one character over others without good vs. bad component or aggressive component—emphasis is on power and strength

___ **devouring** this is a stop beyond aggression/rage—one figure eats or devours another figure

___ **seeking** consulting a power figure such as a judge, parent, teacher, boss, or a wise archetype such as a wizard, good witch, God, or another religious figure

Control and Safety by Being in Control

___ **fire play** something is burning or on fire

___ **burying or drowning** buries figures/objects in sand or under other objects in room, characters drown

___ **broken play** a character or house is broken, sick, hurt

___ **fixing play** something is broken and needs repairing, gluing, hammering, doctoring a non-endangered figure—differs from rescue play in that a character is not endangered first

___ **failure to fix**

___ **self-fixing**

___ **bridge building play** the child builds a structure that serves as a bridge between two places, objects, or characters—shows evidence of empowerment

___ **instability play** characters are falling, stumbling, tipping things "accidentally," spilling—falling off roofs, walls of house fall down, things fall apart, balancing things precariously as if going to fall, child is in danger of falling or pretends to be about to fall off something

___ **cleaning** washing, sweeping, cleans up area, rearranges objects so they are "just so," arranging playroom or rectifying changes made by other children using the room

___ **messing** making a mess, pours water/sand around room, characters "make a mess"

___ **sorting** lines items up, categorizes, groups, splitting (good characters lined up on one side & bad characters on the other, putting animals in family groups)

Safety, Security, Protection Play—focus on establishing safety for the child or identified characters

___ **containing** building cages, rooms, jail, or house of large blocks, focus is on keeping something inside or outside a space—includes secrets—differs from hiding play, which emphasizes interaction, not containment

___ **danger themes** potential danger is identified and needs to be responded to—dangerous figures, places, events, objects or situations—a character alone abandoned, lost, homeless

___ **protective** keeping something out of danger, keeping things safe, needing the therapist to hover to keep climbing play safe, or hiding a character in a drawer or other 'hiding place' to be safe

___ **rescue** an endangered character is rescued, the rescuer may be an action figure, an authority figure, public helper or someone who adapts an abandoned figure

___ **escape** a character escapes from a bad situation without help from a rescue figure

Family and Nurturance

___ **constancy** activities to establish identity of self or other, attachment, and stability of those identities such as hide and seek, naming games, mirror play, taking "pictures" of things for permanency and separation, games such as "catch me"—includes child needing to take a toy from the playroom as a transitional object

___ **reunion** includes reunions or returns after separation

___ **nurturing** positive activities such as one character feeding, holding, hugging, caring for other; giving gifts

___ **self-nurturing/soothing** common in parentified kids who don't allow selves to be nurtured—using baby things to comfort self-rocking, stroking, feeding self, taking a bottle, putting self to bed

___ **failed nurturance** deprivation—one figure withholds from other, abuses, neglects, punishes, poisons

___ **neglect, abuse, or punishment of the self** child withholds nurturance from self, hurts self when doing something child thinks is wrong, places self in dangerous situations

___ **store and shopping** set up a store, goes shopping, has the therapist be the storekeeper

___ **adult activities** playing caregiver, role activities/behaviors, negative—positive; appropriate—inappropriate

Sexualized Play (also labeled as Victimization, Re-enactment, Re-empowerment)

___ **sexual activity** with dolls or animals including sexual acts or contact between those figures; re-enactment

___ **sexual behaviors directed at therapist** exhibitionism, sexualized contact such as rubbing/fondling, exploration such as looking up skirt or down shirt; attempting to engage via sexual contact (role playing perpetrator)

___ **masturbation** in secret behind play room furniture, on/with toys with goal of self-soothing; arousal

___ **sexual talk** slang, body part words, sexual innuendo

___ **sexual curiosity** looking at body parts, undressing dolls

Death, Loss, Grieving, Abandonment Play

___ **death play** characters die of natural or aggressive causes—categories include anger-death, separation-death, overwhelmed and harmed death, safety-death, dependency-death, control-death, devouring eating death

___ **abandonment** a character leaves, goes away, or moves from someone wise or protecting, or the character is left by that person

Meta Themes

___ **doing and undoing** plays out a theme, then it's opposite, such as death/life, fixing/breaking, giving/taking, messing/cleaning, aggression/nurturance

___ **repetition** child plays the same theme over and over within session or across sessions

___ **life stage mix** plays roles from different periods of the lifespan simultaneously such as putting on a wedding dress while drinking out of baby bottle

___ **role mix** playing two incompatible roles simultaneously such as good person and bad person

Play Therapy Themes by Factor Analysis

Based on factor analysis research by Laura Hillman. She studied play therapy cases of 352 preschoolers, aged 3–6 years; 64% males and 36% females; 37% Black-Americans, 35% Caucasian, 16% Hispanic, 3 % multi-ethnic; 6% unknown. The factor analysis occurred using the Benedict Play Therapy Research Database (41 play themes, 19 interpersonal-codes, two process codes).

1. Empowerment/Loss of Self-Control
   - fail, imitation control, independence, messing play, art and drawing, rejection themes
2. Safety
   - boundary setting, protective and containing play, rescue play, burning themes
3. Violent Violations
   - boundary violations, anger, imitation play themes
4. Parentified Internalizing
   - sadness, self-fixing, self-nurturing, control, nurturing play, adult activities, affection themes
5. Hyperarousal/Dissociation
   - mastery play, exploration, and sleeping themes
6. Maltreatment Communication
   - fixing play, sexual curiosity, failed nurturance with abuse themes
7. Attack/Protect from Self
   - aggression, protect, good guy versus bad guy, positive connection themes
8. Uncertainty/Loss
   - danger, reunion, broken play, instability play, separation play themes
9. People Pleasing
   - natural death (by natural causes), seeking or consulting a power figure, helping themes

REFERENCE: Hillman, L. (2014). *Underlying constructs in play therapy themes: An exploratory factor analysis*. [ProQuest Information & Learning]. In *Dissertation Abstracts International: Section B: The Sciences and Engineering* (Vol. 76, Issue 6—B(E)).

Play Therapy Themes That Merit Special Attention

Eric Green, David Crenshaw, and Cynthia Lubin Langtiw indicated that in a play therapy setting some themes warrant special attention when working with children. The descriptors and possible implications are listed here.

1. Death Themes
   a. possible conflicts with anger or separation anxiety
   b. may be rooted in trauma, loss, grief, or rage
   c. 'safety death'—child kills character to keep others safe
2. Failed Nurturance
   a. nurturing play becomes negative and hostile activity
3. Separation Themes
   a. clinging behavior to attachment figures, panic or aggression on anticipated separation
   b. play out animals being lost and unable to locate mothers; so same with human figures
4. Aggressive Play
   a. seen in children of severe early neglect; physical abuse
   b. devouring play, relationship aggressive play (isolate or berate imaginary friend in play)
5. Boundary Violations in Play
   a. dollhouse play where there are no doors; demonstration of little privacy
6. Safety Themes
   a. sign of very disordered family unit
   b. importance to play therapist maintaining safe therapeutic environment for child's anger play
7. Sexualized Play Themes
   a. authors caution that sexualized play is rare (6% of children with sexual abuse history) and 36% of preschoolers with "disordered behavior problems" (implied sexual play); may have other causes
8. Stage-mix
   a. playing out contradictory developmental stages
   b. child is confused about where they fit and belong

REFERENCE: Green, E. J., Crenshaw, D. A., & Langtiw, C. L. (2009). Play theme-based research with children. *The Family Journal*, 17(4), 312–317. DOI: 10.1177/1066480709347358

Play Therapy Session
Cues & Clues: Other Useful Scales

Child's Overall Play Behavior:

Child's Activity Level LOW	1	2	3	4	5	6	7	8	9	10	Child's Activity Level HIGH
Intensity of Play LOW	1	2	3	4	5	6	7	8	9	10	Intensity of Play HIGH
Inclusion of Therapist LOW	1	2	3	4	5	6	7	8	9	10	Inclusion of Therapist HIGH
Destructive	1	2	3	4	5	6	7	8	9	10	Constructive
Messy/Chaotic Disorganized	1	2	3	4	5	6	7	8	9	10	Neat/Orderly

Child's Affect and Play:

Sad/angry/depressed/fearful	1	2	3	4	5	6	7	8	9	10	Content/satisfied appropriate affect
Anxious/insecure	1	2	3	4	5	6	7	8	9	10	Confident/secure
Low frustration tolerance	1	2	3	4	5	6	7	8	9	10	High frustration tolerance
Dependent/clingy/needy	1	2	3	4	5	6	7	8	9	10	Autonomous/independent
Immature/regressed hypermature	1	2	3	4	5	6	7	8	9	10	Age appropriate
External locus of control	1	2	3	4	5	6	7	8	9	10	Internal locus of control (self-controlled)
Impulsive/easily distracted	1	2	3	4	5	6	7	8	9	10	Purposeful/focused
Inhibited/constricted	1	2	3	4	5	6	7	8	9	10	Creative/expressive/ spontaneous/free
Isolated/detached	1	2	3	4	5	6	7	8	9	10	Connected/sense of belonging

Ongoing Parent Consultations

Weekly Parent Feedback Form

Weekly Parent Feedback Form—Sample

Parent Consultation Preparation Form*

Parent Consultation Preparation Form—Sample

Parent Consultation Session Note*

Parent Consultation Session Note—Sample

*These forms are also available on the Routledge Website. See Appendix A for detailed instructions.

Source: Weekly parent feedback form

Weekly Parent Feedback Form

Date: _____ Child Client: _____ Parent/Rater: _____

Behavior at Intake   **Current Rating**   **Desired Behavior**

Treatment Plan #1   1 2 3 4 5   Treatment Plan #1

Treatment Plan #2   1 2 3 4 5   Treatment Plan #2

Treatment Plan #3   1 2 3 4 5   Treatment Plan #3

Other comments you want to share with your child's counselor:

Weekly Parent Feedback Form—Sample

Date: _____

Child Client: _Noah_____   Parent/Rater: *Alicia/Mom*_____

Behavior at Intake	**Current Rating**	**Desired Behavior**
Aggression between siblings	1 2 3 4 5	Typical sibling relationship
6 X's daily/3 X's daily— physical attacks		1–2 arguments a day
Melt-down response 4–6 times a day family rules/parents	1 2 3 4 5	Able to comply 1 tantrum a week
Day care aggression	1 2 3 4 5	No peer attacks at day care & 2–3 peer relationships

Other comments you want to share with your child's counselor:

Source: Parent consultation preparation form

Parent Consultation Preparation Form

Client Name: _____ Date of Session: _____

Number of Sessions with Child:_____

Goal of Session_____

Conceptualization of Parent(s):_____

Treatment Plan Goals:

1.

2.

3.

Therapeutic Progress of Treatment Plan Goals:

Play Therapy Themes or Theory Concepts to Share:

Follow-Up Questions to Ask:

Parenting Skill to Teach (if parent is ready):

Encouraging Comments About the Child:

Parent Consultation Preparation Form—Sample

Client Name: *Noah*

Date of Session: *July 21, 20XX*

Number of Sessions with Child: 8

Goal of Session: *Provide feedback, link play therapy progress to behaviors at home.*

Conceptualization of Parent(s):
Mom: *Ideal Self—peaceful, no negative feelings in the home*
Dad: *Conditions of worth—I am a good dad when my children behave*

Treatment Plan Goals
1. *Reduce sibling arguments to 1–2 a day and no attempts*
2. *Compliance with family rules*
3. *Develop peer relationships and no attacks on peers at school*

Therapeutic Progress
1. Parent feedback form reports progress

   Week 5: #1: 5; #2: 3; #3: 2
   Week 6: #1: 5; #2: 4; #3: 3
   Week 7: #1: 5; #2: 4; #3: 3
   Week 8: #1: 5; #2: 4; #3: 3

2. *In session, Noah's compliance with limits has improved, he has begun to limit his own behavior.*
3. *Continued aggressive behavior in session.*

Play Therapy Themes or Theory Concepts To Share:
Noah's play themes are centered around his need for control, he seems to feel chaotic at home with all the changes and his play is focused on his need for control. Within that need for control, he is beginning to comply more with limits so it seems his need for control is beginning to be met in therapy. I think we need to figure out some ways at home to help him feel seen and to help him feel like he has age-appropriate amounts of control in his life.

Follow-Up Questions To Ask:
How do teachers at school discipline Noah for aggression toward peers?

Parenting Skill To Teach (if parent is ready)
Reflection of feeling (see Reflection of Feeling Practice Worksheet in Appendix F)

We use reflection of feeling to help him feel seen and understood. It is critical that your reflections have a genuine tone of voice, that they are short and make a statement.

Encouraging Comment About the Child
Noah experiences great joy in working to solve problems, he is so proud when he figures out how to do something.

Parent Consultation Session Note

Client name _____ Parent/Guardian present_____

Date of session/session number _____

Parent report of client behavior and progress:

Therapist report of session progress: (play or verbal themes, significant insights, etc.)

Therapeutic parenting skills or insights shared:

Recommendations, homework/action plan:

_____   _____
Play Therapist Signature & Credentials   Date

© 2023, *The Guide to Play Therapy Documentation and Parent Consultation*, L. Homeyer & M. Bennett, Routledge.

Parent Consultation Session Note—Sample

Client name: *Noah* _____   **Parent present**: *Alicia, mother*

Date of session/session number: *July 21, 2022/#3*

Parent report of client behavior and progress:

Alicia reported Noah continues to struggle with compliance, however he is able to comply with requests occasionally.

Therapist report of session progress: (play or verbal themes, significant insights, etc.)

Therapist reported Noah's play includes themes of control and mastery that are consistent with his need for more control in relationships outside of session.

Noah has reached Goal #1 on the treatment plan.

Therapeutic parenting skills or insights shared:

Therapist explained the Window of Tolerance to parents and made the connection of Noah's growing Window of Tolerance with his ability to be compliant and more flexible at times.

Recommendations, homework/action plan:

Notice Noah's Window of Tolerance. Assist Noah in returning to his window, with up- and down-regulation activities discussed in this session while maintaining their own ability to stay regulated. Acknowledge when Noah complies and follows through with parental requests, such as "thank you, Noah, for picking up your toys before bedtime."

Linda E. Homeyer _____   November 11, 20XX

Linda E. Homeyer, PhD, LPC-S, RPT-Ss   Date

Appendix F

Therapeutic Parenting Skill Practice Worksheets

Reflection of Feeling Practice
Worksheet—Instructions

This practice sheet is part of the *teach-demonstrate-do model.* These examples can be used in session with parents in a role-play situation to provide opportunities for parents to practice therapeutic skills. Parents tend to follow-through and use these skills at home if they have experienced success in practice in a parenting consultation.

When teaching reflection of feeling, see Chapter 6: Ongoing Parent Consultations for a detailed description of teaching these skills to parents. Focus mainly on: Genuine tone of voice, touching the child's heart and keeping it short. To communicate Landreth and Bratton's (2020), the Be-With Attitudes: *I'm here, I hear you, I understand, I care, and I delight in you.*

Reflection of Feeling Practice Worksheet

Reflection of Feeling Tips:
Match your child's emotion with your tone of voice and facial expression
Short and to the point—You feel _____
Let your child respond, then reflect again!

Asia came running into your office to tell you her class got a pet today. A lizard named fuzzy!
How does Asia feel? *Excited*
Reflection of feeling: *You are so excited!*

1. Jamal comes in after school and says, "Well I played football today with the other boys and I scored two touchdowns."

   How does Jamal feel? _____

   Reflection of feeling: _____

2. Grace puts her head on the math paper with a loud, "UGH!"

   How does Grace feel?_____ _____ _____

   Reflection of feeling: _____

3. Amir says, "Jeffery told me I wasn't funny. So I told him he wasn't very funny."

   How does Amir feel? _____

   Reflection of feeling: _____

4. At bedtime, Slone says, "Don't go, leave the light on, stay with me."

   How does Slone feel? _____

   Reflection of feeling: _____

5. Karis says, "Tomorrow is pajama day at school, I'm going to wear my unicorn pajamas!"

   How does Karis feel? _____

   Reflection of feeling: _____

6. Evan is yelling at Joseph, "Don't knock down my tower! You can't do that!"

   How is Evan feeling? _____

   Reflection of feeling: _____

Limit Setting Practice Worksheet—Instructions

This practice sheet is part of the *Teach-Demonstration-Do Model*; these examples can be used in session with parents in a role-play situation to provide opportunities for parents to practice therapeutic skills. The play therapist helps the parent keep their tone of voice neutral and when possible allow the child to gain control of self in order to comply with limits before the parent presents a choice or consequence.

ACT Limit Setting Practice Worksheet

Developed by Landreth (2012)

Acknowledge the feeling, wish, need or want (remember to have a compassionate tone of voice)

Communicate the limit

Target an Alternative

Example: Noah throws a truck against the wall.

>   Noah, I see you are angry. (Acknowledge the feeling)
>   But toys are not for throwing. (Communicate the limit)
>   You can hit the couch or hit the pillow. (Target an alternative)

Zara is standing on the kitchen chair while working on an art project at the table.

A_____

C_____

T_____

Junior grabs Jessie's truck out of his hand.

A_____

C_____

T_____

Liam is begging to go to the park but it is dinner time.

A_____

C_____

T_____

Mom says, "It's time for a bath." Tanner says, "No!" and runs and hides.

A_____

C_____

T_____

Adlerian Play Therapy Limit Setting Practice Worksheet

Developed by Kottman & Meany-Walen (2016)

Example: Noah throws a truck against the wall.

    Step 1: Noah, the rule at home is toys are not to be thrown. (stating the limit)

    Step 2: I see you are angry at me. (reflecting the feeling) or You are testing me to see what I will do when you throw toys. (metacommunicating)

    Step 3: I bet you can think of something else you can do to show me you are angry.

    Step 4: (if necessary) Noah, what do you think should happen if you throw the truck again? We agree then, if you choose to throw the truck then you choose not to play with it for the rest of the day.

Zara is standing on the kitchen chair while working on an art project at the table.

_____

_____

_____

_____

Junior grabs Jessie's truck out of his hand.

_____

_____

_____

_____

Liam is begging to go to the park but it is dinner time.

_____

_____

_____

_____

Mom says, "It's time for a bath." Tanner says, "No!" and runs and hides.

_____

_____

_____

_____

Termination

Play Therapy Termination Summary*

Play Therapy Termination Summary—Sample

*This form are also available on the Routledge Website. See Appendix A for detailed instructions.

Source: Play therapy termination summary.

Play Therapy Termination Summary

Client Information

Client Name:

Client Age:

Client Address:

Parent Name:

Treatment Data

Intake Date:

First Session Date:

Final Session Date:

Number of Sessions:

Counseling Modalities Implemented:

DSM Diagnosis:

Termination Information

Reason for Termination (check the appropriate option)

☐ Met treatment goals

☐ Parent terminated; treatment goals not met

☐ Referral for relocation of client

☐ Referral for other treatment intervention

☐ Referral for failure to comply

Post-treatment Recommendations:

_____

_____

_____

_____

_____

_____

_____

_____

_____

_____

_____

_____

_____

_____

_____   _____
Play Therapist Signature and Credentials   Date

Play Therapy Termination Summary—Sample

Client Information

Client Name: Noah Rodriguez

Client Age: 4 years

Client Address: 782 Sunset Drive, Somewhere, TX

Parent/Caregiver Name: Alice & Juan Rodriguez

Treatment Data

Intake Date: September 10, 20XX

First Session Date: September 14, 20XX

Final Session Date: February 20, 20XX

Number of Sessions:

14 individual play therapy; 10 sibling play therapy; 6 parent consultations

Counseling Modalities Implemented: Adlerian Play Therapy

DSM TR-5 Diagnosis: *F43.24, Adjustment Disorder, Disturbance of Emotions and Conduct, Persistent*

Termination Information

Reason for Termination: Met treatment goals
Post-treatment Recommendations: None.

Linda E. Homeyer   February 21, 20XX
Linda E. Homeyer, PhD, LPC-S, RPT-S   Date

Index

Note: Page numbers in *italics* indicate figures. Page numbers in **bold** indicate tables.

Made in the USA
Middletown, DE
22 April 2023

29324974R00144